❧ BIBLE PROPHECY ❧

Dedication

To my wife Bonnie who has inspired me through
her own struggle with religion and who has enlivened
our marriage with her active mind and probing curiosity.

❖ BIBLE PROPHECY ❖

Failure or Fulfillment?

Tim Callahan

MILLENNIUM PRESS
ALTADENA, CALIFORNIA

Copyright © 1997 by Tim Callahan

All rights reserved. No part of this book may be reproduced of transmitted in any form, or by any means, electronic or mechanical, including photocopying , recording, or by any informa-tion and retrieval system, without permission in writing from the publisher.

Published in the United States by Millennium Press, 2761 North Marengo Avenue, Altadena, California, 91001.

Phone: 818/794-3119; Fax: 818/794-1301; e-mail: skepticmag@aol.com

Library of Congress Cataloging-in-Publication Data
Callahan, Tim
Bible Prophecy: Failure or Fulfillment?
Includes Bibliographical References and Index.

ISBN: 0-9655047-0-0

Library of Congress Catalog Card Number: 96-078368

1. Biblical prophecy. 2. Biblical criticism. 3 Ancient History I. Title.

Book design, illustrations, charts, maps, and jacket design by Pat Linse
Cover: *The Death of Sardanapalus* by Eugene Delacroix
courtesy Louvre Museum, Paris, France. © Photo RMN—Hervé Lewandowski
George Washington as a Freemason courtesy of the Library of Congress

9 8 7 6 5 4 3 2 1

Printed in the United States of America on acid-free paper
First Edition

Table of Contents

Preface: How Dare I?   ix

Introduction
Without Presupposition: How to Test a Biblical Prophecy   1

Chapter 1
Who Wrote the Bible?: How the Bible Was Written and Organized   9

Chapter 2
How to Think About the Bible: An Introduction to the Prophetic Books   33

Chapter 3
"Behold the Days Are Coming": The Prophets of the Assyrian Period   49

Chapter 4
Prophecy or False Prophecy?: Prophets of the Chaldean Period   71

Chapter 5
"And the Word Became Flesh and Dwelt Among Us":
Do Old Testament Prophecies Foretell the Life of Jesus?"   111

Chapter 6
From Prophecy to Catastrophe:
The Post-Exilic Prophets and the Growth of Prophetic Literature   133

Chapter 7
Head of Gold, Feet of Clay: The Book of Daniel   149

Chapter 8
The Last Days: Apocalyptic Writings of the New Testament   179

Chapter 9
The End of the World: The Rapture and the Second Coming   203

Chapter 10
Black Helicopters, Hong Kong Gurkhas, and Other Signs
of the New World Order: Secular Conspiracy Theories   231

Epilogue   253

Bibliography   257

Index   260

Timeline Charts

Assyrian Prophets 48
Chaldean Prophets 72-73
Persian Prophets 132

Illustrations

The Death of Sardanapalus 78
Assyrian Atrocities 82
The Great Seal of the United States 234
The Seal of the Knights Templars 234
George Washington as a Mason 240

Maps

Israel Under David and Solomon 40
The Assyrian Empire with Inset:
The Divided Kingdoms of Israel and Judea 58
The Lydian, Median, and Chaldean Empires 74
Nineveh 80
Jerusalem 88
Tyre 96
Babylon 100
Palestine In the Time of Christ 112
The Persian Empire 134
The Enemy from the North 142
Alexander's Empire 154
The Diadochian Wars 321 B.C.E. 156
Alexander's Successors 240 B.C.E. 158
The Growth of the Maccabean Kingdom 178
The Roman Expansion 190 B.C.E. 180
The Roman Expansion 89 B.C.E. 182
The Roman Expansion 62 B.C.E. 184
The Cities of the Christian Era 192
The Parthian Empire 196

Notes on Dating and other Abbreviations

While the author grew up using and is quite comfortable with the abbreviations B.C. and A.D., the fact that the stand for, respectively, "before Christ" and *Anno Domini*, (L. "in the year of the Lord") causes discomfort in some due to the inherently Christian bias of those titles. Therefore this book uses in their place B.C.E. ("before the Common Era") and C.E. ("Common Era"), respectively.

Unless specifically stated otherwise biblical quotes are from the Revised Standard Version of the Bible. The abbreviations of various Biblical translations used in this book are:

RSV . . . . .Revised Standard Version

OAB or OAV . .Oxford Annotated Bible (or Version), an annotated edition of the RSV.

NASB . . . . . . .New American Standard Bible

NIV . . . . .New International Version

KJV . . . . .King James Version

MT . . . . .Masoretic Text, the final redaction of the Hebrew Scriptures.

JPS 1955 . . . . .English Translation of the MT by the Jewish Publication Society in 1955.

JPS 1988 . . . . .English Translation of the MT by the Jewish Publication Society in 1988.

LXX . . . . .The Septuagint, Hebrew Scriptures translated into Greek in the third century B.C.E. The Catholic Douay Bible is largely based on the LXX as opposed to the MT.

Acknowledgments

I would like to acknowledge the debt I owe to my late parents for providing me with a house full of books and for engendering in me a respect for knowledge and scholarship. I also owe a debt to the public library systems everywhere, repositories of knowledge whose existence has not only provided all of us with books to read but has made possible the writing of so many others.

I would also like to thank my wife for her constant support and inspiration, Dr. Michael Shermer for suggesting this project, and Betty McCollister for editing the manuscript. I particularly wish to thank Pat Linse who, by dint of tireless labor and artistic competence, is largely responsible for the professional quality of the graphics and layout of this book.

In addition I wish to acknowledge the role of Bob Wheeler, my creationist opponent in a duel of letters to the editor, whose ardent yet friendly antagonism first piqued my interest in the phenomenon of fundamentalism, to the *Pasadena Star-News* and Larry Wilson, its opinion page editor at the time, for putting up with our prolonged debate, and to all those who joined in on both sides of the issue.

I would particularly like to thank Dr. Gerald Larue and Dr. Randal Helms for reading and critiquing my manuscript. In addition I wish to thank Mlle. Bernadette Letellier, Conservator-in-Chief of the Department of Egyptian Antiquities, *Musée de Louvre*, for taking the time to respond to my request for information on the inscription on the statue of Nes Hor (Louvre A90).

HOW DARE I!

W RITE A BOOK THAT LOOKS AT AN IMPORTANT PART OF THE BIBLE with a jaundiced eye? How dare I indeed! Even among people so secular that it is problematic as to whether they will make it to church on either Christmas or Easter, there is an uneasiness about saying anything against the Bible. This is true even of people who have never opened a Bible. In fact, I suspect that their very lack of familiarity with the book is the main source of its mystique. Read the Bible with any degree of intellectual independence and it soon becomes evident that it is full of internal contradictions, faulty history, and ideas seen as ethical that we in the 20th century would find abhorrent. As examples of the later, consider the glorification of genocide in the book of Joshua and the acceptance of slavery found in many of the Pauline epistles. One problem of dealing with the Bible in an objective manner is that when people do read it, they often do so with an attitude of reverence such that if one points out a pernicious idea the Bible ascribes to God, they will rationalize it or assume that it doesn't really mean what it so plainly says. Much the way an oyster makes a pearl, they coat the harsh message in layer after layer of symbolic meanings until the hard corners of the offending contaminant no longer tear at their innards. Let us consider just one of these as an example. In 2 Kings 2:23-24, there is a curious incident involving the prophet Elisha:

> He went up from there to Bethel; and while he was going up on the way, some small boys came out of the city and jeered at him, saying, "Go up, you baldhead! Go up, you baldhead!" And he turned around and when he saw them, he cursed them in the name of the Lord. And two she-bears came out of the woods and tore forty-two of the boys.

This little tale stands alone. Nothing in the preceding verses leads up to it and what follows is the story of a war between the Israelites and Mesha, king of Moab. So here we have a little moral tale meant to scare children into respecting their elders, particularly if those elders are holy men. Since Elisha was just a man, God's approval of his curse is implicit in its grim fulfillment. There is really no way to interpret this story other than that God sanctions the killing or at least mauling of children for a sin as trivial as making fun of a bald-headed man. Is this a God anyone would care to worship?

In his *Encyclopedia of Bible Difficulties*, Gleason A. Archer Jr. gives the following defense of this incident (1982, p. 205):

> A careful study of this incident in context shows that it was far more serious than a "mild personal offense." It was a situation of serious public danger, quite as grave as the large youth gangs that roam the ghetto sections of modern American cities. If these young hoodlums were ranging about in packs of fifty or more, derisive toward respectable adults and ready to mock even a well-known man of God, there is no telling what violence they might have inflicted on the citizenry of the religious center of the kingdom of Israel (as Bethel was), had they been allowed to continue their riotous course.

Earlier, Archer had spoken of Elisha's tormentors as "young men." In examining a number of editions of the Bible, including a direct Hebrew to English translation of the Hebrew Bible, I have found the boys described as "children," "small boys" and, in one footnote, boys of at least 12, implying that they should have known better. Yet, in order to rationalize the text, Archer has to transform them from ill-bred children into young men and then, through the agency of an invented context (yet the story isn't set in any context) from young men into a youth gang. Having done so, he is free to magnify their bratty behavior into a "riotous course." The allusion to the street gangs of modern cities roaming in "packs" of 50 or more sets up the potential for readers to fill in the blanks with their own imaginations. Though not specifically brought up, images of Crips and Bloods and drive-by shootings lie at the edge of one's consciousness. (Presumably, the gangs of Elisha's day would have whipped by in hot chariots discharging arrows.) Yet there is nothing in the actual story to justify anything in Archer's interpretation. What the good professor is avoiding is the fact that the message of this passage was acceptable to the harsh society in which Elisha lived, but is appalling to us. That it represents something that can't possibly be the word of God is unacceptable to Archer, because the freedom to hold such a view would allow people the right to judge what in the Bible they will or will not believe. I suspect that this unwillingness to consider such an unattractive possibility, held openly by fundamentalists such as Archer, is also held implicitly by many people who, if confronted with the verses above, would find them outrageous. In essence it lies beneath the surface of their consciousness and causes them to react with a certain distress toward biblical criticism. For, secular though they might be, society has drummed into their heads through a thousand subtle messages that the Bible is the "Good Book" and must contain the thoughts and intentions of God.

Another group of people who might be inclined to ask me how I dare write a work on biblical criticism are those who demand credentials before they will listen to what one has to say. As someone holding only a Bachelor of Fine Arts degree, how do I presume to write a book on the interpretation of biblical prophecy? First of all I would point out that it is easy enough for a layman like myself to check a prophecy that fundamentalists claim is true against actual historical fact. As an example of this, consider the prophecy in Jeremiah 25:11 that the Jews would be exiled and in captivity at Babylon for 70 years. So pitiful is the teaching of history in our schools that I have heard of the Babylonian captivity casually referred to as lasting 70 years from a number of secular sources. Yet the captivity lasted from the fall of Jerusalem in 586 B.C.E. to the fall of Babylon to the Persians in 538 B.C.E., a period of not quite 49 years. There are several possible interpretations of Jeremiah's prophecy, including the possibility that the number 70 was meant to be symbolic (a sabbath of decades), that it meant the length of a human life (three score and 10 years) or that it was figurative language for "a long time." One thing that it *cannot* mean is the literal 70 years fundamentalists claim as the period of the Babylonian captivity.

Several of those who accept the 70-year captivity are, like Gleason Archer, Ph.D.s. It would seem that a doctorate is no defense against sloppy thinking and erroneous conclusions. Nor is scholarship limited to those with degrees. A love of history, particularly ancient history, plus extensive readings in comparative mythology have helped me see such gaps in the scholarship of those with doctorates. An all too common tendency of many scholars in the field of biblical interpretation is to be influenced by the strictures of their belief systems. Put simply, fundamentalist reasoning, even among those whose level of knowledge should tell them otherwise, is that the Jews *had* to have been captive 70 years in Babylon because the Bible says they were

Finally my layman's status may actually be a benefit in that I have the ability to relate the findings of biblical scholars with a clarity they themselves often lack, due to the use of professional jargon inexplicable to many outside their field. The idea to write this book came about largely because there is a lack of anything accessible to the lay person regarding the interpretation and criticism of biblical prophesy. Late in 1994 Michael Shermer accepted an article of mine for *Skeptic* magazine, debunking Hal Lindsey's "end-time" speculations concerning Russia as fulfilling the role of Gog and Magog in Ezekiel 39 and the "Enemy from the North" in Daniel 11. Dr. Shermer suggested at that time that my writing had a certain clarity that would be useful in a book on the subject of biblical prophecies and their interpretation by various fundamentalist authors such as Lindsey. The end result of that suggestion is this book, in which I not only dare to interpret Bible prophecy with a skeptic's eye, but invite the reader to do so as well.

Pasadena, May 1995

WITHOUT PRESUPPOSITION

How to Test a Biblical Prophecy

BEFORE WE TAKE A SKEPTICAL LOOK AT BIBLE PROPHECY it is important to understand just what skepticism is. For many the word is synonymous with cynicism, and it is important that we dispel that idea immediately. To be a skeptic means to take nothing on faith. The converse of this is to never automatically eliminate any possible explanation, regardless of how far-fetched it may seem. If someone claims to have evidence of the existence of sea-serpents, the skeptic, while maintaining a "show me" attitude, nonetheless accepts the possibility that the claimant has valid evidence for the existence of sea-serpents, hears the claim out and weighs the arguments based on their own strengths, regardless of the claimant's credentials or lack thereof. The skeptic, then, approaches all questions and issues, as far as humanly possible, without giving in to presuppositions.

The problem, of course, is that all of us hold presuppositions—ideas that we assume to be axiomatic without considering that they may be nothing more than bias. Since our presuppositions can cause us to automatically slant our interpretation of data, the scientific method includes as its final test the requirement that independent researchers performing a given experiment under the same strictly controlled conditions will achieve the same results. Likewise, the interpretation of scripture depends a great deal on one's presuppositions, and subjecting one's interpretation to open debate is a way of rectifying the bias of presupposition. I found one example of presuppositional bias when, in the process of researching this book, I read *The Bible Handbook*, an atheist critique of the Bible. Though I found the volume quite useful, the atheist presupposition that the Bible is something not only full of error, but is a document to be scorned as impeding human progress flavored the critique to the degree that it became petty, even attacking the Bible for less than euphemistic descriptions of such things as sexual relations and childbirth. In fact, if the Bible had skirted such issues, it could be faulted for its prudery. As an example of how presupposition blinds one to the significance of a subject, consider the atheist objection, in a section of the book called "Bible Immoralities, Indecencies and Obscenities," to what they refer to as "Ezekiel's filthy cookery" (p. 239). The verses in question are Ezekiel 4:12-15, in which God tells Ezekiel to bake bread over a fire fueled by human dung. So caught up are the atheists with the "filthy" aspects of the passage that they fail to consider it in context. The entirety of Ezekiel 4 is a series of commands by God to Ezekiel to indulge in what we might call a form of performance art as visual demonstrations of God's anger toward his people. The baking of bread with human dung is the culmination of these and is meant to show the Jews how they will be forced to eat unclean things when they are scattered among the nations.

Of course, atheists have no corner on presupposition. The assumption by fundamentalists that all who disagree with them are automatically in error, a presupposition that precludes honest debate, is as arrogant in its way as is the atheist position. For example, in his *Encyclopedia of Bible Difficulties*, Gleason Archer lists eight procedures for dealing with Bible difficulties. While most of these are well-reasoned, at least two of them are based on presuppositions which indicate that, for fundamentalists, even the possibility of biblical error is excluded before any given verse is examined. Consider Archer's first recommendation (1982, p. 15):

> Be fully persuaded in your own mind that an adequate explanation exists, even though you have not found it. The aerodynamic engineer may not understand how a bumble bee can fly, yet he trusts that there must be an adequate explanation for its fine performance since, as a matter of fact, it does fly! Even so we may have complete confidence that the divine Author preserved the human author of each book of the Bible from error or mistake as he wrote down the original manuscript of the sacred text.

The presupposition of inerrancy precludes considering the possibility that some of the books or at least verses in them were less than divine in origin. It assumes that no material that was not of divine origin could have been allowed into the canon in spite of the fact that the editors were, after all, finite, error prone humans subject to political and religious bias. To accommodate such a view, not only must the authors of Scripture be inspired, but the people involved in choosing which books were allowed into the canon had to have been under divine guidance as well. Here we run into problems, since there are distinct differences between the Catholic and Protestant canons. If God inspired Jerome's compilation and translation into Latin of the Vulgate, why didn't he inspire the man to use the Hebrew canon to the exclusion of the Septuagint, which contained such books as Judith and 1 and 2 Maccabees, not admitted to the Jewish canon? But if Jerome was wrong, hence not inspired, and the proper inspiration did not come until the Protestant canon, why did God let Christianity drift for nearly 1500 years with an erroneous version of the Bible? Further, we are given no particular reason why, for example, the Book of 1 Maccabees was not considered inspired, at least by Protestants, despite its proven historicity, while the Book of Esther, which is demonstrably fictional in spite of purporting to be historical, was allowed into the Jewish, Catholic and Protestant canons.

The other inerrantist presupposition in Archer's procedures is that in the case of parallel passages, harmonization of the various versions is the only method that can be justified. He goes on to state that, in the interest of justice, jurors at a trial would have to assume the truthfulness of each witness, regardless of the variance of their testimonies, i. e. that they were each telling the truth from their perspective, said assumption to hold except in cases where the witness has been demonstrated to be of questionable integrity (p. 16). Archer must have a rather odd view of how juries deliberate if he thinks they harmonize varying testimonies. More than likely, a jury will discard the conflicting testimonies of equally reputable witnesses and consider the matter on which there is disagreement as beyond the jury's power to fathom—specifically *because* reputable witnesses can't agree on it. The jury will then concentrate on the material on which there is agreement. Harmonization of testimony might work if two witnesses disagree by describing someone as wearing either a red shirt according to one witness, or a purple shirt according to the other. However, if one witness describes the shirt as red, and the other witness says it was green, the jury can hardly harmonize the two colors as brown. If one verse in Judges says that the Israelites took the town of Jebus from the Canaanites and another verse says that they failed to take it, the two verses can no more be harmonized than can a red shirt with a green shirt (see

Judges 1:8, 1:21, 19:11-12 and 2 Samuel 5:6 8). In any case, the presupposition that harmonization of varying accounts is the only method that can be justified is totally unsupported. It also runs afoul of Archer's earlier inerrantist presupposition. How can we accept that "the divine Author preserved the human author from error," if two human authors of canonical works disagree? Wouldn't keeping them from error result in their complete agreement and eliminate conflicting parallel accounts?

Despite these rather obvious objections to inerrancy, the doctrine that the Bible is true in all that it says is a basic presupposition of fundamentalist biblical interpretation. So too is the position that inerrancy has been the historical position of the Christian church from its inception. As Archer puts it (p. 19):

> Except for heretical groups that broke away from the church, it was always assumed that Scripture was completely authoritative and trustworthy in all that it asserts as factual, whether in matters of theology, history, or science.

In his foreword to Archer's book, Kenneth S. Kantzer backs this position (p. 7):

> Readers will soon discover that the view of inerrancy set forth by Dr. Archer is the historical position of the church in all of its major branches. Behind it stand the illustrious names of Augustine, Aquinas, John of Damascus, Luther, Calvin, Wesley and a host of others.

It is interesting that the first name on Kantzer's list of church fathers is Augustine. Protestants, particularly fundamentalist Protestants, derive much of the emphasis of their beliefs from Augustine, while Catholics tend more toward Aquinas. In point of fact, were he alive today, Augustine would not support Archer's view of inerrancy. In Book VI of his *Confessions*, Augustine tells how Ambrose removed one of the great barriers to his accepting Christianity by pointing out that Scripture isn't always to be taken in a literal sense. In Book XIII, Augustine gives an allegorical interpretation of the six-day creation story in Genesis 1. He clearly did not think that this tale, so hotly defended by fundamentalists, was the literal truth. Augustine is not the only early church father who felt he could be a devout Christian and still not embrace inerrancy. Jerome, for example, accepted the view put forth by the pagan philosopher Porphyry that the book of Daniel was written at the time of Antiochus Epiphanes, between 175 and 163 B.C.E., rather than during the Exile (587-538 B.C.E.) as the book purports. He did not have to believe in

Daniel's historicity to accept that Jesus was God incarnate. Another name on Kantzer's list was that of John Calvin. Yet Calvin, who was greatly influenced by Augustine, also rejected the inerrantist view as necessary for accepting the Bible as the word of God (Rogers and McKim, 1979):

> Just as Calvin did not expect the Bible to be a repository of technically accurate information on language or history, neither did he expect that biblical data should be used to question the findings of science. The purpose of Scripture was to bring persons into a right relationship with God and their fellow creatures. Science was in another sphere and was judged by its own criteria.

Calvin's view is often referred to as accommodation. This is the idea that God accommodated his word to the limitations of the scientific understanding of those to whom he revealed it, a view which avoided forcing theologians to defend as scientifically valid statements in the Bible that said the sun rises and sets; and would, if it were used by modern-day fundamentalists, allow them to believe in the Bible without having to champion creationism.

As an exercise in how we might avoid such presuppositions as those Archer and Kantzer have fallen prey to let us consider the full range of possible truths regarding the divinity or even the historical existence of Jesus. It is possible that (1) Jesus never existed, that he is nothing more than an amalgam of fertility god death and resurrection myths; (2) that he was historical but had no supernatural powers; (3) that he did indeed have supernatural powers but was not a god; or (4) that he was and is God incarnate. Neither the divinity nor the existence of Jesus is a major concern of this book. But if it were, the skeptic's position would be to accept all alternatives as possible. The existence of supernatural powers and agencies would not be automatically discounted, as would be the case in an atheist critique; nor would the possibility that there never was a real Jesus, a position automatically excluded in fundamentalist presuppositions.

Looking at prophecy without presuppositions—the aim of this book—means that in considering any given prophecy we have at least three possibilities as to its validity: (1) it is true; (2) it is false; (3) it is so vague as to be open to many interpretations. For an example of (1), Isaiah's prophecies in 7 and 8, predicting the imminent destruction of the kingdoms of Israel and Syria at the hands of the Assyrians, were clearly true. For an example of (2), Isaiah 17:1 says that Damascus will cease to be a city and become a heap of ruins. The context of Isaiah's prophecies concerning Damascus and Israel is the expansion of the Assyrian empire, which Isaiah repeatedly prophesies will destroy both Syria and Israel. While the Assyrians did give Damascus a good sacking, the city is still thriving today, some 27 centuries after Isaiah predicted it would be reduced to rubble. The prophecy is clearly false. Finally, as an example of (3), the Gog and Magog prophecy of Ezekiel 39 is an example of a prophecy too vague to be interpreted. Gog has been interpreted as Gyges, king of Lydia, the Goths, and even a modern or future leader of Russia. Magog has been interpreted as the Scythians, the Chaldeans, the Huns and modern-day Russia, among others.

If a prophecy is true it could be divinely inspired, but only if it was actually made before, rather than after, the fact. As an example, consider a prophecy made by an unnamed prophet who predicts to King Jeroboam that a descendant of the house of David named Josiah would burn the bones of Jeroboam's pagan cultic priests on Jeroboam's altar. The prophecy is in 1 Kings 13:2, and the fulfillment is in 2 Kings 23:15-18, about 300 years later. However, as the notes in the Oxford Annotated Bible point out, a verse in the same chapter as the prophecy (1 Kings 13:32) refers to the northern kingdom as Samaria. Yet, Israel was not referred to by the name of its capital until after it had fallen to the Assyrians in 721 B.C.E. In any case the Book of Kings—originally 1 and 2 Kings were a single book—was not finally edited until well into the Babylonian Exile (after 586 B.C.E.). Thus, the prophet crying out against Jeroboam's idolatry, which took place around 900 B.C.E., was inserted into the text hundreds of years after the fact and the supposedly fulfilled prophecy was not a prophecy at all.

If we can establish that what purports to be a prophecy was not only true but was made before the fact, then there are a number of possible explanations for it. It could have been directive or deliberately fulfilled by someone attempting to claim a supernatural role; it could be a reasonable guess based on a logical interpretation of current events; or it could be an actual divinely inspired prophecy. As an example of a directive consider how Michal, daughter of Saul, became barren after David became angry with her (2 Samuel 20-23). There is an implication here that God made Michal barren because she was contemptuous of David. However, no supernatural agency is required to explain Michal's barrenness. David could insure that she remained childless simply by refusing to have sexual relations with her. Another example of a directive is the prophecy given by Samuel to Saul in 1 Samuel 10:5,6 that Saul would meet a band of prophets in a state of prophetic frenzy and that the spirit of God would possess him, causing him to fall into the same frenzy. It is hardly surprising that in 1 Sam. 10:10 things turn out exactly as the prophet said they would. Any Pentecostal minister could probably duplicate Samuel's feat amongst his gullible flock, suggesting at the outset of a prayer meeting that many of them will be "slain in the spirit" that very night. An example of deliberate fulfillment of a prophecy could easily be found in Jesus's entry into Jerusalem on an ass on Palm Sunday (Mt. 21:1-9, Mk. 11:1-10, Lk. 19: 28-38, Jn. 12:12-18). As Matthew puts it (Mt. 21:4): "This took place to fulfill what was spoken by the prophet...." The prophecy in question is Zechariah 9:9 where the Messiah comes to Jerusalem riding on an ass. Since Jesus was aware of the prophecy, it is quite possible that he deliberately chose to enter Jerusalem in the manner that would fulfill the prophecy as opposed to doing it in ignorance and fulfilling the prophecy supernaturally.

An example of a prophecy being a logical inference from current events would be Isaiah's prophecies concerning the conquest of Israel and Syria. Given the alliance the two nations were making against Assyria and the latter's increasing might and westward expansion, the logical inference was that Assyria would soon conquer them.

Only after we have eliminated all these possibilities can we prove that a prophecy was supernaturally fulfilled. Therefore, as we examine prophecies in detail, I will subject each of them to the following four questions:

(1) Is it true, and, if so, to what degree?

(2) Was it made before or after the fact?

(3) Was it either directive or deliberately fulfilled by someone with knowledge of the prophecy?

(4) Was it a logical guess?

At this point I must confess that I know of no prophecy that passes the test by eliminating the non-supernatural alternative explanations. As such and for the sake of intellectual honesty, I must confess my own presuppositions. First of all, I assume a natural explanation for seemingly fulfilled prophecies until such explanations can be eliminated as possibilities. Perhaps I am wrong to do this. Whether Jesus' entry into Jerusalem on Palm Sunday was a genuine fulfillment or a deliberately staged affair is, after all, not provable, and a decision to see it one way or another might well be nothing more than a matter of faith, regardless of which choice is made.

Another presupposition of mine is that I have a problem reconciling the concept of long range prophecies with the concept of free will. It is one thing to say that God will do a certain thing, such as become incarnate in a child who will be born in Bethlehem at a later date. It is quite another to say that people as yet unborn will act in a specific manner. If the history of an empire or nation is already part of a divine plan, how can God hold the leaders, and indeed the peoples themselves, accountable for their actions? Yet, the same prophecies usually include the visitation of God's wrath on these empires. If their actions are not part of a divine plan, but are predictable given the nature of the people involved, then their thoughts and actions are so preordained as to render them devoid of free will. In spite of these two presuppositions, I have attempted to make my judgments on Bible prophecies based entirely on history, scholarly Bible criticism, and logic.

Ultimately, my readers, acting as review panel of my peers, will have to judge the validity of my objectivity. Whether their judgment be gracious or harsh, I hope that they too will subject their own views to a review of their peers.

WHO WROTE THE BIBLE?

How the Bible was Written and Organized

SINCE THE BIBLE IS PRESENTED TO MOST OF US as a single document with two major divisions—the Old and New Testaments—and since it is often presented with a tacit understanding that it is not to be questioned, the majority of us have no concept of how it was written or edited. To the untrained and uncritical eye, the Old Testament appears by and large to be a linear document built up over a long history with some legendary material in Genesis and perhaps some elaborations or fictions not to be taken literally, but generally a document whose writings occurred and were edited in the order they appear in the Christian editions of the Bible. But the Old Testament is, in fact, a Jewish document. Thus, it should logically be presented as it is in the Hebrew Bible or *Tanakh*. The word Tanakh is an anagram for the divisions of the Jewish Bible. These are the *Torah* or Law (literally "that which was laid down"), meaning foundational material—Genesis, Exodus, Leviticus, Numbers, Deuteronomy, the *Nevi'im* or Prophets, and the *Kethuvim* or Writings.

The Torah and the Documentary Hypothesis

In spite of the great antiquity of much of its material, the Torah was not completely edited until about 400 B.C.E., well after the return of the exiles from Babylon, and it was not in its finalized canonical form until the Hebrew scriptures were codified in the Masoretic Text (MT) between 600 and 900 C.E. Nor was the Torah or, as it is also called, the Pentateuch (Gr. "five scrolls") written by Moses. It must be remembered that in ancient times it was common to attribute certain kinds of literature to an author of that type of material as a way of legitimizing it. Since Moses was the law-giver all books pertaining to the law were attributed to him. Not only were the various books the work of different authors, each individual book was the work of numerous writers and redactors (editors). This view, held by most scholars who are not fundamentalists, is called the Documentary Hypothesis. Since our main focus in the Old Testament is on the prophets, I will treat this subject only briefly. The main importance of the hypothesis for us is the validity of modern scholarship. Accordingly, my central concern is with the fundamentalist objections to the hypothesis.

Briefly stated, the history of the compilation of the Torah, as seen in the hypothesis, is as follows. The earliest holy writing of the Jews, embedded in Genesis, Exodus and Numbers was the work referred to by Biblical scholars as the "J," or Yahwist document (the German spelling of Yahweh being Jahveh), probably written in the reign of Solomon between 960 and 920 B.C.E. or during the reign of his son Rehoboam and probably written at the court by a Judahite official with a strong bias toward the Davidic line of kings. The J document starts with the second creation story, and God is portrayed in very human, anthropomorphic terms.

A rival document, the E—Elohist or Ephraimite material—was written in the northern kingdom, at the court in Samaria *circa* 850 B.C.E. The name of God in this document was Elohim as opposed to Yahweh, and the writings have a bias favoring Israel over Judah, and particularly favoring the tribe of Ephraim. It starts with the covenant of Abraham and focuses on Jacob. Most of the stories of Joseph, ancestor of the Ephraimites, who dominated the northern kingdom, derive from this document. After the conquest of Israel by the Assyrians in 721 B.C.E., the E document was brought to Jerusalem by refugees. The material was blended by various redactors who attempted, with limited success, to harmonize the two documents.

Independent of these documents were the writings of those reformers we know of as prophets, particularly Hosea, Amos, the first Isaiah, and Jeremiah. They wrote in a time period from just prior to the Assyrian conquest of Israel to the Babylonian captivity. The prophets represent a faction urging the purification of the worship of Yahweh and the expulsion of the rival cults of Baal and Astarte. One might wonder why such a purification would be necessary, since the children of Israel are represented in the book of Joshua as having practically exterminated the Canaanites before the origin of the monarchy. In fact, the purification was essential to establish the monotheistic worship of the god variously referred to as Yahweh and Elohim, because the deity in question was originally one of the gods of the Canaanite pantheon. The Canaanite gods were themselves variants of Sumerian and Babylonian deities. Elohim is the plural of El, a word that can merely mean "god," or can mean the name of a specific deity. El was a sky god, creator and the gray-bearded patriarch of the Canaanite gods. Likewise, Yahweh was also original-ly a Canaanite deity. Variants of his name are found on inscriptions going back as far as the 15th century B.C.E. In later inscriptions, Yahweh's name in the form of Yaw is found in association with two Canaanite goddesses, Anath and Astarte (see Langdon 1931, p. 44). Astarte is the western Semitic variant of the Babylonian goddess Ishtar. A coin from 4th century B.C.E. Gaza actu-ally depicts Yahweh, with the inscription YHW (Yahu or Yaw, three of the let-ters of the tetragrammaton YHWH for Yahweh), as a bearded man holding a hawk and sitting on a winged wheel, much the way Sumerian deities were portrayed. Even though this depiction of God probably did not fit the view held by the post-exilic Jews of that time, we must remember that Gaza was a Philistine city and that the Philistines had, even during the period of the Judges, accepted the Canaanite pantheon. Since they were not exposed to the pressures of the Exile, which forced the Jews to transform their view of God, the Philistines depicted Yahweh as he was originally viewed by the Canaanites and Sumerians. The Sumerian gods were essentially exalted humans, much like the Olympians of ancient Greece. Further, the Sumerians had a rather technological view of how the gods could do miraculous things. How did the gods fly? They could not do this by themselves. Instead, they had winged chariots. The graphic short-hand for a winged chariot was a winged wheel on which the god sat.

The purification of the worship of Yahweh and its separation from the Canaanite fertility cults was a long and arduous process that often pitted the prophets against both king and people. However, the prophets did constitute a powerful faction that could exert a great deal of influence over kings of the Yahwist persuasion. So it was that when, during the lifetime of Jeremiah, as repairs were being made on the Temple (621 B.C.E.), a book of laws was found mysteriously hidden in its walls and was brought to King Josiah. Once he had read it, Josiah tore his clothes and ordered the nation to beg mercy of God for having previously transgressed God's laws. This was eventually considered the second giving of the law, so the document was named Deuteronomy. Just why God would allow his law to be hidden from the time of Moses to the time of Josiah is never explained, and it seems rather odd that God would allow his people to sin in ignorance all those years. While the material in Deuteronomy undoubtedly reflects traditional law and religious codes of the Yahwist cult already in existence, most biblical scholars feel the book itself (hence the codification of these laws) was written at the time of its "discovery" and was not, as its so-called discoverers claimed, from the time or from the hand of Moses. The authors of Deuteronomy, most probably members of the prophetic faction, were referred to collectively as the Deuteronomists (their material being designated D). In addition to writing Deuteronomy they also compiled what is referred to as the Deuteronomist history: Joshua, Judges, 1 and 2 Samuel, 1 and 2 Kings. After the fall of Jerusalem to the Chaldeans in 586 B.C.E., and the deportation of the Jews, another major addition and revision occurred, paralleling the already ongoing Deuteronomist work. This is the P or Priestly material. The Jewish community in the Exile was held together by leaders from the priestly class, starting with Ezekiel and ending after the return of the exiles with Ezra and Nehemiah. Much material that had previously been passed down orally was written during the Exile. Many of the Psalms date from this period as well. Along with adding to and re-editing existing material, particularly Exodus, the priests wrote virtually all of Leviticus and most of Numbers. The priestly writers placed particular stress on the strict observance of ritual purity, dietary laws and observance of the Sabbath. All of these were probably necessary to maintain the separate identity of the Jews in exile. Reflections of these concerns are seen in stories stressing the importance of Sabbath observance. The story of the six-day creation, containing certain Mesopotamian motifs such as the world starting out covered with water, is also a priestly document, largely aimed at establishing the divine origin and ordination of the Sabbath. Finally, after the Exile, editors from the priestly class blended the various traditions, adding bridging material in the process. This material has been labeled R for redactor.

Fundamentalists object to this view of how the Old Testament was built up. While generally acknowledging that the Chronicles, Ezra and Nehemiah were the work of one post-exilic author, they claim that the other narrative books were historical, that Moses wrote the Torah, and that the books were written as they appear, not built up by merging and re-editing of the J, E, D and P material. They point out that nobody has ever actually found the Book of J, for example. However, they are forced to acknowledge that we also lack the original autographs of any of the books of the Old Testament. Another objection raised by fundamentalists is that the Documentary Hypothesis is arbitrary and is nothing more than an attempt on the part of "liberal theologians" to discredit the Bible. They see the higher criticism of the 19th century as being the work of intellectuals with an anti-Christian agenda. The reference to the higher criticism and modern scholars as "liberal"—a pejorative among fundamentalists—is a give-away that what is being referred to is politics and not scholarship. The number of times fundamentalist apologists refer to their opponents as "liberal theologians" indicates to me that the term is not used casually; its repeated usage is a deliberate tactic aimed at tying the views of those who differ from the inerrantist position to a buzz-word calculated to provoke an antagonistic response among the faithful. Consider the company "liberal theologians" are keeping in the following quote from the late Dr. Walter Martin, founder of the CRI, or Christian Research Institute (1988, tape 1):

> The faith of Christ, what was necessary for our salvation, the living of the Christian life, edification and evangelism already existed, complete. You didn't need Mary Baker Eddy. You didn't need Charles [and] Myrtle Filmore. You didn't need Joseph Smith and Brigham Young. You didn't need Charles Russel and Jehovah's Witnesses. You didn't need Madam Blavatsky and Theosophy or the Fox sisters and Spiritism. You didn't need the kingdom of the cults, and you didn't need liberal theologians and destructive higher critics in order for you to arrive at the truth, because the faith was "once for all delivered to the saints."

Without specifically mentioning inerrancy, Martin has here implied that the canon is not to be interpreted critically and has classed anyone who disagrees with that implied position as being either a "liberal theologian" or a "destructive higher critic," said categories being as anathematized in Martin's view as Christian Scientists, Mormons, Jehovah's Witnesses, Theosophists, and Spiritists. In short, Martin's view, and thus that of CRI, is that those who vary from the inerrantist position are in the same camp with cultists and heretics.

In point of fact, the views of theologians who are not inerrantist vary widely, resulting in a range of biblical interpretation from quite conservative to quite radical. By casting the debate in terms of inerrancy vs. liberal theology, the fundamentalists obscure two important facts that tend to undermine their position. First, because there is a multiplicity of views on biblical interpretation, inerrancy is only one of many strands of thought, whereas fundamentalists have implied a scenario involving only two views. Second, since liberal is often synonymous with a departure from tradition, the implication is that fundamentalism, by contrast, represents the traditional view held by the church for centuries. In reality, both fundamentalism and inerrancy are recent developments in Christianity rather than ancient traditions.

Still, the fundamentalists do have a point. How do we know that the J, E, D, and P documents or redactional material actually existed? And if it is of recent invention, why was it that nobody prior to the 19th century noticed the clues that gave rise to the Documentary Hypothesis?

In point of fact, the origins of biblical criticism go back to the early middle ages. As I said in the introduction, Jerome (340-420 C.E.), one of the most important architects of Christian doctrine, and one respected nearly as much as his contemporary and ally, Augustine, accepted the view that the book of Daniel was written later than 200 B.C.E. although the book itself purports to have been written over 300 years earlier. At about 500 C.E. Jewish scholars were having doubts about the Mosaic authorship of the Torah because certain expressions in it obviously came from periods well after the death of Moses. In the 11th century Isaac ibn Yashush, court physician to a Muslim ruler in Spain, pointed out that the list of Edomite kings in Genesis 36 included kings who lived long after Moses had died. Though he was a devout Orthodox Jew, Ibn Yashush's contemporary, Abraham ben Meir Ibn Ezra (1092-1167), a scholar and poet from Moslem Spain, also had some doubts about certain passages in the Torah. Despite having castigated Ibn Yashush and saying that his book should be burned, Ibn Ezra suspected that the Book of Isaiah was actually the work of two different authors.

With the invention of the printing press access to the Bible, and with it biblical criticism, increased. Andreas Karlstadt (1480-1541), Protestant reformer and close ally of Martin Luther, noted in 1520 that since the death of Moses takes place near the end of Deuteronomy (Deut. 34:5). the verses from 34:6 through 34:10 had to have been written by someone else. However, he also noted that there was no change in the style in those last verses. Since it appeared that the verses before and after Moses's death were by the same author, Karlstadt reasoned that the author of Deuteronomy could not be

Moses. Catholic scholars of the period also found problems with the Mosaic authorship of the Pentateuch. In his commentary on the book of Joshua (1574), Andreas Du Maes (1514-1575) conjectured that the Pentateuch was actually compiled by Ezra, who he assumed had edited ancient documents, including those written by Moses. Du Maes noted that the cities of Dan and Hebron were referred to by those names in Genesis, even though they were not given their names until after Moses's death. Previously they were known as Laish and Kirjah-arba, respectively. The conquest and renaming of Laish by the Danites is described in Judges 18. The Church did not take kindly to what Du Maes had to say and placed his book on the Catholic Index of Prohibited Books

The Jewish Dutch philosopher Baruch Spinoza (1632-1677) published a thorough critical analysis of the Torah showing that it simply could not have been written by Moses. Having already been excommunicated from Judaism, Spinoza now found his work condemned by Protestants and Catholics as well, the latter placing it in the Index of Prohibited Books. In addition, an attempt was made on his life. Writing to refute Spinoza, Catholic priest Richard Simon (1638-1712) stated that the Pentateuch was compiled from several documents, some inspired and some of purely human origin. His contemporary Jean Le Clerc (1657-1736) believed that the author of the Pentateuch lived in Babylonia during the exile.

Though these persistent suspicions stretch clear back to the beginnings of the middle ages, it was not until the 18th century that the first Documentary Hypothesis came into being. French physician Jean Astruc (1684-1766) noticed not only that there were often two different versions of incidents in the Pentateuch (i.e. two creation stories, two versions of how many animals of each kind were taken on Noah's ark, etc.) but that God was referred to in different verses as either Yahweh or Elohim. He also noted that the Yahweh and Elohim verses tended to occur in clusters in which one or the other name predominated. Separating the Yahweh (J) material and the Elohim (E) material into different strands, he noticed that each strand made a fairly coherent story and reasoned that Moses had compiled the Pentateuch from two or more traditions. Though most scholars now agree that the J and E documents were written well after the time of Moses, Astruc did come up with the basic idea of the Documentary Hypothesis. Independent of Astruc, J. G. Eichhorn of Leipzig came up with a similar hypothesis in 1785.

In 1800 an English Catholic priest named Alexander Geddes came up with the Fragment Hypothesis. He believed that the Pentateuch was made up of a great number of fragmentary documents compiled at the time of Solomon. Like Astruc and Eichhorn, he argued that there were two basic circles of authors from which the fragmentary documents were drawn. These circles referred to God as Yahweh and Elohim respectively. Writing in 1805, J. S. Vater, in a three volume commentary on the Pentateuch, gave the opinion that it was not finished until the period of the Exile. Other scholars of the first half of the nineteenth century, such as W. M. L. De Wette and F. Bleek, elaborated certain variations on the origin of the Pentateuch. Though Bleek felt that Moses was the author of some of the chapters, he believed that there had been two major redactions of the original work, one during the time of Solomon and one just before the Exile.

In 1853 H. Hupfeld came up with the first version of the Documentary Hypothesis in which he postulated two E sources and one J source. Hupfeld's work was followed and expanded on by A. Dillman and Franz Delitzsch. In 1866, K. H. Graf demonstrated among other things that the book of Leviticus was a later work than the material in Samuel and Kings. His work was elaborated upon by J. Wellhausen between 1876 and 1884. By the end of the 19th century, most scholars had accepted what was called the "Graf Wellhausen" theory of the origins of the Pentateuch, which I summarized earlier. Thus, we see that from the 1500's on there was increasing critical study of Bible, resulting eventually in the Documentary Hypothesis. The fundamentalist claim that it and similar biblical criticism are a recent invention simply is not true. Nor was it the growth of materialism that led to critical analysis of the Bible. It was the printing press and greater access to the Bible itself—the same thing that gave impetus to the Protestant Reformation—that sparked the analysis and critique of the Bible.

Another source of biblical criticism was increasing freedom of thought. When Richard Simon wrote in 1678 that he thought that some of the material upon which the Pentateuch was based was not divinely inspired, it cost him his position as priest in the Congregation of the Oratory and, as with Du Maes and Spinoza, his work was placed on the Index of Prohibited Books. All but six of the 1300 copies of his book were burned. The work was also attacked by Protestants, and when an English translation of it was published, the translator, John Hampden, was imprisoned in the Tower of London until 1688, when he recanted any views held in common with Simon. Even in 1753, Astruc was careful to submit his thesis as a suggestion subject to the approval of the church. Thus, it was only the increasing freedom from religious censure following the Enlightenment that made it possible for the critics of the 19th and 20th centuries to fully develop biblical criticism.

To understand how it is that modern scholars determine the date and authorship of various biblical narratives, let's explore how their techniques are applied to a more neutral subject. Both the *Iliad* and the *Odyssey* are attributed to Homer, as at one time were the so-called Homeric hymns. The two epics describe mythic versions of events that took place *circa* 1200 B.C.E., during the Mycenaean period. Did Homer write during that period or much later? And how do we know, given that the original manuscripts have been lost, when the epics were originally written?

First let us consider the style of writing. There is a unity of meter in both the *Iliad* and the *Odyssey*. By contrast, the supposedly "Homeric" hymns do not have a similar meter, even though there are invocations of the gods in both epics that could be viewed as hymns. Thus the difference in meter and style cannot be attributed to a deliberate use of a separate mode to suit a different purpose. Similar poetic images and phrases occur in the two epics as well. Children are always "innocent"; women are "deep-girdled" and bronze is "sharp and pitiless." Words are "winged" or go through the barrier of the teeth. Ships are "hollow" and they sail on a "wine-dark sea." When telling of a warrior's death in battle, similar descriptions, such as "he fell thunderously," are used in both epics. Thus, if the two epics were not written by the same author, they were written by two poets of the same school.

Homer's descriptions of the world include certain anachronisms that indicate that he wrote at a much later time than the period of the Trojan War (ca. 1200 B.C.E.) For example, he speaks of Dorian Greeks in Crete. Since the Dorians did not penetrate to Crete until between 1100 and 1000 B.C.E. the epics could not have been written at the time of the War itself. Idiosyncrasies in the grammar and spelling also give clues to the date of composition. As the *Encyclopaedia Britannica* points out:

> Certain elements of the poetic language, which was an artificial amalgam never exactly reproduced in speech indicate that the epics were not only post-Mycenaean in composition but also substantially later than the foundation of

the first Ionian settlements in Asia Minor of about 1000 B.C.E. The running
together of adjacent short vowels and the disappearance of the semi-vowel
digramma (a letter formerly existing in the Greek alphabet) are the most significant indications of this. (Encyclopaedia Britannica 1995 Macropaedia vol.
20, p. 636)

Since this critique does not involve anyone's religious material, we do not
hear any howls of outrage about "destructive higher critics" or "liberal theologians" from fundamentalists. Yet the very same methods used to date Homer,
to verify the shared authorship of the *Iliad* and the *Odyssey* and to invalidate
the Homeric Hymns are what modern Bible critics use to separate the threads
of the source documents of the Torah, to judge the different authorship and
dates of the first and second parts of Isaiah, and to date Daniel some 300 years
later than it purports to have been written—in short all of the things that have
so upset fundamentalists. Just as Homer's referring to Dorian Greeks in Crete
shows that he wrote after 1000 B.C.E., so the description of Abraham's home
city in Genesis 15:7 as "Ur of the Chaldeans" betrays an authorship far later
than Moses, since the Chaldeans did not conquer Ur, originally a Sumerian
city, until some time between the 10th and 7th centuries B.C.E. In fact the reference to the Chaldeans implies not only that the verse was written after 800
B.C.E. but that it dates from the time of the Exile (587-538 B.C.E.). Other
anachronisms include Philistines living in Canaan in the time of Abraham
(Genesis 21: 32, 34) and Isaac (Genesis 26: 1, 8, 14, 15, 18), while history tells
us that they invaded Canaan from the sea during the period of the Judges, well
after the time of the Patriarchs.

It is also the same type of scholarship that tells us that the early Christian
work *The Apocalypse of Peter* was probably written in the second century,
hence was not written by the apostle Peter, as it claims to be. Since this work is
not considered canonical, fundamentalists do not object to its dating. Yet, since
the second epistle of Peter is canonical, fundamentalists reject the scholarship
that says that it, like the *Apocalypse* is probably from the second century and
not written by the apostle Peter. Biblical criticism is not always destructive,
however. In his introduction to the first epistle of Peter, Bruce M. Metzger,
New Testament Editor of the Oxford Annotated Bible, supports the Petrine
authorship of the epistle and points out that it was likely to have been written
in Rome at the time of Nero's persecutions in C.E. 64.

The Nevi'im

The Nevi'im or Prophets is divided between the early prophets, which includes the history of the kingdoms of Israel and Judah (Joshua, Judges, 1 and 2 Samuel, 1 and 2 Kings), and the later prophets, which are themselves subdivided between the major prophets (Isaiah, Jeremiah, Ezekiel) and the minor prophets (Hosea, Joel, Amos, Obadiah, Jonah, Micah, Nahum, Habakkuk, Zephaniah, Haggai, Zechariah, Malachi). As I said earlier, the Deuteronomists appear to have compiled the books of the the Nevi'im that related to the history of the nations of Israel and Judah. One of the documents they used in the compilation was the original form of the Books of Samuel (originally one book), possibly written at the court of Solomon, or possibly by the high priest Abiathar and, appropriately enough, referred to as the Early Source. This was coupled with the Late Source, thought to have been written between 750 and 650 B.C.E.

That there were different, sometimes mutually contradictory source materials for the books of Samuel can be seen by examining the story of David and Goliath. This will also give us insight into why biblical scholars have separated the J and E material of the Torah into separate stories. Since most of us do not read Hebrew, we cannot tell which verses refer to God as Yahweh and which refer to him as Elohim. But all we need is an English translation to see that there are two stories of how David met King Saul and became a hero by killing Goliath. We first hear of Saul and David meeting when the king is looking for a musician who can soothe his fits. One of his men tells him (1 Sam. 16:18): "Behold, I have seen a son of Jesse the Bethlehemite, who is skillful in playing, a man of valor, a man of war, prudent in speech and a man of good presence; and the Lord is with him." Here David seems to have already made himself a reputation as a warrior and has considerable sophistication. David is sent for, enters Saul's service and becomes his armor bearer, a position of some honor, and Saul sends to Jesse requesting that David remain in his service (I Sam. 16:21-22). However, the next mention of David (1 Sam. 17:12) introduces him as though he had not been mentioned before, telling us that he was the son of Jesse of Bethlehem, who had eight sons. We are then told that three of Jesse's sons, Eliab, Abinadab, and Shammah, have followed Saul into battle, but that David went back and forth from Saul's camp facing the Philistines to tending his father's sheep (1 Sam. 17:13-15). Jesse dispatches David with food for his brothers and their commander (vs. 17). David greets his brothers, hears Goliath give his daily challenge, asks what will be done for whoever kills the Philistine champion and is told that Saul will give his daughter and riches to whoever kills Goliath. This provokes his brother Eliab (1 Sam. 17:28-30):

> Now Eliab his eldest brother heard when he spoke to the men; and Eliab's anger was kindled against David, and he said, "Why have you come down? And with whom have you left those few sheep in the wilderness? I know your presumption and the evil of your heart; for you have come down to see the battle." And David said, "What have I done now? Was it not but a word?" And he turned away from him toward another, and spoke the same way; and the people answered him as before.

Here David is clearly unfamiliar with what Saul has said concerning Goliath. Further, his eldest brother does not seem to know that David is Saul's armor bearer. From Eliab's words it would seem that David is a rather spoiled little brother who really ought to be back home tending the sheep. David's response of "What have I done now?" also smacks of chronic, petty sibling rivalry. This is not the king's armor bearer, known as a man of valor and prudent in speech, talking. This is an upstart shepherd boy. Following Eliab's rebuke, verse 31 says that Saul has heard that David is asking about the reward for killing Goliath, and sends for him. This seems a bit unlikely. If David is his armor bearer, he would not be running around the camp pestering the soldiers about what the reward would be for killing Goliath, something he would already know, after all. If he's just a shepherd boy, Saul would not take notice of him.

Starting with 1 Sam. 17:32 David again appears sophisticated and able. He boldly tells Saul that he has killed lions and bears, so why should he fear this Philistine? Saul is impressed enough to lend David his armor (vs. 38), but David declines using it because he is not used to the feel of it. David kills Goliath, taking the head to Jerusalem, but keeping Goliath's armor in his tent (vs. 54). Then, starting with the very next verse, Saul does not seem to know who David is. Neither does Saul's general, Abner (1 Sam. 17:55-58):

> When Saul saw David go forth against the Philistine, he said to Abner, the commander of the army, "Abner, whose son is this youth?" And Abner said, "As your soul lives, O king, I cannot tell." And the king said, "Inquire whose son this

stripling is." And as David returned from the slaughter of the Philistine, Abner took him and brought him before Saul with the head of the Philistine his hand. And Saul said to him, "Whose son are you, young man?" And David answered, "I am the Son of your servant Jesse the Bethlehemite."

After that we are told (1 Sam. 18:2): "And Saul took him that day, and would not let him return to his father's house." Yet Saul had already taken David into his service and had told Jesse that he wanted him to stay at court. Clearly, we have two stories here with only a minimal attempt made to bridge them (1 Sam. 17:31). If we separate these two strands, just as Astruc did with the J and E material, we get the two following coherent stories:

Story A

1) David is summoned to Saul's court because of his reputation as a warrior and musician. He is already known as someone who knows how to act at court (1 Sam. 16:18-20).

2) David lives up to his reputation and advances to the position of Saul's armor bearer. Saul tells Jesse he wants David to stay at the court (1 Sam. 16:21-23).

3) Upon hearing the challenge of Goliath, David assures Saul that he can kill the Philistine. Saul sends him out as the champion of Israel, even offering David his armor. David refuses the armor because he is not used to wearing it (1 Sam. 17:32-39).

4) After killing Goliath, David bears his head to Jerusalem, but keeps the Philistine's armor in his tent (1 Sam. 17:54).

Story B

1) David, Jesse's youngest son, is tending his father's sheep. Jesse sends him down to Saul's camp with provisions for his older brothers, who are in Saul's army (1 Sam. 17:12-23).

2) Upon hearing Goliath's challenge, David asks what the reward will be for the one who kills Goliath. The soldiers tell him that Saul will give the man riches and his daughter in marriage. David's oldest brother, Eliab, gets mad at David for his presumption and accuses him of neglecting the sheep so he could come down to see the battle (1 Sam. 17:24-30).

3) After this unknown shepherd boy has killed Goliath, King Saul asks his

general, Abner, who this stripling is. Abner does not know. On the king's orders he brings David, still carrying Goliath's head, to Saul. David tells Saul he is the son of Jesse the Bethlehemite (1 Sam. 17:55-58).

4) Saul takes David into his service (1 Sam. 18:1-2).

Considering that it does not take a Ph.D. to see the inconsistencies of David being Saul's armor bearer one minute and a total stranger to the king the next, how can fundamentalists still say that each book of the Bible was a single inspired message, rather than a compilation of sometimes contradictory legends? Gleason Archer tries to make Saul's question, "Whose son are you?" into something rhetorical, since Saul was amazed at David's prowess. Previously all he had seen was his artistic side. But the first report Saul had of David from the young men of his court, in 1 Sam. 16:18, was that David was, "a man of valor, a man of war." Besides that we have so many inconsistencies between what are obviously two separate accounts. Thus, despite Archer's impressive credentials, including a degree in divinity from Princeton Theological Seminary and a Ph.D. from Harvard Graduate School, his argument is sheer sophistry, as is the fundamentalist denial of the Documentary Hypothesis. As to the books of Samuel, what I called "Story A" is considered part of the Early Source, while "Story B" is from the Late Source.

After the death of Solomon circa 920 B.C.E., the two kingdoms set down kingly chronicles, referred to as the Chronicles of the Kings of Israel and Chronicles of the Kings of Judah. These chronicles, alluded to in 1 and 2 Kings, were lost, but served as source material for those books. They are not to be confused with the Books of Chronicles now in the Bible.

Both Joshua and Judges, though they disagree on many points concerning the conquest of Canaan, appear to have been written by the Deuteronomists. Judges, seemingly only a collection of folk tales about the early leaders of the children of Israel, follows the theology of the prophets and Deuteronomists. Most stories begin with foreigners oppressing the Hebrews, because of their apostasy. They repent, and God raises up the necessary deliverer.

Of the later prophets, Jeremiah is probably the most free of later tampering, since the prophet dictated the work to his devoted scribe, Baruch. Nevertheless, the last chapter of 2 Kings, describing the kind treatment of Jehoiachin, Judah's erstwhile king, by the Chaldean ruler Amel-Marduk (Evilmerodach in the Bible), has been tacked on to the end of Jeremiah. Since by biblical chronology this happened 37 years after the fall of Jerusalem, that is in 541 B.C.E., and since it probably was not written down and edited until well after that date, it is graphic evidence of later tampering. Chapters from 2 Kings were also added to 1st Isaiah. Thus, speculations that prophecies were inserted into these books are based on solid evidence of later tampering, rather than vain hopes of avoiding the implications of divine authorship, as fundamentalists claim. I will go into the origins of the prophetic books and their historical context in the next chapter. For now, let us consider the later books of the Bible and the problems of canonization.

The Kethuvim and the Strictures of Canonization

The Kethuvim, or Writings, consist of Psalms, Proverbs, Song of Solomon, Lamentations, Ecclesiastes, Ruth, Esther, Job, Daniel, Ezra, Nehemiah and 1-2 Chronicles. If all the narrative books of the Christian canon had been written down at the time of the history they purport to record, we would expect the Book of Ruth to be part of the Nevi'im and that it would fit in the Jewish canon where it does in the Christian Bible, between Judges and 1 Samuel. Also, if all books purporting to be prophecy were originally conceived of as prophetic by the Jews, we would expect the Book of Daniel to be grouped with the major prophets, as it is in the Christian canon. Yet both Ruth and Daniel are grouped among the Writings. Clearly, the Jews did not originally consider apocalyptic literature such as Daniel to be the same thing as prophecy and they clearly did not accord Ruth the historical validity they accorded to the early parts of the Nevi'im.

After the return of the Jews from exile in the years following 538 B.C.E., the leaders of the priestly class struggled to keep the worship pure and to keep the Jewish nation from mixing with other peoples. When the Assyrians had carried the population of the northern kingdom off into exile and eventual oblivion, they had also transported strangers into the depopulated area. These new inhabitants feared that if they did not worship the god of their new land, he would harm them. Thus, they ended up practicing an impure form of Judaism (2 Kings 17:24-41). Since the province was now named for its capital, Samaria, these people came to be known as the Samaritans. During the Babylonian captivity, they had also moved into Judah along with other peoples. The returning Jews refused to acknowledge the Samaritans as co-religionists and barred them from helping to rebuild the Temple. For their part, the Samaritans, and other "peoples of the land" responded by trying to hamper the resettlement of the Jews.

A large work written in this time included a rewrite of the Books of Kings as well as a history of the rebuilding of the Temple under priestly leaders such as Ezra and Nehemiah. The author of this work is referred to as "the Chronicler," and the work itself was eventually divided up into the two Books of Chronicles and the Books of Ezra and Nehemiah. It is interesting at this point to reflect on Gleason Archer's assertion that God kept the human authors of the various books of the Bible from error, since it would appear that the Chronicler did not think that the authors of the books of Samuel and Kings had been so inspired. For example, 1 Samuel 17 tells how David killed Goliath of Gath. But 2 Sam. 21:19 says that one of David's captains, Elhanan, slew Goliath during a later war with the Philistines. The verse makes it clear that this Goliath is the giant by comparing his spear shaft to a weaver's beam. Faced with this inconsistency, the Chronicler amended Elhanan's deed. Thus 1 Chronicles 20:5 says that Elhanan slew Goliath's brother, Lahmi. Archer claims that the Chronicler rectified an error in 2 Samuel by substituting Lahmi for Goliath and invents a whole series of events to show how this happened. Arguing that the earlier manuscript the copyist for 2 Samuel was working from had been blurred or damaged, he reconstructs a three-step error by which the copyist first mistakes a "t" appearing just before "Lahmi" as "b-t," hence "beth." Therefore, Lahmi is added to it to get "Bethlehemite," referring to Elhanan. The error-prone copyist then makes two other mistakes. However, the Chronicler managed to repair the error or found a better manuscript from which he made his own copy. A number of objections to Archer's explanation come immediately to mind. First of all, in constructing this scenario Archer is using a method that he would scoff at were it used by advocates of the Documentary Hypothesis. Second, there is no particular reason to favor his scenario over a more simple and direct one of a later writer trying to resolve an inconsistency. Third, this whole reconstruction of a copyist's error directly contradicts his original assertion that God kept the authors of the books, and by logical extension the editors of the canon, from error. To accept Archer's tale of the erring copyist, we have to believe that God protected the authors and editors of the Bible from error, but overlooked the copyists.

In any case, this is not the only time Chronicles clashes with earlier books.

For example, in 2 Kings 16, Ahaz, king of Judah, makes himself the vassal of Tiglath-pileser III of Assyria in order to enlist his help against Israel and Syria, which are warring on Judah. When Ahaz appeals for help, the Assyrians do come to his aid, and Tiglath-pileser takes Damascus. However, 2 Kings is very clear that Ahaz "did what was evil in the eyes of the Lord," including offering his own son as a burnt offering, presumably to Moloch. Apparently the Chronicler could not let God allow an evil king to prosper. Thus 2 Chronicles 28:20 says: "So Tiglath-pileser king of Assyria came against him [Ahaz] instead of strengthening him." This is not only at variance with 2 Kings, it is at odds with history as well. Tiglath-pileser never attacked Judah.

The harsh codes of the priestly community epitomized by the Chronicler, which included exclusion of Jews of mixed ancestry, and tended toward the view of earthly rewards and punishments based on the level of holiness in one's life, seem to have provoked a number of writings which had elements of protest. Notable among these were, according to some scholars, the Books of Job, Ruth, and Jonah. The Book of Job addressed the smug assumption of earthly rewards and punishments as part of its examination of the reason for evil and suffering. The exclusion of people of mixed ancestry was addressed by the Book of Ruth, which made the point that King David would have been excluded from the community for being the descendant of a Moabite woman. Both Ruth and Job were based on older legendary material. Jonah, while using the name of an obscure prophet attached to the court of the northern kingdom, is a wholly post-exilic creation aimed at pointing out God's love for all peoples, even the hated Assyrians.

Other books added to the canon after the exile were the wisdom literature, such as Ecclesiastes and Proverbs, and poetry, such as the Song of Songs, Lamentations and more of the Psalms. Many of these were attributed to David and Solomon to establish their canonical validity, but were written between 200 and 300 B.C.E. As with Job and Ruth, some of this material is based on ancient texts. According to Herbert May, Old Testament editor of the Oxford Annotated Bible (OAB), the third section of Proverbs seems to he modeled on "The Instruction of Amen-em-ope," an Egyptian book of wisdom dating from before 1000 B.C.E. Esther, Second Isaiah, Daniel, the later prophets, and certain bridging material from various redactors round out additions to the Old Testament from this time.

It was in the post-exilic period that the Jewish Bible was put into its canonical form, and this process involved rigorous editing and re-editing, a fact seemingly not recognized by fundamentalists. Hank Hanegraaf, Walter Martin's successor at CRI, often makes the following argument concerning the divine inspiration of the Bible (this is a general paraphrase of Hanegraaf's argument often made on the *Bible Answerman* Show):

> Here's how you prove that the Bible was divine rather than human in origin. You can prove it through the science of statistical probability. Here you have forty different authors writing over sixteen hundred years, on three continents, in three languages, on hundreds of different subjects, yet with complete agreement. How is that possible unless God inspired them?

As I have already shown, there are numerous inconsistencies, even within the individual books of the Old Testament, and these constitute a mere sampling. Thus, there is hardly the complete agreement Hanegraaf claims. I should point out, lest I be accused of a personal attack, that other fundamentalists use this same argument as well, including Dr. James Dobson (*Focus on the Family*, April 5, 1993).

The idea that the Bible was written on three continents is pure sophistry. Technically, if one either assumes the Mosaic authorship of Exodus or accepts the tradition that the gospel of Matthew was written in Alexandria, one could say that the Bible was indeed written in Africa (i.e. Egypt), Asia and Europe. However, the grand sweeping phrase "on three continents" implies writers separated by vast distances and diverse cultures miraculously coming up with a unified body of work. In reality, most of the Bible was written in Israel and Judah. Significant additions were made in Mesopotamia during the exile. Only if one accepts the inerrantist view that Moses wrote at least part of Exodus in Egypt can we consider Africa as a source of the Old Testament, unless we include some of the editing that was done in Alexandria to produce the Septuagint. In any case, the distance from Jerusalem to the Nile Delta is hardly continental in scale. Europe can only be included as a source of the New Testament, mainly for the Pauline epistles. Thus, the Bible was written within an area encompassed on the west by the city of Rome, on the south by the city of Alexandria, on the east by the city of Babylon and on the North by the city of Philippi on the Aegean Sea. In short, even allowing for the broadest interpretations, it was written in a contiguous area of the eastern Mediterranean and Mesopotamia, an area roughly equivalent in size to western Europe. Most of the Bible was, of course, written in Palestine, an area roughly equivalent in size to the Netherlands.

The argument that the Bible was written over a period of 1600 years by many different authors likewise implies miraculous agreement by disparate sources and cultures. However, only if what the authors had written had been sacrosanct from the moment the ink was dry and only if they had not had access to the tradition of earlier books would there be anything miraculous about their general agreement and unity of theme. And, of course, the unity of thought was effectively enforced by later redaction and canonical exclusion.

The Torah seems to have been canonized by about 400 B.C.E., the Nevi'im by about 200 B.C.E. and the Kethuvim by about 90 B.C.E. However, even with these attempts to formalize the Tanakh the canon was not in its final form until after the time of Jesus. For example, the Masoretic text, in which vowels were added to the Hebrew and final clarifications were made as to divisions between words, was not completed until between 600 and 900 C.E. As evidence of this, consider the differences between the final canon and the Septuagint. Following the death of Alexander the Great a number of Jews were induced to settle in Alexandria. More followed when the tolerant Ptolemies lost Palestine to the Seleucids, who were dedicated Hellenizers. After a time, the Jews in Alexandria ceased speaking Aramaic, which had succeeded Hebrew as the language of the Jews. Thus, the Jewish scriptures were translated from Hebrew and Aramaic into Greek, supposedly under the editorship of 70 elders, hence referred to as the Septuagint (L. *septuaginta* seventy). In this translation a number of books were included that were later excluded from the final canon. Notable among these are first and second Maccabees, Judith, and additions to the book of Daniel (Susanna, Bel and Dragon, the Prayer of Azariah, and the Song of the Three Young Men). These books among others are now relegated to the *Apocrypha*. However, since most of the Gentile converts of the early Christian church spoke Greek, the Septuagint was their Bible. When Jerome compiled the Vulgate toward the end of the 4th century, he used both the Hebrew canon and the Septuagint as sources for the Old Testament. Thus these books were included in the Catholic canon, but excluded from the Protestant canon. In part, their exclusion was based on a return to the original Hebrew canon. But at least part of the reason for excluding Maccabees was that it includes an incident where the Jews pray for the souls of the dead. To the Protestant reformers, this smacked too much of the doctrine of praying for the souls in Purgatory that resulted in the selling of indulgences. This was, after all, the flash point that ignited the Protestant Reformation. Considering not only this point, but the fact that Esther, which is part of the Protestant, Catholic and Jewish canons, is as fictional as Judith, which is excluded from the Protestant and Jewish canons, we are led to the question of who decides what is canonical and why.

New Testament Formation and Canonization

The earliest manuscript evidence for any of the gospels is the Rylands fragment, which, though it is a mere 2 1/2 by 3 1/2 inch piece of papyrus, establishes the Gospel of John as having been written within a century of the time of Jesus. On this papyrus, discovered in Egypt in the 1920s, but not effectively studied until 1934, is written the Greek text of John 18: 37-38:

> Pilate said to him, "So you are a king?" Jesus answered, "You say that I am a king. For this I was born, and for this I have come into the world, to bear witness to the truth. Every one who is of the truth hears my voice." Pilate said to him, "What is truth?" After he had said this, he went out to the Jews and told them, "I find no crime in him...."

The fragment can be dated by the style of lettering as having been written between 100 and 125 C.E. Since the fragment was originally found in Egypt, and since the gospel of John was thought to have been originally written in Ephesus, it is a fair assumption that it was originally written around C.E. 90. Thus, the same modern Bible scholarship, so abhorred by fundamentalists when it shows that parts of the Pentateuch could not have been written by Moses, proves that at least one of the gospels was written at a date much earlier than previously assumed in the 19th century by the higher critics of the University of Tübingen. Another assumption of Bible scholars has always been that the other three gospels, called the synoptic gospels, were written earlier than that of John. If this is true, then the gospel of Mark may have been written at about the time of the destruction of the Temple at Jerusalem in 70 C.E., with the gospels of Luke and Matthew being written about a decade later.

While the gospels were all probably written within the first century C.E., they were all probably written by people who were not eyewitnesses to the life of Jesus. For example, Mark was supposedly a sort of secretary to the apostle

Peter. But it is unlikely that any such office existed among Jesus' disciples. Thus Mark would have written the gospel under Peter's direction in Rome. He displays a considerable ignorance of the geography of Galilee and the surrounding areas. For example, in Mark 7 Jesus and the disciples go from Tyre through Sidon to the sea of Galilee, a rather odd route, considering that Sidon is north of Tyre and the Sea of Galilee is southeast of the city. Furthermore, in the time of Jesus there was no road from Sidon to the the Sea of Galilee, only one from Tyre. Also, Mark 5 refers to the eastern shore of the sea as being in the country of the Gerasenes. The city of Gerasa (now called Jerash) is actually over 30 miles to the southeast of the sea. In Mark 10:12 Jesus says, "...and if she divorces her husband and marries another, she commits adultery." Yet under Jewish law a woman had no right to divorce her husband. Jesus, since he was addressing a Jewish audience, would not have used those words. On the other hand, Roman women did have the right to divorce their husbands. Thus, it would seem as though the author of Mark had no compunction about altering the words of Jesus to fit a Gentile audience. While this change is minor it, along with the faulty geography, indicates two things. First, the writer was not an eyewitness. Second, gospel authors saw nothing wrong with altering the words of Jesus, gained second-hand at best. It is quite possible then that, though the basic message of the gospels remained true to the teachings of Jesus, very human errors and idiosyncrasies crept into the specifics of the text. Thus, basing an entire doctrine on one gospel statement is a risky and error-prone practice.

The gospels of Mark, Matthew, and Luke are referred to as "synoptic," a word coined in 1774 by German scholar Johann Griesbach from Greek words meaning "seen together" (because they would seem to be variants of the same text and are often studied by what is called the parallel passage technique). The gospel of John, however, omits many of the incidents reported in the synoptic gospels. Had the synoptic gospels been written independently of each other, we would not expect as much material in common as they actually possess. Among the reasons for considering Mark to be the source of the common material are the following: Mark contains little that is not in the other two synoptics. When Matthew disagrees with Mark in sequence of events, Luke is closer to Mark, and when Luke disagrees with Mark, Matthew and Mark are closer to each other. Further, Matthew and Luke never agree on a sequence in opposition to Mark. Also the Greek of Luke and Acts, which was written by

Luke, is far more polished than that of Mark, indicating someone who was a Greek as opposed to an Aramaic-speaking Jew writing in a second language. As such, Luke not only was not an eyewitness, but would likely have borrowed much of his material from an earlier source. In fact, Luke says as much at the beginning of his gospel. In the 1920s and 1930s Canon Burnett Streeter of Queen's College, Oxford and, following him, Professor Charles Dodd developed, based on these and other observations, a kind of Documentary Hypothesis of the Gospels. Since there is material common to Luke and Matthew that is not in Mark, Streeter hypothesized a source document for this material, which he called "Q" from the German word *Quelle*, meaning source. Mark seems to have been combined with Q and two other sources, one called "M" for material only found in Matthew and one called "L" for material only found in Luke (see Mack, 1993.)

Of course, fundamentalists scoff at such ideas as lost source gospels. However, there are lost books referred to in the Pauline epistles, such as his letter to Laodicea, and other letters to the Corinthians than are recorded in the New Testament. Here we have a problem. Anything from the hand of Paul would likely have been considered inspired had it survived. Inerrantists are particularly adamant that every line Paul wrote was indeed inspired. That Paul referred to these epistles means that he attested to their existence. In fact, in Colossians 4:16 Paul urges the Colossians have the letter he wrote to them read to the church in Laodicea and to read his letter from Laodicea in their church, indicating that the Laodicean letter was as inspired as Colossians. Yet it was lost. Thus it is not surprising that some Christian scholars interpret the letter in question to be the epistle to the Ephesians. Otherwise they would have to answer this question: How could God allow anything inspired to be lost?

Concerning the Pauline epistles, modern scholars, by comparing the style and content of the letters, have divided them into those thought to be genuinely written by Paul and those written by later followers and attributed to Paul. These latter are called deutero-pauline letters. While there is some variance of opinion as to how many of the Pauline epistles fall into the second category, there is general agreement that 1 and 2 Timothy and Titus were deutero-pauline. Again, fundamentalists scoff at such scholarship. However, in the King James version of the Bible, the epistle to the Hebrews is attributed to Paul. Yet even fundamentalists today agree that Hebrews was written by a separate, anonymous author. Furthermore, the same scholarship that says that

Titus and the letters to Timothy were not written by Paul also says, as I mentioned earlier, that 1 Peter was probably authored at least indirectly by the apostle. Modern scholars also affirm that the three letters attributed to John were indeed the work of the author of the gospel of John.

During the early years of the Christian church it is likely that each Christian community had its own gospel. Excluding such heterodox material as the Gnostic Gospel of Thomas there was a Gospel of the Hebrews, mentioned by both Origen and Jerome, a Gospel of the Egyptians mentioned by Clement of Alexandria, and a Gospel of the Ebionites, a group condemned in the fourth century as heretics for not accepting the divinity of Jesus. In addition, there were a number of apocalyptic works. Besides the canonical Apocalypse of John (Revelation) and the already mentioned Apocalypse of Peter, there was an Apocalypse of Paul. It was not until the Council of Nicaea, convened in 325 by the Emperor Constantine, that basic Christian doctrine was formulated, which finally dictated which gospels, epistles and apocalypses would be accepted and which rejected in the official canon.

Those holding to inerrancy have been extremely critical and even derisive of the seminar of biblical scholars that has been deciding, by vote, which statements attributed to Jesus in the gospels are valid and which are not. This does seem a rather odd way to resolve divergent views, each of which is probably supported by considerable evidence and scholarship. However, the various church councils that decided which books were to be accepted into or excluded from the canon were, in essence, doing the same thing. In fact the trinitarian view, which triumphed over the Arian concept that Jesus was merely a man, was made Christian dogma by the judgment of Constantine, a man barely Christian in his beliefs.

In spite of their eventual exclusion from the canon a number of the Christian apocryphal works continued to be considered semi-authoritative. Writing in the January 11, 1993, issue of *Christianity Today,* Michael Gorman, a Ph.D. in New Testament studies, uses three of the excluded works, the *Didache,* the *Epistle of Barnabas,* and the *Apocalypse of Peter* to demonstrate that the early Christian church held strong views condemning abortion, even though the canonical books of the New Testament do not mention it. This is somewhat curious. As a Methodist, Gorman is part of a body that excludes 1 Maccabees from the canon, even though its historical content is generally considered valid and its message inspiring. Thus, according to the Protestant view, no matter how authoritative its history might be, 1 Maccabees could not be used for teaching church doctrine unless the doctrine found in it was also found in a canonical work. Yet Gorman is willing to use three books excluded from both the Catholic and Protestant canons to argue that opposition to abortion is basic to Christian doctrine, in spite of the fact that abortion is not mentioned in the New Testament canon. While I do not doubt that the early Christian church opposed abortion, the use of non-canonical books to bolster Christian doctrine blurs the distinction between what is and what is not part of the canon. (Although abortion is not the concern of this book, the *Apocalypse of Peter* not only has women who had abortions suffering in hell, it also includes disobedient slaves among the damned.) Given that inclusion of books into or rejection from the canon is a human affair, involving politics and passions, and given that these factors have been motivating those involved in the process since the time of King Solomon, inerrancy seems patently untenable.

2

HOW TO THINK ABOUT THE BIBLE

An Introduction to the Prophetic Books

IN THIS CHAPTER WE WILL EXPLORE THE NATURE OF THE PROPHETS, their function in ancient Jewish society and the historical context of their prophecies. We will also consider the differences between concrete prophecies and apocalyptic passages.

The Nature and Function of the Prophets

The Prophetic movement seems to have originated from ecstatic oracular holy men who went into a trance and prophesied, possibly in a way similar to those who spoke in tongues in the early Christian church. Two parallel stories in 1 Samuel concerning the origin of a saying, "Is Saul also among the prophets?", highlight this aspect of prophesying. In 1 Sam. 10:9-13, Saul, whom Samuel has just anointed king, meets a band of prophets playing tambourines, flutes and lyres, and "the spirit of God came mightily upon him, and he prophesied among them" (1 Sam. 10:10). Later, when Saul is pursuing David, his messengers find Samuel with a band of prophets, prophesying, and are so overcome by the spirit that they join in. Saul sends other messengers, and they too fall into a prophetic trance. Finally, Saul himself comes, only to be overcome by the divine influence along with the others: "And he too stripped off his clothes, and he prophesied before Samuel and lay naked all that day and all that night" (1 Sam. 19:24). This type of behavior is found again in 2 Sam. 6:14 when David, wearing only a linen ephod (a sort of apron covering only the front of the body), dances ecstatically before the Ark of the Covenant. The image of the prophets most of us have have from Bible stories is one of stern, puritanical patriarchs calling down the wrath of God on the wicked. The idea of prophets as roving bands of ecstatics playing music, falling into trances and running about naked sounds more like the followers of Dionysus than those of Yahweh. I suspect that it is rather a disturbing image for modern American Christians in general and for fundamentalists in particular. The closest thing to it in our day are the charismatics, such as Pentecostals who, transported by the spirit, speak in tongues and collapse "slain in the spirit." Some of the more extreme charismatics may indulge in handling poisonous snakes, but none that I know of go naked.

As a tacit example of just how disturbing these images from Samuel are, Gleason Archer claims that only Saul stripped off his clothes as he prophesied before Samuel, because God wanted to humiliate him, though the Bible clearly says, "he *too* stripped off his clothes". Nor does Archer explain how it was acceptable to Yahweh that King David would dance in public displaying his bare backside. Some apologists try to explain that David was not actually naked, merely unadorned, and that Michal upbraided him for not wearing his kingly robes and leading a solemn procession. But Michal's words in 2 Sam. 6:20 give a much different picture: "How the king of Israel honored himself today, uncovering himself today before the eyes of his servants' maids, as one of the vulgar fellows shamelessly uncovers himself." That is the Revised Standard Version. The Catholic Douay Bible is a bit more frank: "How glorious was the king of Israel today uncovering himself before the handmaids of his servants, and was naked, as if one of the buffoons should be naked!" Two things need to be noted concerning these translations. First, the accusation that David "uncovered" himself is very pointed. Whenever the Bible speaks of "uncovering" the reference is not only to nakedness, but implied sexuality as well. This is particularly apparent in the Levitical catalogue of proscribed sexual offenses. For example, Lev. 20:11 says that if a man lies with his father's wife he has "uncovered his father's nakedness." Second, the Catholic Bible is based on the Septuagint, while the Protestant Bible is based more on the Masoretic text. Since the later is a more refined and heavily edited version of what we call the Old Testament, the Septuagint, replete as it is with books and stories later discarded from the official canon, may often give us versions of events that are more frank, as though we were seeing the Bible with its guard down.

Prophecy was not only a matter of oracular trances, however. Another form of oracle was the casting of sacred stones, reminiscent of the casting of runes among Teutonic tribesmen. In fact, there was probably little to separate the early worship of Yahweh from the religions of other gods of that general time and place. Jephthah's sacrifice of his own daughter in thanks for victory (Judges 11:34-40) indicates that on certain occasions Yahweh was thought to accept human beings as burnt offerings. Archer tries to interpret the story in such a way that the girl is given to the Lord's service as a sort of Jewish nun and that the description of her bewailing her virginity was because she would never bear a child, and her father's line would come to an end (see Archer 1982, p. 164). But this defense does not hold water. The Bible is very clear on this point. Jephthah's vow (Judges 11:30) is that if he is victorious, he will offer up whoever comes to meet him as a *burnt offering*, not as someone dedicated to priestly service for the rest of their life. Also, Judges 11:39 is very clear as to how Jephthah fulfilled his vow: "And at the end of two months she returned to her father, who did with her according to his vow which he had made." It is important to note that Jephthah made his fatal vow while under divine influence (Judges 11:29-31):

> Then the spirit of the Lord came upon Jephthah and he passed through Gilead and Menasseh. He passed into Mizpah of Gilead, and from Mizpah of Gilead he passed on to the Ammonites. And Jephthah made a vow to the Lord and said, "If you will give the Ammonites into my hand then whoever comes out of the doors of my house to meet me, shall be the Lord's, to be offered up by me as a burnt offering."

Jephthah's actions really do not seem that different from those of Agamemnon offering his daughter Iphigenea as a sacrifice for fair winds to allow him to attack Troy. Jephthah is not the only one in the Book of Judges upon whom the spirit of the Lord descends. It also comes upon Othniel (Jud. 3:10) and Samson (14:19 and 15:14). It also comes upon Saul once again (1 Sam. 11:6) when he is told of an atrocity threatened against the Israelite town of Jabesh-gilead by the Ammonites. In all these cases the descent of the spirit of God provokes a berserk rage. It is interesting to note that among the Vikings berserk rage, poetry, and prophetic gifts were all imparted by the god Odin. This agrees with the Bible where prophesies are often given in a poetic form, and the spirit of God provokes both a berserk rage and a prophetic frenzy.

Another important point about the early worship of Yahweh is that he was not viewed as the one and only god, but merely as the god who ruled in Israel.

He was in essence a tribal god. This is evidenced by two incidents in 2 Kings. In one of these Elisha heals the Syrian commander, Naaman, of leprosy. As Naaman is leaving, he begs permission to take two mule-loads of earth from Israel back with him to Syria, upon which to build an altar to make burnt offerings to Yahweh (2 Kings 5:17). The reason for this request was that it was believed by the people of that day that one could not worship the god of one land on foreign soil. Naaman's request is for a bit of Israel upon which he can reasonably expect to worship the God of Israel. Fundamentalists might counter that this does not mean that the Israelites believed that foreign lands were ruled by other gods or that Yahweh's rule extended no further than the borders of Israel. After all, they might argue, Naaman, being a Syrian, had a primitive, pagan outlook, which Elisha was merely humoring. Had he been an Israelite, he would have known better. However, earlier in 2 Kings there is an incident that attests to the fact that not only did the people of Israel believe in the territoriality of gods (including Yahweh), but that the authors and editors of the book did as well. The incident occurs at the end of chapter 3. Mesha, king of Moab, has refused to pay tribute to Israel, and the armies of Israel and Judah have invaded Moab, defeated the Moabites and devastated the country-side. After failing to break out of his besieged city, Mesha sacrifices his eldest son on the wall, in view of the Israelites, with the result that: "there came a great wrath upon Israel; and they withdrew from him and returned to their own land" (2 Kings 3:27). How could there be a "great wrath upon Israel," one strong enough to cause the Israelites to withdraw while total victory was in their grasp? Certainly Yahweh would be angry with Mesha for sacrificing his own son to a pagan deity. (The god of Moab was Chemosh, a sun god, the Hebrew for sun being *shamash*). He certainly would not be angry with the Israelites. The only explanation is that the Israelites believed that Yahweh had no power in Moab, at least not in the face of an appeal to Chemosh that involved the sacrifice of the crown prince. (Archer, by the way, fails to address either of these incidents.) While there were glimmerings of the concept of a universal God during the time of two kingdoms, it was the Babylonian exile that forced a dramatic change in the thinking of the Jews. Had they not been able to formulate the idea that Yahweh could succor them, even in a foreign land, then they would not have survived as a separate nationality and would have disappeared from history along with not only their Chaldean captors, but the 10 tribes taken into captivity by the Assyrians. Much is made of the mystery of the 10 "lost" tribes of Israel. Yet their fate is rather obvious. Their language and customs were not that different from any of the other Semitic peoples in the Assyrian empire. And, since they had ceased to worship Yahweh exclusively, those who had not fled south to Judah before the fall of Israel were simply assimilated by the peoples amongst whom they had been settled. By contrast, the Jewish population of the Babylonian Exile retained their identity, and the Jewish community in Babylon was thriving even after the time of Jesus. Thus, the difference between the worship of Yahweh and that of the surrounding religions was not how it started out, but how it ended up.

The forge in which Judaism was purified and hardened was the onslaught of first the Assyrian and then the Chaldean empire. And it was the prophets who, though they started out as ecstatic seers, led the way in transforming Judaism from the worship of a tribal god to one of the first great ethical religions of the Middle East. The prophets were the champions of the worship of Yahweh as a deity separate from the Canaanite pantheon. And it is the worship of Yahweh and Yahweh alone that insured the survival of the Jews in captivity as a people.

How did the prophets become such a force for change? I suspect that the office of divine oracle gave them a leverage with the kings, whom they advised and even rebuked. Nathan carried on the tradition of Samuel as did the prophets Elijah, Elisha, and their followers. Nathan's right to condemn a king for his crimes against a common soldier was magnified by Amos some 200 years later. It is noteworthy that the prophecies of doom against such nations as Egypt, Assyria, and Chaldea, as well as those against neighboring states such as Moab, Ammon, and Edom, the very prophecies that fundamentalists insist were fulfilled to the letter, were all based on God's wrath against unethical behavior, as were the prophecies against the kings and peoples of Israel and Judah. For example, in Amos 1:13 God's wrath against the Ammonites is "because they have ripped up women with child in Gilead, that they might enlarge their border." The prophecies were a cry against brutality, deceit, hypocrisy, greed, the abuse of the poor and weak by the powerful and the worship of other gods than Yahweh. Given their social and political nature, it is worth considering in the light of the failure of so many of the prophecies whether they were ever intended to foretell the future as fundamentalists insist they were. This is a question I will deal with as I consider the prophecies and prophets in detail.

Historical Divisions of the Prophets

The prophetic books of the Bible (including those of Samuel and Kings) fall into four basic periods. The first of these is the period of the early prophets, Samuel, Nathan, Elijah, and Elisha, during the period when the Jews were independent and ruled by kings, a period of about 200 years between ca. 1040 B.C.E. to ca. 840 B.C.E. The second period is the time of the Assyrian expansion and includes 1st Isaiah, Amos, Hosea, and Micah. This period of less than a century, from 760 to 687, saw the total destruction of the northern kingdom of Israel by Assyria and the devastation of Judah by the Assyrians following Hezekiah's revolt. The Jewish kingdom was reduced to little more than a city state of Jerusalem by 687. Even this was lost in 587, when the Chaldeans under Nebuchadrezzar took Jerusalem. The third period of prophecy, which I will call the Chaldean period, includes the ministries of Jeremiah, Ezekiel, Nahum, Habakkuk, Zephaniah, and Obadiah. It covers 64 years, from 627 to 563, during which the Assyrian empire was destroyed by the Medes and Chaldeans, and the Jews were taken into exile in Babylon. The fourth period, following the end of the Exile in 539 and stretching to possibly as late as 350, was a period of restoration under the comparatively kind rule of the Persian empire. The prophets of this period were 2nd Isaiah, Malachi, Haggai, Zechariah and Joel. Jonah, a fictional work, was also probably written in this period.

Following this last period of prophecy there was a period of turmoil starting with the oppression of the Jews by the Seleucid king Antiochus Epiphanes (175-164 B.C.E.), during which the book of Daniel was written, and continuing into the Christian era, with the period of Roman rule. This was a period that produced many apocalyptic works, both Jewish and Christian, the most notable, of course, being the Revelation of John, which seems to have been written during the reign of the Roman emperor Domitian (C.E. 81-96).

I will go into detail about the history of each of these periods as I deal with the specific prophets. However, a brief overview of the history of all the periods seen together shows a pattern explaining the concentration of prophets at specific times in the history of the Jewish people. The ancient history of the Middle East was determined by the ebb and flow of great empires. The first of these, the Egyptian empire, controlled the Nile valley and the Levant. It was countered by the growth of the Hittite empire in Asia Minor. To the east was the kingdom of Urartu (Ararat in the Bible) and the kingdom of Babylonia.

During the period from about 1300 to 1000 B.C.E. the relative stability of the region was shattered. The Egyptian and Hittite empires fought each other to a standstill in a series of wars that ended with a peace treaty in 1271, at which point both empires were too exhausted to effectively control the Levant. Waves of barbaric invaders also disrupted the ancient world. First the Achaean, then the Dorian Greeks destroyed the civilization of Minoan Crete and sent a mixed group of invaders called the "Peoples of the Sea" fleeing ahead of them. They invaded the Nile delta. After being defeated by the Egyptians in 1180, they invaded Canaan from the west some time after the Israelites had invaded from the east. The same wave of invasions that brought the Dorians into Greece brought the Phrygians into Asia Minor, where they destroyed the Hittite empire around 1200 B.C.E. The Assyrians had begun their rise to power during the Egyptian-Hittite wars, but were chiefly occupied in a see-saw struggle against the Babylonians and in campaigns against Urartu.

The retreat of the Egyptians from the Levant, the preoccupation of the Assyrians with Babylonia and Urartu, and the destruction of the Hittites left Syria and Palestine free from imperial domination. After the Israelites emerged victorious over their neighbors under David (ca. 1000 to ca. 960 B.C.E.) and Solomon (ca. 960-920 B.C.E.), the kingdoms of Israel and Judah enjoyed varying fortunes until the Assyrian empire, which had been in a period of decay, revived under Tiglath-pileser III. Previously, an alliance between Syria and Israel under Ahab had checked the Assyrian advance at the battle of Qarqar in 853. But now the still prosperous kingdom of Israel lay in the path of the Assyrians, who during the reign of Sargon II took Samaria, the capital of Israel in 722. Judah became an Assyrian vassal state, but seethed with resentment against their Assyrian overlords. The prophets of the Assyrian period saw the hand of God in Assyria's destruction of Israel and warned Judah against the apostasy that had led the Lord to destroy Israel. Isaiah and the other prophets of his day also warned against entangling alliances that would put Judah in harm's way, particularly those revolts fomented by the Egyptians, who for their own security wanted to disrupt Assyrian rule in Palestine and to detach potential buffer states from Assyrian control. The prophets probably saw clearly that the Egyptians were using Judah as a cat's paw and that they would be of little help in the event of a revolt against Assyria. For a time King Hezekiah seems to have heeded Isaiah's warnings, but following the death of Sargon II Judah joined a revolt which included the Phoenician and Philistine

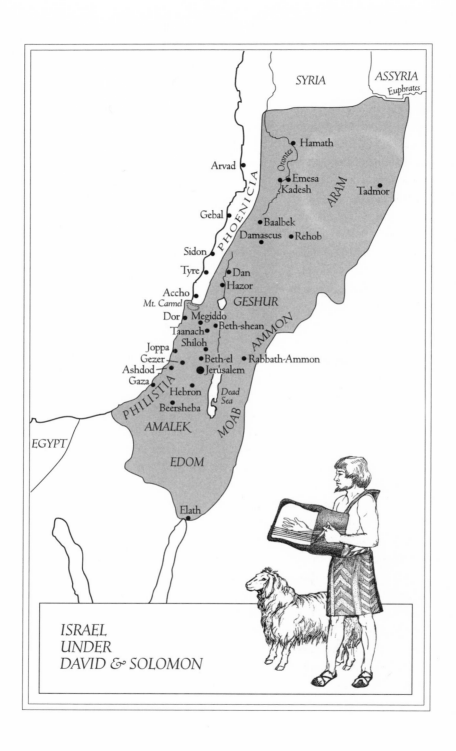

SYRIA

ASSYRIA

Euphrates

• Hamath

Arvad •

• Emesa
Kadesh

Orontes

ARAM

• Tadmor

Gebal •

• Baalbek

Damascus • • Rehob

Sidon •

Tyre • • Dan

PHOENICIA

• Hazor

Accho •

GESHUR

Mt. Carmel

Dor • • Megiddo

• Beth-shean

AMMON

Taanach •

Joppa • Shiloh •

Gezer — • Beth-el • Rabbath-Ammon

Ashdod —

Gaza •

• Jerusalem

PHILISTIA

Hebron •

Dead Sea

Beersheba •

MOAB

AMALEK

EGYPT

EDOM

• Elath

ISRAEL
UNDER
DAVID & SOLOMON

cities and was backed by Egypt. In 701 B.C.E. Sargon's successor, Sennacherib, swiftly and methodically crushed the revolt, defeated the Egyptians when they tried to raise the siege of Jerusalem, and utterly devastated all Judah outside of the capital. Hezekiah finally sent a heavy tribute and hostages to Sennacherib and preserved a remnant of his kingdom, little more than Jerusalem and its surrounding environs.

The Assyrians overextended themselves and were weakened by continual wars. Their attacks on Urartu destroyed a power that had blocked the inroads of steppe barbarians from north of the Caucasus mountains, and the Cimmerians, driven south by the Scythians, invaded the western provinces of the empire in Asia Minor. The weakening Assyrians paid the Scythians to subdue the Cimmerian raiders, much as the Romans later used Germanic tribes on their frontier as *foederatti*. This turned out to be an unwise policy. The Scythians seeing the weakness of the empire launched a series of devastating invasions between 645 and 617. Following the death of Ashurbanipal in 625, the Medes and Chaldeans threw off Assyrian rule and began to divide the empire between them. In 612 their combined forces took and utterly destroyed the Assyrian capitol of Nineveh.

The collapse of Assyrian power gave Judah a brief period of independence under King Josiah. It proved to be spurious, however. Necho II of Egypt marched to the aid of the failing Assyrians since it was in Egypt's best interest to maintain a weak empire rather than facing a new, strong one on its frontier. Josiah unwisely tried to stop Necho and was defeated and killed at Megiddo in 609. Judah was briefly an Egyptian province. But Nebuchadrezzar defeated Necho crushingly at Carchemish in 605. Judah now passed into Chaldean hands. The history of the Assyrian period then repeated itself. Necho's grandson, Hophra, lured Judah into revolt against Chaldea despite the exhortations of Jeremiah against opposing the Chaldeans. The pressures that produced another wave of prophets culminated in the capture of Jerusalem, the destruction of the first Temple and the deportation of the Jews to Babylonia in 586.

The destruction of the Assyrian empire created an uneasy balance of power between the Chaldean, Median and Lydian empires. The Lydian empire was founded in 678 when the Lydians defeated the Cimmerians and began to conquer western Asia Minor. Nebuchadrezzar's successors, particularly Belshazzar, made defensive alliances against the Medes with Lydia, Egypt and Sparta. By this time the Greeks were becoming known as valuable mercenaries and their new form of heavy infantry was considered a potentially decisive weapon. In 560, Cyrus of Persia deposed his Median overlord, Astyages. King Croesus of Lydia seized some of the western provinces of the Median empire, which gave Cyrus a pretext to make war on him. Cyrus moved swiftly and defeated Croesus decisively at the battle of Thymbra in 546 B.C.E. The rapid fall of Lydia left the Chaldeans virtually alone to face the Persians, since neither Egypt nor Sparta was in a position to mobilize effectively. Babylon fell to the Persians in 538, at which point the new rulers allowed the Jews to return to Jerusalem.

During the Persian period, prophets saw in the rebuilding of the Temple and the restoration of the city a new hope and cherished vain fantasies that a new king from the Davidic line would restore Israel to a new period of glory. Instead, the Jews passed from Persian rule to Alexandrian rule. Upon the death of Alexander in 323 his generals divided the empire between them. Initially, Asia Minor, the north of Mesopotamia, Syria and Palestine were held by Antigonus. However, during the struggles between the various generals and the dynasties they founded, the Jews found themselves under the control of the Ptolemies and finally the Seleucids. During a brief interregnum when the Seleucid Empire was being eaten away from the east by the Parthians and from the west by the Romans, the Maccabees founded the Hasmonean dynasty and established an independent Jewish state. They also conquered the surrounding peoples, such as the Idumeans, who were the descendants of the Edomites. In contrast to the exclusion of the "peoples of the land" that had been practiced by Ezra and Nehemiah, the Hasmoneans forcibly converted conquered populations to Judaism. Just as in the time of the Chaldeans, once the Romans had finished absorbing the Seleucids, Jewish independence came to an end. And, as with the Assyrian and Chaldean empires before them, the Jews resented and revolted against the Romans. Repeating the history of the Chaldean period, the Romans took Jerusalem, destroyed the Temple and deported the population.

Prophecies, Apocalypses, and their Interpretation

The same pressures that produced waves of prophetic writing—the threat of imminent destruction and enslavement by a powerful, implacable enemy— also produced apocalyptic literature. Mixed in with the prophecies of Isaiah, Jeremiah, Ezekiel, and virtually all of the minor prophets are apocalyptic passages referring to "the latter days." Along with these passages, all the prophecies of the book of Daniel are apocalyptic. Other Jewish apocalyptic literature includes the book of 2 Esdras, which is part of the Catholic canon, but is consigned to the apocrypha by Jews and Protestants. The main Christian apocalyptic passages are in the Olivet Discourse in the synoptic gospels, certain references to the last days in the Pauline epistles and, of course, the Book of Revelation. Along with these are numerous non-canonical apocalypses.

The main difference between prophecy and apocalyptic literature is that prophecies are concrete predictions to be fulfilled in history and are not spoken of as happening in "the latter days." Apocalyptic literature focuses on either the end of the world or a period far in the future, when God will put an end to the cycle of wars and conquest, that is, an end to history if not the world.

In assuming that prophecies in general are of an apocalyptic nature, fundamentalists often blur the line between the two classifications. Ignoring the historical context, they see, as an example, Ezekiel's prophecy of the destruction of Tyre as being fulfilled in the time of Alexander the Great. But the reason Ezekiel believed that God's wrath would fall upon Tyre was that it had, he felt, drawn Judah into a revolt against the Chaldeans, only to leave the Jews to the mercy of Nebuchadrezzar while the Tyrians sat safely protected behind their fleet in their island city. Nebuchadrezzar's unsuccessful 13 year siege of Tyre began in 586. Alexander took the city in 332. Why would God punish the city 254 years after its people had wronged the Jews? By that time all of the people Ezekiel thought God should and would punish were long dead. One reason fundamentalists cannot accept that Ezekiel was predicting the conquest of Tyre by Nebuchadrezzar is that they cannot accept that Ezekiel's prophecy was wrong. I believe that, along with no small degree of intellectual blindness, fundamentalists suffer from the faulty use of hermeneutics.

Hermeneutics is the discipline of literary interpretation, most commonly used in biblical interpretation. While many books have been devoted to this subject, each one based on the presuppositions of Catholic or Protestant views, liberal or conservative views, or even personal bias, I have chosen to use as an example the principles of hermeneutics as laid down by the late Dr. Walter Martin. I am doing this to show that fundamentalists violate their own reading of these principles in the defense of inerrancy. Martin first lays out a few basics for understanding Scripture. We must understand, he says, the structure and idioms of the languages in which the Bible was written (Hebrew, Aramaic, and Greek), as well as the historical and geographical background and context. Also, we have to understand whether what we are reading is prose, poetry, history, allegory, etc. and whether the language was meant to be taken literally or symbolically.

As an example of how some things in the Bible must be taken symbolically, consider how Matthew 1:17 states that there were 14 generations between Abraham and David, 14 more between David and the onset of the Babylonian captivity, and 14 between that event and the birth of Jesus. Since a generation is computed in the Bible as being 40 years, then the spacing between each of these events would be roughly $14 \times 40 = 560$ years. However, to the degree that Abraham can even be pinpointed in history, there were probably 1,000 years between Abraham and David, who reigned between 1000 and 960 B.C.E. (roughly), and only 373 years between David and the capture of Jerusalem by the Chaldeans, which occurred 587 years before the birth of Jesus. To insist on literalism would make Matthew 1:17 absurd. The separation by equal numbers of generations for each event is probably a way of equating each as a turning point in the relationship between God and his people. Truth, as the author of Matthew probably understood it, was not a matter of literal conformation to history or natural law.

Finally, Martin points out, we must understand the life settings of the biblical authors and look at the world through their eyes. The Bible is, he points out, an eastern book, not based on our Aristotelian views of logic and cause and effect. It is full of paradox and reflects as well God's progressive revelation—that God did not give his people truths they could not comprehend. This fits Calvin's view of accommodation. Yet, like other inerrantists, Martin apparently could not understand that the theory of evolution by natural selection and genetic mutation would fit into this category.

Martin goes on to note the senses in which biblical passages can be interpreted. They are the literal sense, the allegorical sense, the moral sense, and the anagogical sense. The last of these means that heavenly meanings are intended, even though the literal word mentioned refers to something earthly. Any given word or phrase in the Bible can be interpreted in any of these senses. For example, Martin points out that "water" can mean literally water, be allegorically interpreted as baptism, morally interpreted as purity, and/or anagogically interpreted as the Holy Spirit. What Martin is referring to is called the fourfold hermeneutical principle, which was formulated by John Cassian, a contemporary of Augustine. His most common example was the city of Jerusalem, which, like water, could be variously interpreted as the city itself (literal), the church (allegorical), the soul (moral), or the heavenly kingdom (anagogical). How the word or phrase is to be interpreted depends on the context in which it is set. In the absence of specific context, the word or phrase is to be interpreted literally.

These basic principles are quite sound, and Martin's reasoning is reflected by other fundamentalists. As we will see, however, they are enforced inconsistently by inerrantists. Whenever application of these principles threatens to undermine such cherished views as end-times prophecy or creationism, such ideas as setting the prophetic or apocalyptic work in its historical context or applying Calvin's principle of accommodation to creation myths are quickly abandoned. Even the literal sense is abridged in the case of parallel accounts. Where there are two utterly different stories of a given event, a wealth of material is invented to harmonize the two tales. Events that would have to be miraculous are often argued to be scientifically true. And outrageous actions or ideas are glibly explained away or buried in verbiage without really coming to grips with the philosophical and theological implications of such concepts as predestination and original sin.

We have already seen examples of some of these in Gleason Archer's attempt to turn the sacrifice of Jephthah's daughter into an involuntary assumption of holy vows, a symbolic reading of the text, when it was quite obviously meant to be taken as a literal blood sacrifice and burnt offering. Archer's problem would seem to be an unwillingness to come to grips with the fact that in allowing Jephthah's vow to be carried out, God was either accepting a human sacrifice or allowing an innocent girl to be killed for no good reason. Other explanations are that the story is fictional or that there is no God. Of course, Archer would have to reject the last possibility on the basis of his belief. Curiously enough, he could accept the story as fictional and still believe in the validity of the Bible. If the story is read as a moral tale—a caution against making rash vows—then it would serve a moral purpose. Yet that path is fraught with danger for fundamentalists. It allows people to pick and choose what they will and will not accept as factual in the Bible. So Archer is caught in a dilemma. He must accept the story as true, but then make it only true in a symbolic sense, lest it show God as either uncaring or accepting human sacrifice.

Despite fudging embarrassing stories such as Jephthah's sacrifice of his own daughter or Elisha's deadly curse on the bratty little boys, fundamentalists insist that Old Testament prophecies have been literally and specifically fulfilled, even if this means a deliberate misreading of history, as in Jeremiah's prediction of a 70-year Babylonian captivity, which in reality lasted only 49 years. As I said in Chapter l, there are a number of symbolic meanings for the term 70 years that make far more sense than insisting that the Jews were indeed captive in Babylon for a literal 70 years in the face of historical evidence to the contrary. The reason I suspect that fundamentalists insist on such a rigid view of historical fulfillment of prophecy is that they can then use that as a basis for validating their particular interpretation of the as yet unfulfilled end-times prophecies of the apocalyptic writings.

Since fundamentalists must make prophecies work out to the letter, they go through some rather extraordinary lengths to make them come out right. As examples of how this reasoning process works let us consider a few supposedly fulfilled prophecies from a four-page tract by Hugh Ross entitled "Fulfilled Prophecy: Evidence for the Reliability of the Bible." Ross, a physicist turned minister and an advocate of old-earth creationism, sets up 13 prophecies that he believes were specifically fulfilled. Then, ever the physicist and mathematician, he estimates what the probabilities are that they could have been fulfilled entirely by chance and comes up with astronomically low numbers such as a one in a billion, thus "proving" divine fulfillment. At this time I will only deal with those prophecies that are from the first period, the time of independent kingdoms before the Assyrian invasions.

Two of Ross's prophecies are self-referencing, i.e. the supposed fulfillment of the prophecy is part of the biblical story of the prophecy itself, hence without non-biblical corroboration and thus totally unfalsifiable. These are the prophecies by the "sons of the prophets" to Elisha that his master, Elijah, would be taken from him that very day (2 Kings 2:3-11) and the prophecy by Jahaziel that King Jehoshaphat and his tiny army would be supernaturally delivered from an attacking force of Moabites and Ammonites (2 Chronicles 20). Two others of Ross' 13 were written after the fact and thus are not prophecies at all. One of these is the fulfillment of Joshua's curse on whoever would rebuild Jericho, that he would build it at the cost of his eldest and youngest sons, the first to die at the beginning of the work, the second at the end. The fulfillment is in 1 Kings 16:33-34, when Hiel of Bethel rebuilt the city and seems to have sacrificed two of his sons, burying them under the foundations as part of a pagan rite. Both the passages in Joshua and 1 Kings seem to be the work of the Deuteronomist editors of King Josiah's time. But even if this prophecy in Joshua had been written before the fact, there is no way to tell for sure whether it was divinely fulfilled or even if it was true. Hiel upon deciding to rebuild Jericho might well have deliberately sacrificed his sons in order to fulfill the prophecy and thus be in accord with God's word. Another possibility is that a later redactor, finding the story of Hiel rebuilding Jericho and not finding any mention of the fulfillment of Joshua's curse, might have added the story of the sacrifice to make things come out right. In any case, without an extra-biblical source we have no way of either corroborating or falsifying the prophecy, as we do in the case of predictions supposedly fulfilled in history. The other prophecy is on the part of an unnamed prophet who predicts to King Jeroboam that a descendant of the house of David named Josiah would burn the bones of the pagan priests on Jeroboam's altar, which I alluded to in my introduction. The prophecy is in 1 Kings 13:2, and the fulfillment is in 2 Kings 23:15-18, about 300 years later. Since 1 Kings 13:32 refers to the northern kingdom as Samaria and since Israel was not referred to by the name of its capital until after it had fallen to the Assyrians in 721 B.C.E., the prophet crying out against Jeroboam's idolatry, which took place around 900 B.C.E., was inserted by the Deuteronomists hundreds of years after the fact.

This is the only time I will deal in any detail with the early period of prophecy because of its lack of extra-biblical references for corroboration or falsification. I will deal with the prophecies of the later prophets grouped by their period (i.e. 1st Isaiah and his contemporaries; Jeremiah, Ezekiel, and their contemporaries; etc.) with the exception that the prophecies of the fall of Tyre and Babylon, which were made by prophets of both the Assyrian and Chaldean periods, will be dealt with in the chapter dealing with the Chaldean period. Old Testament prophecies seen as referring to Jesus, which come from many periods, have been given their own chapter. After I have dealt with supposedly fulfilled prophecies I will deal with the apocalyptic books and their various interpretations, a brief history of millennial movements, and a critique of such modern doomsayers as Hal Lindsey.

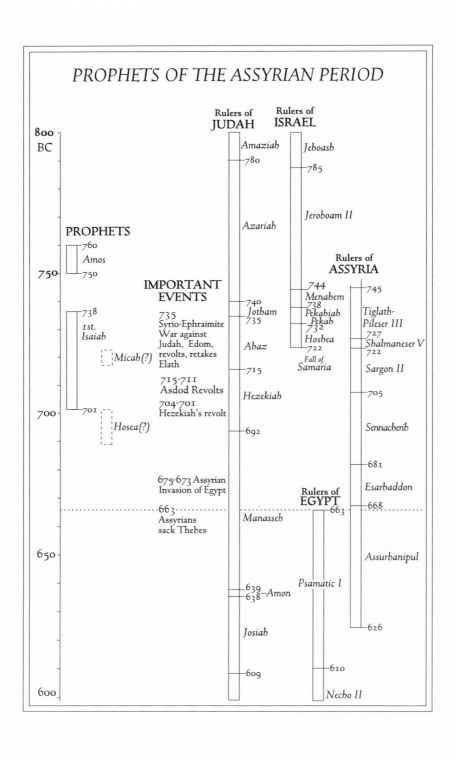

PROPHETS OF THE ASSYRIAN PERIOD

Rulers of
JUDAH

Rulers of
ISRAEL

800
BC

Amaziah	Jeboash
—780	—785
	Jeroboam II
Azariah	

PROPHETS

—760
Amos
750— —750

Rulers of
ASSYRIA

**IMPORTANT
EVENTS**

—738
1st.
Isaiah

735
Syrio-Ephraimite
War against
Judah, Edom,
revolts, retakes
Elath

Micah(?)

715-711
Asdod Revolts

704-701
Hezekiah's revolt

—701
Hosea(?)

700—

—740	744		—745
Jotham	Menahem		
735	—738		Tiglath-
	Pekahiah		Pileser III
	—732		
Ahaz	Pekah		—727
	Hoshea		Shalmaneser V
	—722		—722
—715	Fall of		Sargon II
	Samaria		
Hezekiah			—705
—692			Sennacherib

675-673 Assyrian
Invasion of Egypt

—681

Esarhaddon

Rulers of
EGYPT

663··················—663·
Assyrians
sack Thebes

Manasseh

—668

650—

Assurbanipul

Psamatic I

—639—Amon
—638

Josiah

—626

—609

—610

600—

Necho II

3

"BEHOLD, THE DAYS ARE COMING"

The Prophets of the Assyrian Period

THE MOST IMPORTANT PROPHET OF THE ASSYRIAN PERIOD was Isaiah ben Amoz, author of chapters 1 through 39 of the book of Isaiah, and I will deal chiefly with the prophecies of 1st Isaiah in this chapter. I will also deal with the prophecies of Amos, Hosea, and Micah. However, fundamentalists do not as often use their prophecies as proof of God working in history, as they do with Isaiah. Thus, they are not as important for the purpose of this book. Considering that we will be dealing with the most controversial prophecies of Isaiah, the fall of Babylon and the rise of Cyrus of Persia, in another chapter, the most important point of contention and one I will deal with immediately is the reasoning behind dividing Isaiah into two different books authored by prophets living in different centuries.

The Divisions of the Book of Isaiah

As they do with the Documentary Hypothesis, fundamentalists charge that the division of Isaiah into two or more works—one being the writings of Isaiah ben Amoz during the Assyrian period and one or more being written either late in the Exile or after the Exile—is the work of those biased against the very concept of divine authorship and inspiration. In the case of Isaiah they claim that what they see as an artificial division comes from a bias on the part of the scholars against believing in even the possibility of predictive prophecy. As I said in Chapter 1, as early as the 1100s Ibn Ezra expressed doubts about the authorship of chapters 40 through 66. But it was J. C. Doederlien (1745-1792) who, in his exegetical work on Isaiah, initially formulated the Deutero-Isaiah theory. Certainly, Ibn Ezra, a pious Jew, did not base his doubts on a material-istic disbelief in the possibility of predictive prophecy. In fact, regardless of what Doederlien or any modern scholars may feel about prophecy, there are ample reasons for believing that chapters 40 through 55 are the work of a dif-ferent author than Isaiah ben Amoz and that this author was from a much later time. Chapters 56 through 66 seem to be the work of a third writer (or writ-ers), often referred to as Trito-Isaiah. Some scholars feel that chapters 56-66 are a mix of pre-exilic and post-exilic prophecies edited together.

Speaking of just two of the many stylistic differences between the two Isaiahs, Reverend T. K. Cheyne said (1895, p. 256):

> But it is only in chaps. xl-lv [40-55] that we find that subordination of the infinitive to a previous verb which reminds us so forcibly of Arabic and Syriac idiom...All the passages in which adjectives and participles in the feminine plural are used as if neuter substantives occur in chaps. xl-lv.

Both of these peculiarities are significant. The use of words in Hebrew in a manner that would be more fitting in Syriac (i.e. Aramaic) mirrors one of the clues that the writers of the gospels of Mark, Matthew, and John were Jews writing in a second language. When their Greek is translated into Aramaic, their phrases flow in a much more natural and even poetic manner, much as Dante's *Inferno* does when the verses rendered in English translations are translated back into Italian. That chapters 40-55 are written in what seems to be an Aramaic idiom indicates they were written by an Aramaic-speaking Jew writing in Hebrew. And this in turn indicates a post-exilic writer, since Aramaic was not commonly spoken by the Jews before the Exile. We have striking evidence from 2 Kings 18 and Isaiah 36 that most of the Jews in Isaiah's time were ignorant of Aramaic. During the Assyrian siege of Jerusalem, Sennacherib s official, the Rabshakeh, has been telling Hezekiah's courtiers that his revolt will be crushed and that the Egyptian aid he has counted on will be of no avail to him. He has been speaking in Hebrew and the courtiers are worried that his words will panic the people (2 Kings 19:26-29 and Isaiah 36: l l-14):

> Then Eliakim the son of Hilkiah and Shebna and Joah said to the Rabshakeh, "Pray speak to your servants in the Aramaic language, for we understand it; do not speak to us in the language of Judah within the hearing of the people who

are on the wall." But the Rabshakeh said, "Has my master sent me to speak these words to your master and you, and not to the men sitting on the wall, who are doomed to eat their own dung and drink their own urine?" Then the Rabshakeh stood and called out in a loud voice in the language of Judah: "Hear the word of the great king, the king of Assyria! Thus says the king: 'Do not let Hezekiah deceive you, for he will not be able to deliver you out of my hand.'"

While it is probable that Isaiah, like Hezekiah's courtiers, understood Aramaic, his first language was Hebrew and he would not have spoken or written Hebrew in an Aramaic idiom.

Cheyne's second point, regarding the use of adjectives and participles which are in the feminine plural being used as though they were neuter substantives, may well be lost on most of us, who probably have forgotten the finer points of grammar dealing with parts of speech and who, as English speakers, are unfamiliar with the idea of words having a particular gender. A little review, even an admittedly oversimplified one, will help us understand how important this peculiarity of language is. First of all, a participle is a form of a verb used as another part of speech, often an adjective. For example, in the phrase, "a battered suitcase," battered, a past tense of a verb, is used to describe a noun (the suitcase) and, as such, is used as an adjective. A substantive is an adjective used as if it were a noun, as in "The flower is blue." Ordinarily, the word blue will, if used as an adjective, come before the noun as in "blue flower." Now let us consider gender. In English it is virtually pointless to ask what a noun's gender is. However, in Latin, and most other languages, every noun and every adjective describing that noun is either masculine, feminine, or neuter. For example, in Latin both *vir* (man) and *gladius* (sword) are masculine, while both *femina* (woman) and *vagina* (sheath) are feminine. *Ferum* (iron) is neuter. The gender of words, however, does not always follow the logic of these examples. Since swords are associated with males, it would seem logical that a word for sword would have a masculine gender. But, while *gladius* is masculine, a particular type of long sword used in the later periods of the Roman empire, the *spatha*, is feminine. Also, *nauta* (sailor) and *agricola* (farmer), which were meant to describe men, are both feminine. Sometimes the masculine or feminine ending in Latin affects the meaning of a word. For example, *animus* (masculine) means mind, and *anima* (feminine) means spirit. Thus, gender is very pervasive in language and very important. Now let us get back to those chapters in question in Isaiah. It is a notable peculiarity in chapters 40-55 that adjectives and verb forms used as adjectives, both of which are feminine, are being used in these chapters as if they were neuter nouns. That this oddity is limited to these chapters is just one of many clues that they were written by a different author than were the first 39 chapters.

Other clues include other differences in syntax, difference in the frequency of certain words and phrases, a different emotional tone and a different style of writing. Syntax is the pattern of formation of phrases and sentences in a given language. It varies greatly from one tongue to another. For example, in English we put the adjective before the noun as in "hot water." But in Spanish they say *aqua caliente* or "water hot." In English we structure sentences such that the subject comes first, then the verb, then the object, as in, "Jim says hello to Fred." But in Latin the order was subject, object, verb, as in *Publius Marco salutum dicit* which, if translated without changing the syntax, reads, "Publius to Marcus salutation speaks (says hello)." This is reminiscent of the old joke about the Pennsylvania Dutch saying such things as, "Throw the cow over the fence some hay." Within the same language there are more subtle changes in phrase and sentence structure between different writers. One author may frequently use crisp, short sentences with active verbs, while another may use more ponderous sentences with subordinate clauses and passive verbs. For example, compare the style of the sentences below:

> Isaiah wrote the first 39 chapters of the book of Isaiah during the time the Assyrians were expanding into Syria and Palestine. His text reflects the tensions of this period.

> Written at the time of the Assyrian expansion into Syria and Palestine, the text of the first 39 chapters of Isaiah, the work of Isaiah ben Amoz, has reflected in it the tensions of the period.

Another aspect of style is the repeated use of certain phrases and words. Let us consider a few examples. In Isaiah 40-55 the phrase "Fear not" occurs in chapter 41 verses 10, 13, 14; chapter 43 verse 5; chapter 44 verse 2 and chapter 54 verse 4. "I am the first and I am the last" occurs in chapter 44 verse 6, and chapter 48 verse 12, and a similar phrase, "I am Yahweh (rendered in English as "the Lord") and there is none else," is found in chapter 45 verses 5, 6, 18 and 22; and in chapter 46 verse 9. None of the phrases above occur at all in chapters 1-39. God is referred to in chapters 40-55 in such terms as "I am the Lord, who stretches out the heavens." On the other hand, in chapters 1-39 God is repeatedly referred to as the "Lord of hosts." There is little of comfort in the message of Isaiah 1-39. But Isaiah 40-55 is full of words of healing and comfort, as in the above mentioned, oft-repeated phrase "Fear not."

These are but a few of the many clues that tell us that chapters 1-39 and 40-55 were written by different authors. By themselves each of these clues would be of little importance. But taken together they cannot be ignored. Again, this is the type of scholarship that experts use to test the validity of assigning both the *Iliad* and the *Odyssey* to Homer. If Isaiah were not part of the Bible there would not be any controversy about assigning everything after chapter 39 to another author. Since there is such a controversy, let us consider some of Gleason Archer's objections to the Deutero-Isaiah theory. First, Archer points out that the name of Isaiah's eldest son, Shear-jashub, meaning "a remnant will return," is part of a prophecy. How, asks Archer, could Isaiah have known of the Exile and that only a remnant of the Jewish people would return from Babylon except by divine inspiration? Thus, it is reasonable to assume that Isaiah's prediction of the rise of Cyrus of Persia in 2nd Isaiah was also divinely inspired. Of course, the main reason for the division is not based on what prophecies are in it, particularly since there is a prophecy of the destruction of Babylon in chapter 13, part of 1st Isaiah. However, Archer's challenge should be answered. Because we in a later period of history know of the Exile and the return of the Jews after the fall of Babylon, we tend to think of *that* remnant returning when we hear Isaiah 10:20-21:

> In that day the remnant of Israel and the survivors of the house of Jacob will no more lean upon him that smote them, but will lean on the Lord, the Holy One of Israel, in truth. A remnant will return, the remnant of Jacob, to the mighty God.

However, when we put the prophecy back in the context of chapter 10, we find that it is not speaking of a captivity in Babylon under the Chaldeans, but that most of the chapter relates to the Assyrians. Starting with verse 10:5 God says that Assyria, "the rod of my anger," has become boastful, thinking that its own strength is its source of power, when in reality it is an instrument in God's hands. Next God says that when he has finished his work in Jerusalem, he will punish the king of Assyria for his pride (10:12). The prophet describes God's punishment of Assyria as a forest fire, saying that the remnant of trees left in Assyria's forest will be so few that a child will be able to count them (10:19). It is at this point the prophet says "In that day the remnant of Israel...will no more lean upon him that smote them" (10:20). Clearly, when the prophecy is put in context, "him that smote them" is Assyria, not Chaldea, and the remnant that will return are those that the *Assyrians* had deported from the northern kingdom of Israel, in Isaiah's day, not those the Chaldeans would later deport from Judah. Perhaps the failure of fundamentalists to put this prophecy in context results from the embarrassing fact that those deported by the Assyrians did *not* return.

More to the point of comparing style and other clues, Archer says that Isaiah 1:15 and 59:3,7 have similar phrasing as do 10:1-2 and 59:4-9, and that these argue for a unity of the entire book. Let us compare the first pair 1:15 and 59:3,7

> 1:15: When you spread forth your hands, I will hide my eyes from you; even though you make many prayers, I will not listen; your hands are full of blood.
> 59:3: For your hands are defiled with blood and your fingers with iniquity; your lips have spoken lies, your tongue mutters wickedness.
> 59:7: Their feet run to evil and they make haste to shed innocent blood; their thoughts are thoughts of iniquity, desolation and destruction are in their highways.

Verse 1:15 and verse 59:3 are somewhat similar in that they refer to hands filled with blood or defiled with blood. Verse 59:3 only says that they make haste to shed innocent blood, a phrasing significantly different from those referring to blood-stained hands. So we have a slight similarity between 1:15 and 59:3, and not much else. Now let us compare 10:1-2 and 59: 4-9:

> 10: 1-2: Woe to those who decree iniquitous decrees, and the writers who keep writing oppression, to turn aside the needy from justice and to rob the poor of my people of their right, that widows may be their spoil and that they make the fatherless their prey!
> 59: 4-9: No one enters suit justly, no one goes to law honestly; they rely on empty pleas, they speak lies, they conceive mischief and bring forth iniquity. They hatch adders' eggs, they weave the spider's web; he who eats their eggs dies, and from one which is crushed a viper is hatched. Their webs will not

serve them as clothing; men will not cover themselves with what they make. Their works are works of iniquity and deeds of violence are in their hands. Their feet run to evil and they make haste to shed innocent blood; their thoughts are thoughts of iniquity, desolation and destruction are in their highways. The way of peace they know not, and there is no justice in their paths; they have made their roads crooked, no one who goes in them knows peace. Therefore justice is far from us, and righteousness does not overtake us; we look for light, and behold, darkness, and for brightness, but we walk in gloom.

If anything this pair, the first so crisp and concise, the second so overblown and wordy, makes my point better than it makes Archer's. Other than a general outcry against corruption, the two blocks have nothing in common. The same is true of one last comparison Archer uses, 29:13 and 58:2,4 which read as follows:

29:13: And the Lord said: Because this people draw near with their mouth and honor me with their lips, while their hearts are far from me, and their fear of me is a commandment of men learned by rote;
58:2: Yet they seek me daily, and delight to know my ways, as if they were a nation that did righteousness and did not forsake the ordinance of their God; they ask of me righteous judgments, they delight to draw near to God.
58:4: Behold, you fast only to quarrel and to fight and to hit with wicked fist. Fasting like yours this day will not make your voice heard on high.

Here again we have a similar sentiment, but not much else. And this sentiment was shared by all of the prophets. So, for comparisons of style between 1st and 3rd. Isaiah, Archer has one match only.

Next, Archer points out that idolatry is alluded to in verses 57:4-5 and 65:2-4. This could not be from after the Exile, he says, because those that returned from Babylon were very pious, while idolatry was a problem in the time of Isaiah ben Amoz. This would seem to be a solid argument. However, in his *Introduction to the Old Testament*, Robert H. Pfeiffer says (1941, p. 458):

From the fact that whoever wrote 57:1-13; 65:1-15; 66:15-17 saw with his own eyes Jews practicing idolatry, it cannot be inferred that these sections were written before 586...for we know that the attraction of heathenism persisted in some Jewish circles at least until the Maccabean period.

Pfeiffer's point is well taken. We read in 1 Maccabees 1:52 that many of the Jews at the time of Antiochus Epiphanes (175-164 B.C.E.) were quite willing to go along with his edicts forbidding Jewish worship and instituting both idolatry and emperor worship. So, Archer's point does not hold up, and the reference to idolatry in the later chapters of Isaiah does not date them as being before the Exile.

However, fundamentalists might point out that later lapses into idolatry did not involve infant sacrifice, which is specifically referred to in Is. 57:3-13. Yet in Nehemiah 13:23-27 that priest and governor tells how he forced the breakup of mixed marriages between Jewish men and women of the Philistine city of Ashdod, as well as women of Ammon and Moab. He complains that the children of these mixed marriages do not even speak the language of the people of Judah. Since both Trito-Isaiah and Nehemiah are post-exilic, it is quite possible that the invective against pagan rituals in Is. 57:3-13, a block of verse that seems out of place with the material preceding and following it, may have been aimed at this mixed population, whose leanings were more toward the old paganism than toward the refined beliefs of the returning exiles.

Finally, Archer argues that the trees referred to in verses 41:19 and 44:14 would be unknown to an author living in Mesopotamia, which is where 2nd Isaiah is thought to have been written. The trees referred to are cedar, acacia, myrtle, olive, cypress, plane, and pine trees, which in 41:19 God says he will cause to grow in the desert; and in 44:14 cedars, holms, and oaks, which carpenters can fashion into idols. Archer says that such trees are unknown to Babylonia. But there is a great difference between what is native to a land and what is known to it. I could envision the Sahara Desert being irrigated so that mangoes and papaya as could be grown there even though I have never seen either a mango or papaya tree. Besides, the epic of Gilgamesh, the legendary king of Uruk, a city just south of Babylon, was undoubtedly written in Mesopotamia. Yet in chapter 2 of the epic, Gilgamesh and Enkidu journey to the Land of Cedars to do battle with Humbaba. In order to accept Archer's contention that the author of 2nd Isaiah could not have known of the trees he refers to if he were living in Babylon, we would have to believe that an educated author, living in that society and most likely being familiar with the epic, would not have ever heard of cedars or have any concept of what they were. That, of course, is simply ridiculous. Archer also argues that 2nd Isaiah speaks of mountains which a dweller in an alluvial plain would not be familiar with.

Yet, there are mountainous areas just to the east of Mesopotamia. The author would have some knowledge of what mountains were even if he did live in a river valley, just as someone living along the Mississippi river today could easily speak of either the Rockies or the Appalachians. Thus, like Archer's other arguments, this one disintegrates upon examination.

The Prophecies of 1st Isaiah

Other than the prophecy against Babylon in chapter 13 and one against Tyre and Sidon (also relating to the Chaldean period) in chapter 23—both of which will be covered in a separate chapter—the most important and historically verifiable prophecies in 1st Isaiah are those against Israel and Syria, those against Assyria, those against Egypt, those against Judah's neighbors (Philistia, Moab, and Edom) and the prophecy regarding the Babylonian embassy from Merodoch-baladan. For the fundamentalist view, when it is given I have used Gleason Archer's *Encyclopedia of Bible Difficulties* and the chapter on fulfilled prophecy from Josh McDowell's *Evidence that Demands a Verdict*. I have used these two books because both of them are classic works of fundamentalist apologetics and echo the arguments and sentiments of fundamentalism in general

Before we deal with these, let us consider the historical setting of Isaiah's day in some detail. Just like Nathan, who could upbraid King David for his adultery, and Elijah, who preached against the idolatry of King Ahab, the prophet Isaiah was mainly concerned with his own time and was essentially preaching a "social gospel." The period of his prophecies, 738-701 B.C.E., was a time of profound social changes in the kingdom of Judah. The old pastoral way of life was giving way to an urban society with an agricultural base. It was a period of prosperity which included the rise of a class of wealthy landowners and merchants at the expense of great numbers of free men. It was a time marked by corruption, exploitation and idolatry. The last of these was possibly the result of influences from already urbanized cultures including those neighboring Judah, particularly Israel and the Phoenician city-states, as well as the influence of the Canaanite pantheon, of which Yahweh was originally a member. Judah's wealth was due to the conquest of Sela by King Amaziah (798-780, see 2 Kings 14:7), followed by Azariah's (780-740) conquest of the rest of Edom, including the port of Elath on the Red Sea. These conquests gave

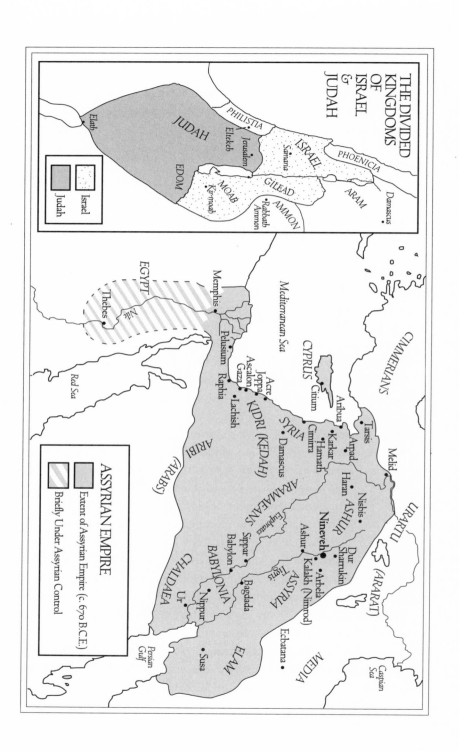

THE DIVIDED
KINGDOMS
OF
ISRAEL
&
JUDAH

Israel
Judah

PHILISTIA
JUDAH
ISRAEL
Jerusalem
Eltekeh
Samaria
PHOENICIA
EDOM
GILEAD
MOAB
AMMON
Kirmoab
Rabbath
Ammon
ARAM
Damascus
Elath

ASSYRIAN EMPIRE

Extent of Assyrian Empire (c. 670 B.C.E.)
Briefly Under Assyrian Control

EGYPT
Memphis
Thebes
Nile
Red Sea
Mediterranean Sea
Pelusium
Raphia
Gaza
Ascalon
Joppa
Acre
Lachish
KIDRI (KEDAH)
ARBI
(ARABS)
CYPRUS
Citium
Aribua
Arpad
Karkar
Hamath
Cimira
SYRIA
Damascus
ARAMAEANS
Euphrates
CIMMERIANS
Tarsis
Melid
URARTU
(ARARAT)
Haran
Nisibis
ASHUR
Dur
Sharrukin
Nineveh
Ashur
Kalakh (Nimrod)
Arbela
ASSYRIA
Tigris
Sippar
Babylon
Bagdada
BABYLONIA
Nippur
CHALDAEA
Ur
Persian
Gulf
ELAM
Susa
Echatana
MEDIA
Caspian
Sea

Judah control of the copper mines of Arabath and a seaport on a sea not con-trolled by the Phoenicians. From Elath, Judah's ships bore copper to Arabian ports and returned with oriental merchandise. Egypt was in anarchy at the time and posed no threat to Judah's security. In the north, Israel under Jeroboam II (785-744) had restored the borders of the time of Solomon, and Israel too was enjoying a period of great wealth.

The prosperity of the two kingdoms was overshadowed by ominous inter-national events. After a period of ineffectual kings, Assyria revived with the accession in 745 of Tiglath-pileser III (745-727). During the time of Ahab, an Israelite-Syrian alliance had checked the advance of Assyria at the battle of Qarqar in 853. However, Tiglath-pileser's conquest of Arpad in 740 gave him control of most of Syria. Rezin, prince of Damascus, along with the other princes of Syria and King Menahem of Israel, became an Assyrian tributary in 738. Between 737 and 735 Tiglath-pileser was distracted by wars in Media and Urartu, at which time Rezin organized an alliance against Assyria. Menahem's pro-Assyrian son, Pekahiah, had been assassinated by Pekah, his captain of the guard, who became king and joined Rezin's revolt.

Pekah and Rezin demanded that Judah become part of their alliance and jointly attacked Jerusalem upon the accession of King Ahaz in 735 to force the issue. The Edomites took advantage of Judah's plight and recaptured Elath (2 Kings 15:6), thereby cutting off the source of Judah's wealth. Shaken by these two disasters, Ahaz panicked and, against the advice of Isaiah, made himself the vassal of Tiglath-pileser, thereby putting Judah under Assyrian protection.

The Oracles Against Israel and Damascus

This is the background of the first set of Isaiah's prophecies that we will con-sider. Urging Ahaz to simply stand firm and not send to the Assyrians for help, Isaiah says that Ephraim (Israel) will be destroyed and cease to be a people within 65 years. (Is. 7:8). To help convince the king, the prophet then gives him two signs, the Immanuel sign (Is. 7) and the Maher-shalal-hash-baz sign (Is. 8). The first sign is that a child named Immanuel ("God [is] with us") will be born shortly. Before that child is old enough to know good from evil the two kingdoms attacking Judah will be deserted and Judah will be oppressed by both Assyria and Egypt. The second sign is that Isaiah's wife bears him a son, whom he names Maher-shalal-hash-baz ("the spoil speeds, the prey hastes"). Before that child can say "father" or "mother" the king of Assyria will carry off the wealth of Damascus and Samaria. Isaiah's prophecy that both kingdoms would be swept away was fulfilled to some degree when Damascus fell in 732 B.C.E. and Samaria fell in 722 B.C.E. If one takes the fall of Syria as fulfillment of the prophecy, then indeed the child Immanuel, then only three, would scarcely know good from evil. However, the prophecy said that *both* lands would fall to the Assyrians before the child would know good from evil, and Israel fell 13 years after the prophecy was pronounced. The child Maher-sha-lal-hash-baz would have spoken his first words even before the fall of Damascus. Therefore, the prophecy that Israel would be destroyed within 65 years is true; the Immanuel sign is half true and half false; and the Maher-sha-lal-hash-baz sign is a totally false prophecy. Of course, the general truth that both Israel and Damascus would soon fall does not depend on all of these prophecies being exactly fulfilled. However, fundamentalists claim that Bible prophecies are fulfilled to the letter. The failure of Isaiah's two signs to work out exactly is one of many reasons for assuming that their basic truth was of human rather than divine origin. Another is that, considering the reason for the Syrio-Ephraimite attack on Judah was to bolster their alliance against Assyria, against whom they were rebelling, it was logical to assume that both kingdoms would soon be attacked and destroyed by Tiglath-pileser. Isaiah was trying to point out that there was no need for Ahaz to send Tiglath-pileser tribute money to do what he intended to do any way. It was also reasonable to assume as Isaiah did in the Immanuel prophecy that the Assyrians would gobble up Judah as well as Israel and that Egypt might take advantage of the situation and occupy parts of Judah from the south (Is. 7:18). The latter did not happen, however.

In chapter 17 Isaiah resumes his oracles against Israel and Syria for their attack on Judah. He says of Damascus (17: 1-2):

> An oracle concerning Damascus. Behold, Damascus will cease to be a city, and will become a heap of ruins. Her cities will be deserted forever; they will be for flocks which will lie down and none will make them afraid.

Well, here it is some 27 centuries since Isaiah made that prophecy and Damascus, arguably the oldest continuously inhabited city now extant, is still thriving. It has been sacked numerous times, to be sure. But the prophecy explicitly states that it would cease to be a city forever, and the prophecy is explicitly wrong. Curiously, neither Gleason Archer nor Josh McDowell mentions this failed prophecy.

The Oracles Against Assyria

We have already looked into the oracle on Assyria's pride in chapter 10. Isaiah 30:31 says that Assyria will be terrified at the sound of God's voice. Neither of these is specific enough to either verify or falsify historically. Predicting that Assyria would be humbled is merely showing some knowledge that human states are finite not only geographically but temporally. Certainly, I could correctly foretell that America will fall—some day.

The main prophecy concerning Assyria is that of the destruction of the Assyrian army besieging Jerusalem and the death of Sennacherib. The history leading up to this prophecy concerns Hezekiah's revolt. Following the capture of Damascus, Tiglath-pileser occupied all of Israel except Ephraim. Upon his death in 727, Hoshea, king of Israel, revolted. The new Assyrian king, Shalmaneser V (727-722), overran Ephraim and besieged Samaria. He died before the city was taken, but his successor, Sargon II (722-705), did take the city in 722. Sargon deported, according to Assyrian records, 27,290 Israelites—probably the leading families—and brought in foreigners to populate the land. More Israelites were undoubtedly carried off as slaves later, and others fled south to swell the population of Jerusalem, while those who stayed probably intermarried with the foreigners and lost much of what made them Jewish. Even Ephraim ceased to exist as a tributary kingdom, and all Israel became the province of Samaria. At about this time Hezekiah (720 or 715?-686) succeeded Ahaz as king in Judah. He was eager to be out from under the Assyrian yoke, but appears to have followed Isaiah's advice not to get involved in two disastrous, Egyptian-sponsored rebellions. The first was in 720. The cities of Damascus, Samaria, Arpad, and Gaza all revolted, with the Egyptian army backing Gaza in the south. Sargon quickly crushed this revolt with victories at Qarqar and Raphia. The second revolt occurred in 713, when an Ionian Greek adventurer seized control of the Philistine city of Ashdod and tried to induce the tributary kingdoms of Palestine to revolt. One of Sargon's generals broke this revolt in 711.

What finally induced Hezekiah to risk his fortunes in the third revolt was a mix of an embassy from the Chaldean, Marduk-apal-iddina (Merodoch-bal-adan in the Bible), who had usurped the throne of the native Babylonian prince and was temporarily holding the city, and the death in 705 of Sargon II. The Chaldeans were probably organizing a revolt in Palestine in hopes that it would distract the Assyrians while they (the Chaldeans) consolidated their control over southern Mesopotamia. However, Sargon's son, Sennacherib (705-681), installed a native Babylonian ruler and drove the Chaldeans out of Babylon in 704. The Chaldeans returned in 703 but were promptly driven out again. By this time the revolt was already moving forward. Egypt, under the Ethiopian pharaoh, Shabaka (712-700), was enlisted to support this new venture in place of the Chaldeans. Tyre, Sidon, most of the Philistine cities, Edom, Moab, Ammon, and Judah all rose in revolt. Sennacherib moved quickly and besieged Tyre in 701. Sidon and the other Phoenician cities capitulated. Sennacherib then took most of the cities in Philistia and routed the Egyptians at Eltekeh (near Ekron). With the loss of Egyptian support the revolt collapsed, and, with the exception of Hezekiah, the tributary kings paid an indemnity to Sennacherih at Lachish. It was at this point that the Assyrian king sent his *rab-shaqa* (literally "cup bearer" called the "Rabshakeh" in the Bible) to Jerusalem to demand Hezekiah's surrender. Hezekiah refused, and Sennacherib invaded and devastated Judah. Only Jerusalem was left standing and it was under siege. Sennacherib says that he shut Hezekiah up in his royal city "like a caged bird." Hezekiah finally capitulated and, according to Assyrian records, paid out 30 talents of gold, 800 talents of silver and several hostages from his court. This is in fair agreement with the 30 talents of gold and 300 of silver mentioned in 2 Kings 18:14-16. Curiously enough, the Bible has this occur before the Rabshakeh's interview with Hezekiah's courtiers, thus before the siege of Jerusalem. The story, as told in 2 Kings and Isaiah, is that Hezekiah consults Isaiah, who prophesies that Sennacherib would not take the city, but that he would return to Assyria the way he came (Is. 37:33-35). Next an angel of the Lord destroys the Assyrian army, presumably with a plague (Is. 37:36). Sennacherib goes back to Assyria and is killed there by his sons, Adrammelech and Sherazar.

Was Isaiah's prophecy in fact fulfilled? We have no Assyrian record of such a plague. However, the Assyrians were not terribly honest about admitting failure. For example, their records claim a stunning victory over the allied forces of Israel and Syria at Qarqar in 853. Yet Assyrian expansion into that region stopped abruptly after the battle. What most likely happened was that the allies fought the Assyrians to a draw—no mean feat—whereupon the Assyrians withdrew after being paid tribute. It has been argued that had Sennacherib had the victory he claims over Hezekiah, he would not have contented himself with tribute and hostages, but would have taken Jerusalem and destroyed it as an example. That a plague could have swept through and rapidly decimated a besieging army is entirely possible. Dysentery due to poor sanitation could do it easily. On the other hand, Sennacherib seems to have varied his punishments on the rebellious kingdoms. Tyre was not taken but surrendered under terms favorable to Assyria. Ekron was taken, and the rebel leaders there were tortured and executed. Thus, an example had already been made. Sennacherib might not have thought it necessary to take Jerusalem after having already devastated the rest of Judah. In any case, it seems odd that the Assyrians would accept Hezekiah's tribute and hostages, then invade Judah, as the Bible has it. That would be bad policy, since such treachery would discourage rebels from capitulating. The Assyrians had enough trouble putting down revolts without creating a policy guaranteed to make retaking every rebel city a fight to the death.

As to the sudden demise of Sennacherib, seemingly as a result of his blaspheming Yahweh in his pride, the historical facts are somewhat different. Sennacherib was not murdered until 20 years after his attack on Jerusalem. The verdict on this prophecy has to be this: We have no historical validation. Barring new archaeological discoveries, we have to take its fulfillment or non-fulfillment as a matter of faith.

Oracles Against Egypt

Isaiah's oracles on Egypt are in chapters 19 and 20. In the first of these (Is. 19:2) Isaiah says that God will stir the Egyptians up against each other and that God will also give them up to be ruled by a fierce king (vs. 4). In verses 5-10, Isaiah prophesies in detail how the Nile will dry up. Chapter 19 continues with the prophecy that God will confuse the Egyptians and that (vs. 17), "...the land of Judah will become a terror to the Egyptians." Further, there will be five cities in Egypt that speak the language of Canaan and worship Yahweh (vs. 18). In that day, says Isaiah, a highway will connect Assyria and Egypt, and both will worship the Lord (vs. 23-24).

The first of these oracles was probably not even meant as a prediction, since Egypt was in a state of civil war at the time of Isaiah. The fierce king could either be the Ethiopian Shabaka or could refer to the Assyrians. As to the Nile drying up, while we have no particular mention of a drought in Egyptian records of the time, such things happened regularly enough that there would be nothing supernatural about such an occurrence. The kingdom of Judah never did become a terror to the Egyptians. Nor were five Jewish cities built there. The conversion of Egypt and Assyria and their being connected by a highway sounds apocalyptic rather than prophetic, i.e., something that was to happen in the "latter days" when God sets everything to right. Certainly neither Assyria nor Egypt was ever converted to Judaism.

Chapter 20 is a prophecy set in the year Sargon sent his commander-in-chief to Ashdod and took it. This would fit the revolt of 713-711. During that time Isaiah went about half naked and barefoot, imitating a captive, as a visual demonstration of what would happen to Judah if Hezekiah joined the revolt. Not only did Isaiah predict that the Assyrians would crush the revolt in Ashdod (Is. 20:6), however, he also said that the Assyrians would conquer Egypt and Ethiopia. As to crushing the revolt in Ashdod, this prophecy could easily have been made after the fact since Is. 20: 1-2 says:

> In the year that Tartan came unto Ashdod, when Sargon, king of Assyria sent him, and he came against Ashdod and took it; at that time the Lord spoke by Isaiah the son of Amoz, saying "Go and loose the sackcloth from off thy loins and put thy shoe from off thy foot."

In other words the prophecy against Ashdod was referred to in a chapter that mentions Ashdod being taken by Sargon's general in the past tense.

If Isaiah was prophesying the immediate conquest of Egypt or even one in his time, he was quite wrong. If he meant that eventually the Assyrians would conquer Egypt, he was only partly right. To attack Egypt in those days meant one of two things, either a sea-borne attack on the Nile Delta or a three-day trek across the Sinai Desert. Landing troops in the face of a hostile defender was virtually impossible, and the logistics of providing water for three days for an army were sufficiently daunting to deter most commanders. When the Persians under Cambyses took Egypt (512 B.C.E.) they did so by making deals with the Arabs to provide them with water. Despite having ample reason to invade Egypt, neither Sargon nor Sennacherib seems to have felt such a military adventure worth the cost. It was not until the reign of Esarhaddon (681-668) that the Assyrians finally invaded. Esarhaddon was in Egypt from 675-673 and did not bother to go further than the delta. Shabaka fled up the Nile from him, leaving his family for Esarhaddon to carry off as captives. The Assyrian king appointed various Egyptian princes as tributary rulers, but no sooner had he left then they began to plot against him. The foremost of these was Necho I, whose son Psamatik I (663-610) established the Saite dynasty. Egypt was virtually independent in 668 upon the death of Esarhaddon, and the Egyptians expelled the Assyrians in 658. Thus, the Assyrian rule in Egypt, consisting mainly of establishing tributary princes in the delta, only lasted, with varying levels of control, between eight and 18 years. Esarhaddon's successor, Ashurbanipul (668-626), attacked the delta in 667 and held some control over it for nine years. He also gained control of Thebes in 666, but the Thebans did not acknowledge the Assyrian-sponsored Psamatik I as their ruler until 664, and Ashurbanipul still found it necessary to sack Thebes in 663 to enforce Theban obedience to Psamatik. Even before Ashurbanipal's death, Egypt had won its total independence, and shortly after his death the Assyrian empire was destroyed by the Medes and Chaldeans. Was Isaiah's prophecy of the Assyrian conquest true? To the degree that it took place briefly, perhaps it was. But the prophecy in Isaiah 20 suggests the thorough subjugation of Egypt at the time of the anti-Assyrian uprisings in Palestine (Is 20:4-6):

> "...so shall the king of Assyria lead away the Egyptians captives and the Ethiopians exiles, both the young and the old, naked and barefoot, with buttocks uncovered to the shame of Egypt. Then they shall be dismayed and confounded because of Ethiopia their hope and Egypt their boast. And the inhabitants of this coast land will say in that day, 'Behold, this is what has happened to those in whom we hoped and to whom we fled for help to be delivered from the king of Assyria! And we, how shall we escape?'"

Since this prophecy was made in 713 and the Egyptians were still able to make mischief in 704, and in fact were not invaded until 675, some 28 years after Isaiah's prophecy, it seems doubtful that it was fulfilled as the prophet envisioned it. If, on the other hand, the point of the oracle was that the Egyptians would be hard put to defend themselves, let alone be dependable allies during a revolt, Isaiah was absolutely right. In any case, the possibility that Isaiah could predict the eventual (although temporary) Assyrian conquest of

Egypt without divine inspiration hardly has to overcome astronomical odds.

Oracles Against Judah's Neighbors

Isaiah's oracle against the Philistines in Is. 14:28-31 is set in the year that King Ahaz died, 715. It's historically vague, only saying that an enemy out of the north would destroy even the remnant of Philistia. The same is true of the prophecies against Moab in chapters 15 and 16, and of those against Edom in Is. 21:11-12 and Is. 34:5-17. In the last of these, Edom is spoken of as being soaked with blood in vengeance for Edom's acts against Zion (the mount of Jerusalem). Then the oracle becomes apocalyptic, saying that Edom's rivers would be turned to pitch and her soil to brimstone. Verse 10 says that "its smoke shall go up forever and ever." Following that, Isaiah predicts that Edom will be a deserted wasteland. Isaiah's wrath against Edom could stem from that nation taking advantage of Judah's weakness in the first year of Ahaz, when Israel and Syria were attacking Judah. It could also be that he was angry with all of Judah's neighbors for luring Hezekiah into the ill-fated revolt against Assyria.

To some degree all of these prophecies did come true in that there are no more Edomites, Moabites, or Philistines. However, without historical specifics there is no way to verify or falsify them. Obviously, the land of Edom was not turned into pitch and brimstone, and I think we can safely consider that language to be poetic exaggeration. In fact, other than saying that God would settle Judah's grudges against her neighbors, there is little in these prophecies other than vague but dire threats and poetic embellishment. However, linking Isaiah's oracles against Edom with those of Jeremiah and Ezekiel, Josh McDowell sees in Edom's present desolation a stunning fulfillment of Bible prophecy. In terms of its being fulfilled by chance or by human faculties, he gives a probability of 1 in 10 for Edom's conquest, 1 in 10 for its subsequent desolation and 1 in 100 for its being desolate forever. Multiplying these together, he arrives at a 1 in 10,000 chance that the prophecies could be anything other than divinely inspired. We will deal with Jeremiah's and Ezekiel's prophecies against Edom in the next chapter. For now let us answer this bit of skewed mathematics. Was it a 1 in 10 chance that Edom would be conquered? Considering that it stood in the path of the expanding empires of Assyria, Chaldea, Persia, Alexander the Great and his successors, Rome, the Moslem Caliphates, and the Turkish Sultanates, it would seem to be more of a 10 in 10 chance. In fact, it would be a 1 in 10 chance that any Palestinian state would have anything other than a history of violence and conquest. The same is true of desolation subsequent to conquest, particularly if we add to that the desolation caused by exhaustion of the soil after thousands of years of over-farming and over-grazing. As to the 1 in 100 chance that Edom would be desolate forever, I would remind McDowell and company that forever is not here yet. Fundamentalist speculations on the fate of the Philistines and Moabites fall into the same general pattern as those mentioned above.

The Embassy of Merodoch Baladan

In Isaiah 39 Hezekiah receives the embassy of the Chaldean ruler of Babylon and shows them his royal treasures, presumably as an assurance that he can finance his part in the coming revolt against Assyria. When Isaiah hears of this he tells Hezekiah (Is. 39:5-7):

> "Hear the word of the Lord of hosts: Behold, the days are coming, when all that is in your house, and that which your fathers have stored up till this day, shall be carried to Babylon; nothing shall be left, says the Lord. And some of your own sons, who are born to you, shall be taken away; and they shall be eunuchs in the palace of the king of Babylon."

With the exception that none of Hezekiah's own children were alive at the time of the Exile, this would seem to be a fairly accurate prediction of the Chaldean sack of Jerusalem in 586 and the subsequent Exile. However, there are other possibilities. First, the passage could have been inserted at the time of the Exile or later. Second, it could be merely a warning that involvement with the Chaldean plot would prove disastrous, as it did. In other words, this could be a genuine prophecy, common sense on Isaiah's part or a bit of later editing. Had Isaiah not referred to Hezekiah's descendants serving the king of Babylon, then his remarks about the royal treasure being carried off to Babylon could be interpreted as an ironic way of saying that Judah's wealth would be drained away in a fruitless adventure that would benefit only the Chaldeans. Since Isaiah *did* say that Hezekiah's sons would serve the king of Babylon, however, this second option would seem untenable. Isaiah's other prophecies concerning rebellions named the Assyrians specifically as the masters who would lead nations off into captivity, while this one refers to the "king of Babylon." Since chapter 39 is considered to be part of 1st Isaiah, albeit the last chapter, how can anyone justify dismissing it as later editing? Does not that show a bias against considering even the possibility of divine inspiration?

There are two reasons to suspect later editing. First, if the prophecy is genuine, why is the history garbled? The order of events in Isaiah is: (1) Sennacherib besieges Jerusalem (Is. 36, 37). (2) The angel of the Lord destroys the Assyrian army, and Sennacherib is assassinated by his sons (Is. 37:36-38). (3) Hezekiah falls deathly ill, but is healed by God (Is.38). (4) Hearing of Hezekiah's recent illness, Merodach-baladan sends him an embassy bearing gifts and letters (Is. 39). Historically, this is almost completely backwards. The actual sequence of events is: (1) The Chaldean embassy arrives in 703 to draw Hezekiah into the rebellion. (2) Sennacherib besieges Jerusalem in 701. (3) Some 20 years later, two of his sons assassinate Sennacherilb. As to Hezekiah's sickness or whether the Assyrian army was decimated by a sudden plague, we have no historical record. One would expect that divine authorship would not only provide accurate prophecy but accurate history as well. On the other hand, a later editor, living in Babylon over a century later, at a time when the Assyrians were nothing more than a memory, could easily have garbled the history of Hezekiah's day.

The second reason to suspect later editing is that parts of Isaiah were copied verbatim from 2 Kings. The oracle above from Is. 39:5-7 is identical to 2 Kings 20:16-18. The garbled history is likewise from 2 Kings. The books of 1 and 2 Kings were derived from the lost kingly chronicles of Israel and Judah and were later edited during the Exile. We know this because the history of the aftermath of the sack of Jerusalem, including the kindly treatment of Judah's erstwhile king, Jehoiachin, by Nebuchadrezzar's successor, Amel-Marduk (Evil-merodach in the Bible) in 560 B.C.E. concludes 2 Kings. Since 2 Kings had to have been edited after 560 and the prophecy regarding the Chaldean embassy is derived from 2 Kings, it was likely written after the fact. That material from 2 Kings was inserted into Isaiah demonstrates later tampering to enough of a degree to render all the prophecies in Isaiah suspect of being written, or at least altered, after the fact. Fundamentalists might object that the material common to Isaiah and 2 Kings could have originally come from Isaiah and that it was later copied into 2 Kings. This is unlikely, however, since the common material is in prose and is in the style of 2 Kings, whereas the prophecies of Isaiah were mostly in poetic form. Isaiah could have originally made a prophecy that because because Hezekiah had shown the Chaldean embassy his treasure, i.e. fallen in with their plan for a revolt, the treasure would be carried off to Assyria, along with some of Hezekiah's own sons, who would serve the king of Assyria. The editor would merely have to substitute Babylon for Assyria without further altering the original prophecy.

The Prophecies of Amos, Hosea, and Micah

While Isaiah seems to have been of the Judean nobility, Amos was a commoner. He felt called to leave his home in Judah and prophesy to the northern kingdom of Israel sometime between 760 and 750 B.C.E. during the prosperous reign of Jeroboam II. Most of his prophecies are against Israel and are complaints against social injustice. His prophecies against foreign nations are limited to the first two chapters, have a rote formula and are not specific enough to compare to historical records. Briefly, they are against Damascus and Ammon for wreaking destruction in Gilead (Am. 1:3-5 and 13-15), for which both nations will go into exile; against the Philistine cities, Tyre and Edom for trafficking in slaves (Am. 1:6-12), for which God will send fire on their strongholds; and against Moab for burning the bones of a king of Edom (Am. 2:1-3), though why Amos, (or Yahweh for that matter) should care what harm the Moabites and Edomites did to each other is hard to understand. Like the other prophecies, this one predicts destruction for Moab, without naming the destroyer.

Chapter 2 continues the brief prophecies with one against Judah (Am. 2:4-5) for failing to keep the law. Like the others, it has a rote formula that begins, "For three transgressions of Judah and for four, I will not revoke the punishment;" then continues with a description of the actual sin and ends with the words, "So I will send fire upon Judah and it shall devour the strongholds of Jerusalem." This is vague enough that it could mean divine destruction as with Sodom and Gomorrah, the sack of Jerusalem by the Chaldeans in 586 B.C.E. or its destruction by the Romans in 70 C.E. Anything that can be interpreted that widely is, of course impossible to either verify or falsify.

The only specific prophecy that might be historically verifiable is Am. 5:26-27, which says that because Israel has taken up Assyrian deities (Sakkuth and Kaiwan), God will take them into exile beyond Damascus. Since the Assyrian empire was in a state of torpor until 745, it is possible that this could be a genuine prophecy. On the other hand, Assyria as a not so distant menace that had attacked Israel in the days of Ahab could be a reasonable choice as Israel's executioner from purely human logic. This is particularly true if, despite the fact that Assyria had not roused itself yet, it had enough influence that Assyrian gods were being worshiped in Israel.

Hosea, a younger contemporary of Isaiah, was a native of Israel during its slide from prosperity into subjugation. Thus his prophecy in 11:5 that Assyria would rule Israel was a logical conclusion. His prophecy in that same verse that Israel will return to Egypt, also foretold in 8: 13, need not be taken as false so much as symbolic. Otherwise, Hosea's prophecies are historically vague.

Micah, another contemporary of Isaiah, was, like Amos, a commoner from the Judean countryside. His prophecy that Jerusalem would be destroyed (3:12), like that of Amos, is not specific enough to verify historically. Otherwise, the prophecies are general denunciations of corruption or references to "the latter days."

There are two exceptions to this in the prediction in 2:12 that the remnant of Israel will be gathered up and the prediction in 4:10 that, "you shall go to Babylon. There you shall be rescued, there the Lord will redeem you from the hand of your enemies." The first of these is obviously false. Those taken into exile from Israel by Assyria never returned. The second prophecy is obviously true. It would seem to come down to a matter of faith as to whether one considers this to be a genuine prophecy or a post-exilic addition. Much of the book of Micah, including chapters 4 and 5, refers to the restoration of Israel in the latter days, at which time the Jews will be powerful enough to defeat the Assyrians (5:6) and be to the nations of the world like a lion among the beasts (5:8). Obviously these prophecies are false in the historical sense that the Jews never did become powerful enough to defeat the Assyrians and have yet to be the chief nation state in the world as the lion is chief among all beasts. However, Assyria in this prophecy could merely be symbolic of world power. This sort of apocalyptic symbolism, if that is what it is, is far more typical of post-exilic literature than of the Assyrian period. On the other hand, there is no particular stylistic or linguistic evidence that this prophecy was not written by Micah. I would find it easier to believe in prophecies such as this one if they were supported by other true prophecies and were not encumbered by plainly false ones, such as Micah 2:12. Taken together, the prophecies of Isaiah and his contemporaries present one with too many false prophecies, clear evidence of later editing, and muddled history, to not make one suspicious of any that could be even possibly true.

PROPHECY OR FALSE PROPHECY?

Prophets of the Chaldean Period

WHILE 1ST ISAIAH CLEARLY DOMINATES THE ASSYRIAN PERIOD of prophecy, two great prophets, Jeremiah and Ezekiel, share the limelight in the Chaldean period. Jeremiah's prophecies were made over a period of 47 years, between 627 and 580. They end a few years after the destruction of Jerusalem by Nebuchadrezzar, when Jeremiah was taken to Egypt against his will as a refugee. Ezekiel's prophecies span 30 years between 593 and 563. He was among those deported to Mesopotamia. The minor prophets of the period were Zephaniah, who prophesied during the reign of Josiah (638-609); Habakkuk, active between 608 and 598; Nahum, whose short book deals only with the fall of Nineveh; and Obadiah, whose prophecies are entirely devoted to Edom. Because there is considerable overlap in the prophecies of Jeremiah and Ezekiel, as well as those of the minor prophets of the period, I have decided to deal with them as a group and have divided the prophecies as follows: oracles against Assyria and Nineveh, prophecies of the Exile and restoration, oracles against against Judah's neighbors (the Philistines, Moab, Ammon and Edom), those against Egypt and, finally, those against Tyre and Babylon. Of course, before we can truly understand what these prophecies really dealt with, we need to put them in their historical context.

History of the Chaldean Period

Following the death of Hezekiah, his son Manasseh (692-639) reigned for 53 years. He maintained a servile attitude toward his Assyrian masters, even

PROPHETS OF THE CHALDEAN PERIOD

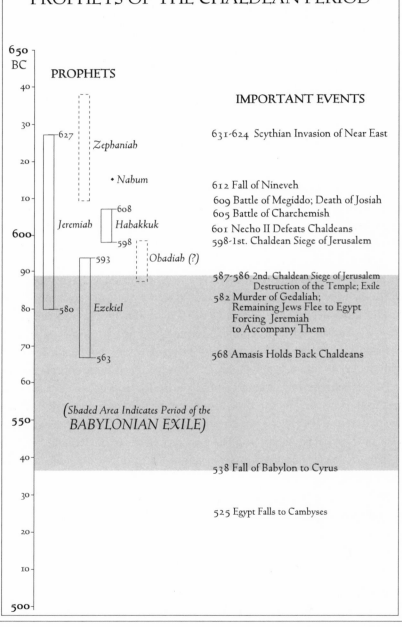

650 BC

PROPHETS

IMPORTANT EVENTS

627 *Zephaniah*

631-624 Scythian Invasion of Near East

• *Nahum*

612 Fall of Nineveh
609 Battle of Megiddo; Death of Josiah
605 Battle of Charchemish

Jeremiah

608 *Habakkuk*

598

601 Necho II Defeats Chaldeans
598-1st. Chaldean Siege of Jerusalem

593 *Obadiah (?)*

587-586 2nd. Chaldean Siege of Jerusalem
        Destruction of the Temple; Exile
582 Murder of Gedaliah;
        Remaining Jews Flee to Egypt
        Forcing Jeremiah
        to Accompany Them

580 *Ezekiel*

563

568 Amasis Holds Back Chaldeans

(Shaded Area Indicates Period of the
BABYLONIAN EXILE)

538 Fall of Babylon to Cyrus

525 Egypt Falls to Cambyses

500

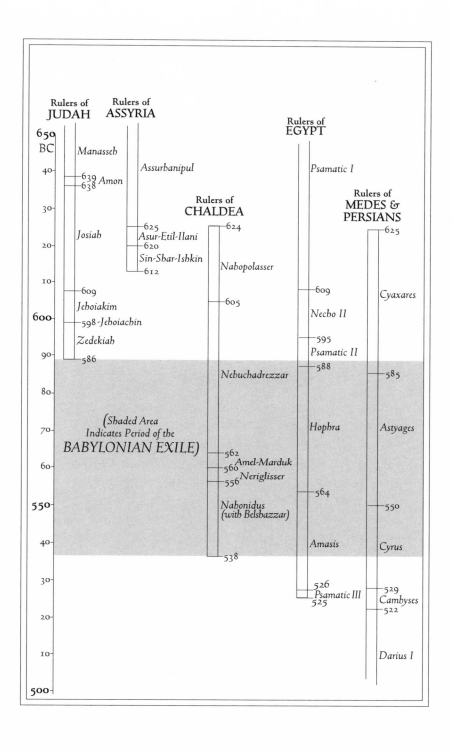

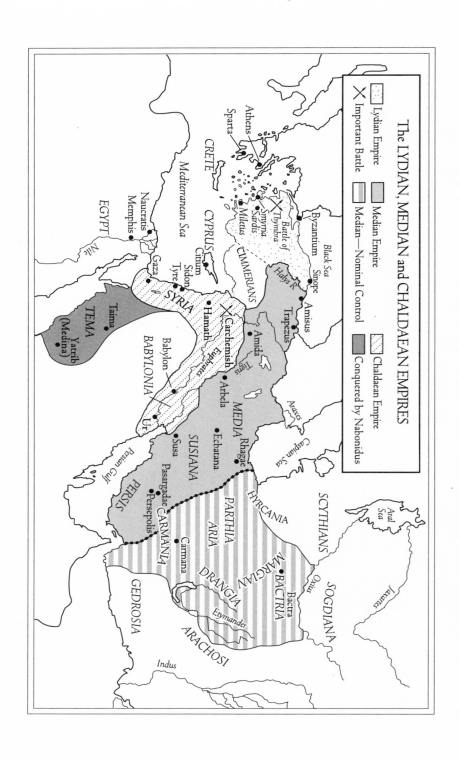

The LYDIAN, MEDIAN and CHALDAEAN EMPIRES

Lydian Empire
Important Battle ✕
Median—Nominal Control
Median Empire
Chaldaean Empire
Conquered by Nabonidus

SCYTHIANS

Aral Sea

Jaxartes

SOGDIANA

Oxus

MARGIANA

BACTRIA
Bactra

HYRCANIA

PARTHIA

ARIA

DRANGIA

Etymander

ARACHOSI

CARMANIA

Carmana

GEDROSIA

Indus

Caspian Sea

Araxes

Rhagae

MEDIA

Ecbatana

SUSIANA

Susa

PERSIS

Pasargadae

Persepolis

Persian Gulf

Amida

Tigris

Arbela

BABYLONIA

Babylon

Euphrates

Ur

Trapezus

Amisus

Sinope

Halys R

Black Sea

Byzantium

CIMMERIANS

Sardis

Smyrna

Miletus

Battle of
Thymbra

Athens

Sparta

CRETE

CYPRUS

Citium

Mediterranean Sea

Tyre

Sidon

Hamath

Carchemish

SYRIA

Gaza

EGYPT

Memphis

Naucratis

Nile

Taima

TEMA

Yatrib
(Medina)

adopting their customs and religion. He also allowed a great deal of corruption to flourish and is spoken of in the Bible with unmitigated vituperation. When his son, Amon, succeeded him in 639 and seemed likely to continue his father's policy, he was assassinated, and the people made Amon's son Josiah (638-609) king. He was only eight years old at the time and was under the control and teaching of members of the prophetic party during his minority years. Thus, he grew up to be a strong advocate of the pure worship of Yahweh.

The Assyrian empire was in a period of rapid decline at this time. Like his predecessors, Ashurbanipal had waged war during most of his reign. The empire was exhausted and had to rely increasingly on foreign allies. For example, the Assyrian presence in the Nile delta was greatly aided by Libyan mercenaries. Another tribe's service to the empire proved to be disastrous. The Assyrian attacks on Urartu had removed a barrier to nomadic tribes from north of the Caucasus mountains. Among those who infiltrated into Asia Minor were the Cimmerians, whom the Assyrians called the Gimmirai, and who are called the nation of Gomer in the Bible. They constantly raided Assyria's western provinces. Since the Cimmerians had been driven from the Caucasus by the Scythians, the Assyrians hired the latter to subdue them again. Realizing that the Assyrians were growing too weak to do their own fighting, the Scythians turned on their erstwhile employers and invaded the empire between 645 and 617. They sacked Damascus, bypassed Jerusalem and were bought off by the Egyptians as they approached the delta. In the east they penetrated as far as Media and Babylon. Unable to remain united in peacetime, the Scythians did not create their own empire and were eventually driven back across the Caucasus by the Medes. Upon the death of Ashurbanipal in 625 the Medes under Cyaxares (625-593) and the Chaldeans under Nabopolassar (625-609) declared their independence and attacked their former masters. Their joint forces destroyed Nineveh in 612 B.C.E.

The ensuing chaos endowed Judah with a spurious autonomy. This was not to last long, however. In Egypt, Psamatik I (663-610) had restored stability and united the kingdom. In 609 his son, Necho II (609-595), decided to take advantage of the power vacuum by occupying Palestine and Syria and aiding the remnant of the Assyrians. To the Egyptians a weak Assyrian state was preferable as a neighbor to a vigorous new empire. Josiah seems to have felt himself allied to the Chaldeans and undoubtedly saw the hand of God in the rapid fall of Assyria. Thus, considering God to be on his side, he opposed

Necho's forces at Megiddo. The result was predictably disastrous. Not only was his army defeated, but Josiah himself was killed. The Egyptians imposed a war indemnity on Judah and swiftly conquered all of Syria.

Necho's conquests proved to be as spurious as Judah's brief period of independence. The Assyrians under Ashur-uballit had made a stand at Harran, but the Medes and Chaldeans took Harran in 609. After a failed attempt to retake the city in 608, the Egyptians and Assyrians fell back on a defensive position on the west bank of the Euphrates at Carchemish. In 605 the Chaldeans under their crown prince Nebuchadrezzar forced a crossing, crushed the Egyptians and drove them in flight almost to their border. At that point Nebuchadrezzar heard that his father had died and hastened back to Babylon to secure his accession. He ruled from 605 to 561. Necho made no further attacks, and Syria and Palestine fell into Chaldean hands.

Following the death of Josiah, the Jews had made his son Jehoahaz king. However, within three months Necho had Jehoahaz sent to Egypt in chains and appointed his brother Eliakim king, naming him Jehoiakim, as a sign that, like his name, his power as king was a gift from the pharaoh. Following the battle of Carchemish, Jehoiakim (609-598) submitted to Nebuchadrezzar. In 598, however, Jehoiakim refused to pay tribute, and the Chaldeans attacked Judah, aided by bands of Arameans (Syrians), Moabites, and Ammonites. Jehoiakim seems to have fallen in battle. His son, Jehoiachin, surrendered to the Chaldeans in 597 and was taken into exile along with at least 10,000 of the leading citizens, iron workers, and other craftsmen. By deporting the leaders and anyone who might be skilled at making weapons, the Chaldeans thought to forestall any further revolts. Nebuchadrezzar put Josiah's third son, Mattaniah, on the throne, changing his name to Zedekiah.

Necho's son Psamatik II (593-588) remained at peace with Chaldea. But upon his accession, Psamatik's son Hophra (also called Apries, 588-569) invaded Palestine, taking Sidon by land and Tyre by sea. Along with Tyre and Ammon, Judah rose in revolt despite Jeremiah's warnings that it was folly. Edom and Philistia remained loyal to the Chaldeans. Nebuchadrezzar quickly besieged Tyre and Jerusalem in 587. The siege of Tyre lasted 13 years. Hophra sent an army to raise the siege of Jerusalem, but Nebuchadrezzar defeated the Egyptians and took Jerusalem after a bitter year-and-a-half siege, during which the city was reduced to starvation. Zedekiah attempted to flee, but was caught. After forcing him to watch the execution of his own sons, Nebuchadrezzar had him blinded and sent in chains to Babylon. The Chaldeans destroyed the city, razed the Temple to the ground and took most of its citizens into exile. Nebuchadrezzar appointed a man named Gedaliah governor of the province. He was assassinated in 582 by Ishmael, a descendant of the Davidic line. This revolt too was crushed, and 745 men and their families were taken to Babylon. Fleeing the Chaldeans, some of the rebels sought sanctuary in Egypt. They forced Jeremiah to come with them, and he ended his days there.

Oracles Against Assyria and Nineveh

Zephaniah, prophesying as he did during the reign of Josiah, foretold that Assyria would fall and that Nineveh would be destroyed (Zeph. 2:13-15). The entire text of the book of Nahum is a poem celebrating the fall of Nineveh, and is generally considered to have been written a few years before the city was destroyed in 612. Both prophecies are obviously true and both were written before the fact. Was divine inspiration required or were these prophecies a matter of common sense? Considering that Zephaniah was active during the reign of Josiah, during the time that Assyria was crumbling, and considering that Nahum was writing at a time when Assyria's enemies were converging on Nineveh, divine inspiration hardly seems necessary for the fulfillment of these prophecies. However, Josh McDowell considers the fall of Nineveh to be one of the prime evidences of prophecy fulfilled in history in a way that could not be predicted by mere human knowledge and insight. He argues that Nahum's prediction that the city would be taken in a state of drunkenness (Nahum 1:10), that it would be destroyed in an overflowing flood (Nahum 1:8, 2:6), that it would be burned (Nahum 3:13), and that it would be destroyed rather than captured (Nahum 3:19) were all specifically fulfilled in history. Before examining McDowell's claims in detail, let us see if Nahum really did say what McDowell claims he said. As to Nineveh being taken in a state of drunkenness, Nahum 1:10 says:

> Like entangled thorns they are consumed, drunken as with their drink, like dry stubble.

Leaving aside for the moment the fact that the first chapter of Nahum seems to be an acrostic psalm tacked on to the poem at a later time, there does seem to be an allusion, however oblique, to drunkenness. As to Nineveh being

Sardanapalus was a king of legend, not of historical fact.
Detail: *The Death of Sardanapalus* by Eugene Delacroix courtesy Louvre Museum, Paris, France. © Photo RMN—Hervé Lewandowski

destroyed by a flood, Nahum's words are:

> 1:8: But with an overflowing flood he will make end of his adversaries. 2:6: The
> river gates are opened, the palace is in dismay;

The first of these could be poetic imagery or it could mean a real flood. As to the second, the opening of the river gates has nothing to do with flooding the city. Of Nineveh's fourteen gates, eight opened on rivers. Thus, the odds of an enemy breaking through at a river gate were rather high. As to the city being burned, the usual fate of cities when they are sacked, Nahum 3:13 says:

> Behold, your troops are women in your midst. The gates of your land are wide
> open to your foes; fire has devoured your bars.

The gates referred to here have to be figurative, since they are the gates to the land rather than the city. It is a bit of a stretch to infer from this that Nahum was predicting the burning of Nineveh. As to the claim that Nahum predicted the total destruction and desolation of Nineveh, Nahum 3: 19 reads:

> There is no assuaging your hurt, your wound is grievous. All who hear the news
> of you clap their hands over you. For upon whom has not come your unceas-
> ing evil?

I have to say that it is a total stretch to make this verse say that Nineveh would be destroyed and remain desolate forever. This is particularly true when one considers that elsewhere in the Bible when prophets want to say this they do so quite explicitly, such as in Isaiah's unfulfilled prophecy of the destruction of Damascus (Is. 17: 1-2).

Ignoring for the moment that McDowell has stretched much of Nahum's prophecy to fit the fulfillment, let us consider his arguments. McDowell claims that Assyria's king Sardanapalus was camped outside his walls and had heard reports that his armies were doing well, though in reality they were being beaten. The king held a victory feast in the camp, and the army got roaring drunk. The Medes then launched a surprise night attack. The Assyrians were driven into the city with heavy losses. Secure behind massive walls and with enough food to last three years, the king did not consider that heavy rains would swell the Tigris river to the point that it swept away much of the city's walls and even flooded the city proper. When this happened Sardanapalus gave up hope, sealed off a portion of his palace, had his concubines killed and burned him-

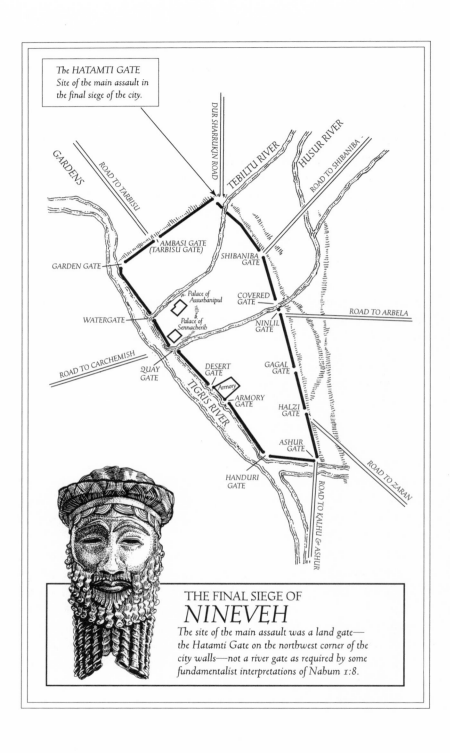

The HATAMTI GATE
Site of the main assault in
the final siege of the city.

GARDENS

ROAD TO TARBISU

DUR SHARRUKIN ROAD

TEBILTU RIVER

HUSUR RIVER

ROAD TO SHIBANIBA

AMBASI GATE
(TARBISU GATE)

SHIBANIBA
GATE

GARDEN GATE

Palace of
Assurbanipul

COVERED
GATE

ROAD TO ARBELA

WATERGATE

Palace of
Sennacherib

NINLIL
GATE

ROAD TO CARCHEMISH

TIGRIS RIVER

QUAY
GATE

DESERT
GATE

Armory

GAGAL
GATE

ARMORY
GATE

HALZI
GATE

ASHUR
GATE

ROAD TO ZARAN

HANDURI
GATE

ROAD TO KALHU & ASHUR

THE FINAL SIEGE OF
NINEVEH

The site of the main assault was a land gate—
the Hatamti Gate on the northwest corner of the
city walls—not a river gate as required by some
fundamentalist interpretations of Nahum 1:8.

self amidst his royal treasures as the Medes, Scythians, and Chaldeans poured into the city through the breach in the walls made by the flood.

What is wrong with this picture? Just about everything. McDowell seems to have gotten his "history" through popular but fictional sources. Despite the legendary tragic end of Sardanapalus, portrayed so graphically and with a touch of perverse eroticism in Delacroix's painting *Death of Sardanapalus,* and despite how well the story of his drunken feast fits his character, there was in fact no Sardanapalus. The Assyrians and their kings had not gotten decadent, drunken, effeminate, and addicted to luxury as the story implies, and as would fit the bias of our democratic ideals as the logical end of a powerful empire. No, though it was torn by dissension and exhausted by constant war, the Assyrian empire died as it had lived, and its kings went down fighting. When Ashurbanipul died, his son and chosen heir, Ashur-etil-ilani (625-620?), had to dispose of a usurper even as the distal provinces of the empire were slipping away. Elam and Egypt had become independent even while Ashurbanipul lived. After Ashur-etil-ilani's brief reign his brother Sin-shar-ishkun took over, first having to dispose of yet another usurper before he could organize the defense of the kingdom. Though the Egyptians and Lydians were his potential allies, neither kingdom had yet roused itself to send troops and he was forced to accept the help of the untrustworthy Scythians. He hoped that they would take on the Medes as he faced the Chaldeans. In 615 the Scythians did relieve a Median siege. However, in 612 the Scythians switched sides and joined the Medes and Chaldeans in their siege of Nineveh. Sin-shar-ishkun *may* have thrown himself on his funeral pyre as the city was being taken, thus providing the kernel for the legend of Sardanapalus. Even if this is true, however, the Assyrians did not give up. Ashurbanipal's youngest brother, Ashur-uballit, led a remnant of Assyrians still bent on resisting the invaders out of the falling city to Harran. It is possible that he fell at the battle of Carchemish.

So there was no drunken feast and no despairing king burning himself and his riches. Was the city taken because of a flood? McDowell claims that the three month siege of the city was too short to be explained by anything other than a catastrophic disaster. Actually, as stated above, the city had been attacked by the Medes in 615. Failing to take it on that occasion, Cyaxares plundered Ashur and other nearby cities. The Chaldeans likewise had been making forays into the Assyrian homeland. What was left of the empire was being weakened by repeated blows, and the people who were besieging

"For upon whom has not come your unceasing evil" (Nahum 3:19). Jewish captives are hanged from stakes by Assyrian soldiers in a stone relief found at Nineveh. Such atrocities earned the Assyrians the animosity of their subject peoples.

Nineveh had learned siege warfare from master teachers—the Assyrians themselves. The only indication that flooding may have helped bring down the city is that the Tigris had risen and was lapping against the walls, enabling the attackers to mount battering rams on rafts and assault areas ordinarily protected by the river. Even so, this was most likely a diversionary attack. The main assault was on the northeast corner, away from the Tigris, and it concentrated on the Hatamti gate. While this gate was close to the Tibiltu river, it was not a river gate. Thus, taken as predictive prophecy, Nahum 2:6 is specifically false. Of course, the book is actually a poem celebrating the end of Assyrian power and was not intended as prophecy in the way fundamentalists see it.

Since McDowell goes on at length about the nearly impregnable defenses of Nineveh, it is worthwhile pointing out how the city was taken so easily. Concentrating the attack on one main point, the Medes and Chaldeans only needed to breach the wall there to take the city. However, diversionary attacks, such as the raft-mounted battering rams, pinned down defensive forces in other parts of the city. Also with Scythian cavalry patrolling the landward walls sorties out of the city to take the attackers in the rear could easily be foiled, even assuming the Assyrians still had the man power to mount such attacks. The much vaunted 100-foot tall, 50-foot wide walls and 200-foot tall towers were of little help once a weak point at a gate was breached with the help of siege towers easily as tall as the walls themselves.

Another point that should be cleared up is the reason for the destruction of the city. Most cities when taken are sacked but not utterly destroyed. Was the fury directed against Nineveh an example of divine wrath? Possibly, though such things are a matter of faith. Actually, human wrath is quite sufficient to account for Nineveh's destruction. As Nahum said, "For upon whom has not come your unceasing evil?" As an example of what the Assyrians were like and why so many peoples risked rebelling against them time and again, consider these excerpts from an Assyrian monument set up by Ashurnasirpal about 883 B.C.E. (in De Camp, 1972, pp. 85-86):

> I destroyed them, tore down the wall and burned the town with fire; I caught the survivors and impaled them on stakes in front of their towns...Pillars of skulls I erected in front of the town...I fed their corpses, cut in small pieces to dogs, pigs [and] vultures...I slowly tore off his skin...Of some I cut off the hands and limbs; of others the noses, ears and arms; of many soldiers I put out the eyes...I flayed them and covered with their skins the walls of the town...The heads of

the warriors I cut off, and I formed them into a pillar over against the city; their young men and maidens I burned in the fire…Three thousand captives I burned with fire. I left not a single one alive to serve as a hostage.

A side note about Nineveh is the use that fundamentalists make of its destruction as yet another proof that the Bible was divinely inspired in all its parts. Hank Hanegraaf regularly claims on the *Bible Answerman* show that the city of Nineveh, which was often mentioned in the Bible, was thought to be mythical by historians until it was unearthed by archaeologists. Therefore, the appearance of Nineveh in the Bible proves the book's historical accuracy and is a point in favor of accepting everything else in the Bible as absolutely true. In reality, the city of Nineveh was generally thought to be lost rather than mythical. Even had it been thought of as a myth, however, using this same line of logic I could point out that the city of Troy was likewise considered mythical until the archaeologist Heinrich Schliemann, using the writings of Homer and other Greek myths as his guide, unearthed it. Should we then, following Hanegraaf's example with Nineveh and the Bible, use the discovery of Troy as validation of the existence of the Olympian gods of ancient Greece?

Oracles of the Exile and the Restoration

Jeremiah foretells the Exile in verses 10:17-18 and verse 25:11. Verse 10:17 refers to the people God is addressing as "you who dwell under siege," which could mean that it was written in either 597 or 587. The superscription of Chapter 25 says that it is an oracle that came to Jeremiah in 605. This would certainly be before either of the deportations. Thus, to the degree that it foretold the Exile before the fact, it is to some degree truly prophetic. Two things argue against its being divinely inspired, however. First, Jeremiah would have known that the Assyrians deported the people of Israel and would have interpreted this as God's punishment for their idolatry. He could easily see that not only was idolatry rife in Judah as well, but the likelihood the Jews would revolt and what the Chaldean response to such a revolt would be.

The second problem with the prophecy as stated in 25:11 is that the Jews would be in captivity to Babylon for 70 years. Since most of us do not follow ancient history that closely, it has become a truism that the Babylonian captivity did indeed last 70 years. Actually, the period from the fall of Jerusalem to the Chaldeans in 586 B.C.E. to the proclamation by Cyrus the Great of Persia in 538 B.C.E., allowing the Jews to return to Judah, is not quite 49 years. So the prophecy, if we take it literally, is just plain wrong. However, in all probability, the time was never meant to be exact. The 70 years could be either an idiomatic or symbolic way of saying "for a long time," particularly by using the mystical number seven. Thus Jeremiah could have been saying that the Jews would be in bondage for a sabbath of decades to expiate their sins.

Such an interpretation, however, is not an option for fundamentalists. Their problem is that 2 Chronicles 36:20-21 says:

> He [Nebuchadrezzar] took into exile in Babylon those who had escaped the sword, and they became servants to him and his sons until the establishment of the kingdom of Persia, to fulfill the word of the Lord by the mouth of Jeremiah, until the land had enjoyed its sabbaths. All the days that it lay desolate it kept sabbath, to fulfill seventy years.

Thus, if the fundamentalist tries to make Jeremiah's 70 years symbolic rather than literal, he makes a liar out of the Chronicler. Indirectly, he runs afoul of Leviticus as well. The land keeping sabbath while the people are in exile refers back to Lev. 25:1-7; 26:27-39. In Lev. 25 the people of Israel are directed to let the land lie fallow every seventh year. The implication often drawn by fundamentalists is that the Jews had neglected this rule for 490 years, hence they were removed for 70 years to make up for the lost sabbatical years. However, there is nothing in the Bible that says that they neglected the practice of sabbatical years. Lev. 26:27-39 says that if the people fail to keep faith with God, he will remove them from the land, and it will enjoy its sabbaths. Was this prophetic? Probably not. Remember that Leviticus is a priestly document, probably written either during the reign of Hezekiah, when the Assyrians had taken the leading people of the northern kingdom into exile and when Sennacherib was menacing Judah, or during the Exile itself. Given the Chronicler's reference back to Leviticus and his statement that the Jews were in exile in Babylon for 70 years, the fundamentalist is caught in what would be a dilemma for most of us. Either he accepts the truth of history and thereby falsifies the Bible, or he accepts Jeremiah 25:11 and 2 Chronicles 36:20-21 as literally true in spite of the historical dates. I said that this would be a dilemma for most of us. It is not a dilemma for fundamentalists: History simply loses. But then what are facts against the Word of God?

Both Jeremiah and Ezekiel prophesied that the Jewish nation would be restored. They obviously did this before the fact. Were these prophecies divinely inspired? To answer that question, let us consider them in some detail. In Jer. 30:3 God tells Jeremiah that the days are coming in which he will restore *both* Israel and Judah. In Jer. 30:9 God says that the Jews will return home to serve him and "David their king." Jer. 31:15 refers to Rachel weeping for her children. Verse 16 says that she will be comforted. Rachel's children were Joseph and Benjamin. Two tribes claimed descent from Joseph, Ephraim and Manasseh, and they were the most powerful of the 10 northern tribes. In fact, Israel is often referred to by the prophets as Ephraim. Therefore, verses 15 and 16 refer specifically to Israel. So Jeremiah's prophecy is that all 12 tribes will be restored and ruled over by a king of the line of David. The same is true of Ezekiel 37. Verses 15-22 refer to the restoration of both Judah and Israel, which, the verses say, will be united in a single kingdom. Verses 24 and 25 refer to a future Davidic king. This clearly did not happen. Judah only was restored and was never again ruled by a Davidic king.

Rather than accept the prophecies as the fond hopes of two prophets who had seen their nation destroyed, fundamentalists often try to make the prophecy a bit apocalyptic, saying that it refers to the modern state of Israel. For example, Hal Lindsey's premillennial bias shows when he states that because Ezekiel 37:21 refers to the children of Israel being returned from exile out of many nations, this could not be the restoration of the Jews after the Babylonian captivity. Had that been the case the verse would have said that God would restore the nation from Babylon. Thus, this restoration refers to the modern state of Israel (see Lindsey, 1970, pp. 51-2 and Lindsey, 1994, 136-7). At first glance this would seem a valid argument. However, when we examine the context of the verse, we find that previous to it in Ezekiel 37:15-20, God has told Ezekiel to take two sticks, one to stand for the 10 tribes of Israel and one to stand for Judah, and to join them together to make one stick. This symbol is to show that God will restore *both* Israel and Judah to the land in one kingdom. In that context, let us look once again at Ezekiel 37:21-22:

> ...Thus says the Lord God: Behold, I will take the people of Israel from the nations among which they have gone and will gather them from all sides, and bring them into their own land; and I will make them one nation in the land, upon the mountains of Israel; and one king shall be king over them all; and they shall no longer be divided into two kingdoms.

In the context of verses 15 through 22, the restoration of Israel, specifically the 10 tribes of the northern kingdom, from many nations refers to their dispersal throughout the Assyrian Empire. Also, we must remember that Ezekiel's work continued on after the fall of Jerusalem and that he knew of the Jews who had gone into exile in Egypt. Thus, even if we consider the people of Israel to consist of not only those from the northern kingdom dispersed through the Assyrian empire, but those in both Egypt and Babylon as well, they could be gathered back to Israel from many sides. Not only does the prophecy not relate to the 20th century, it was another of Ezekiel's many failed prophecies. The stick of Israel was never rejoined to that of Judah—and, of course, modern Israel is not ruled over by a king.

Another supposedly exact prophecy relating to the restoration is found in Jer. 31:38 40. Fundamentalists claim that these verses foretold the exact location and sequence of construction of modern Jerusalem's nine suburbs some 2,600 years ago. Ross gives the odds on chance fulfillment of this prophecy as one in a quintillion (one followed by 18 zeroes). McDowell (p. 314), using the same type of numerical alchemy we saw in the last chapter, says that the probability of the prophecy being fulfilled by purely human insight is 1 in 80,000,000,000.

What the actual prophecy in Jeremiah 31:38-40 says is that some day the city of Jerusalem will be rebuilt, from the tower of Hananel to the Corner Gate and from there to the hill of Gareb, then to Goah, and including the valley of dead bodies and the ashes and all the fields as far as the brook of Kidron and the Horse Gate. The modern city of Jerusalem extends far beyond these landmarks, two of which, the hill of Gareb and Goah, are unknown according to the notes in the *Oxford Annotated Bible*, volume V of the Interpreter's Bible and the *Illustrated Dictionary and Commentary of the Bible*. In fact these landmarks have nothing to do with modern Jerusalem. Rather, they are the boundaries of Old Testament Jerusalem. All that Jeremiah was saying was that Jerusalem would be rebuilt someday. Rather than a prophecy it was the earnest hope of a man who trusted in his God even when it looked as though his nation would be extinguished forever.

How is it then that fundamentalists have arrived at the conclusion that Jeremiah was predicting the boundaries of modern Jerusalem? To understand the twists and turns of their reasoning let us compare the real boundaries with the fundamentalist interpretation of them. First we start with the tower of

Interpreting Jeremiah's Predictions About the Rebuilding of Jerusalem

In order to back their claims that the biblical prophet Jeremiah predicted the step by step growth of Jerusalem from Old Testament to modern times, fundamentalists have conveniently located several unknown sites north of the city where growth has indeed occurred. They have also moved many known sites to the north, in order to accomodate their interpretation of Jeremiah's predictions.

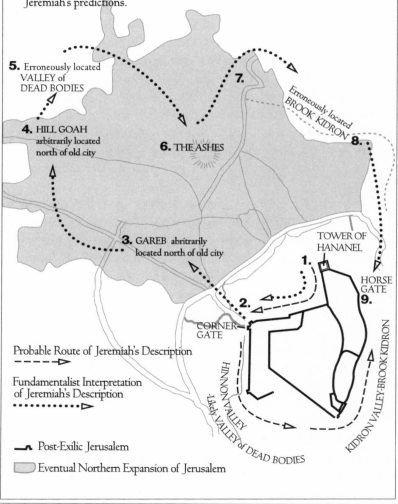

5. Erroneously located VALLEY of DEAD BODIES

7.

Erroneously located BROOK KIDRON

4. HILL GOAH arbitrarily located north of old city

6. THE ASHES

8.

3. GAREB arbritrarily located north of old city

TOWER OF HANANEL

1.

2.

HORSE GATE

9.

CORNER-GATE

Probable Route of Jeremiah's Description
----►

Fundamentalist Interpretation of Jeremiah's Description
••••••••••►

HINNON VALLEY
-likely VALLEY of DEAD BODIES

KIDRON VALLEY-BROOK KIDRON

►◄ Post-Exilic Jerusalem

Eventual Northern Expansion of Jerusalem

Hananel, which was on the northeast corner of ancient Jerusalem. Next we move to the Corner Gate at the northwest corner of Jerusalem. So far the fundamentalist map matches the real one. Now, however, the fundamentalists move north to what they say is Gareb and the hill of Goah, those two landmarks that no one else can identify. Without giving any basis for his reasoning, McDowell simply says that Schneller's Orphanage is the present site of the hill of Goah. He then leads us east to what he claims is the Valley of the Dead Bodies, because it was once a cemetery. In fact, there were also cemeteries southeast of the city. According to the *Interpreter's Bible* the Valley of Hinnom (Gehenna), a place where child sacrifice was performed, was the Valley of Dead Bodies. Thus, from the corner gate we should have turned south instead of north. The fundamentalists now turn south to the brook of Kidron—which is northeast of the tower of Hananel in McDowell's map—and go past the tower to the Horse Gate on the eastern wall of the old city. Thus, they have carved out a considerable section of territory north of the old city. However, in the process of doing this they have had to falsify Jerusalem's geography. In every other map of Jerusalem, whether it be ancient or modern, the Valley of Kidron (which may have had a brook in it thousands of years ago) is southeast of the city, not northeast of the tower of Hananel as McDowell has it. The proper boundaries outlined by Jeremiah run from the tower of Hananel, the northeast corner of the old city, west to the Corner Gate, the northwest corner of old Jerusalem, south to the Valley of Hinnom, southwest of the old city, east to the Valley of Kidron, southeast of the old city, then north to the Horse Gate on the eastern wall. This encloses the old city and nothing else.

Since I cannot read minds, I have no way of knowing whether McDowell's error is deliberate deception, self-deception through wishful thinking, slipshod research, or some combination of any or all of these. I do know it is grossly wrong and that the fundamentalist version of the prophecy cannot come out right without false landmarks.

There is one last possibility that Jer. 31:38-40 is prophetic, however. The city of Jerusalem in Jeremiah's day enclosed a considerably smaller area than is spoken of in the prophecy. The city described in the verses is in fact postexilic Jerusalem. Most scholars see these verses as later material inserted into the text to look prophetic. Fundamentalists could assert that the verses do in fact constitute a genuine prophecy that was fulfilled in ancient times rather than as a description of modern Jerusalem; but should they take that course they would create an insurmountable problem for themselves. The final state-ment in Jer. 31:40 regarding this rebuilt city of Jerusalem is: "It shall never again be uprooted or overthrown." Considering that the Romans under Titus did rather an effective job of overthrowing the city in C.E. 70, even utterly destroying the Temple, this statement in Jer. 31:40 cannot be the word of God.

Oracles Against Judah's Neighbors

As with the prophets of the Assyrian period, many of the oracles of doom and destruction issued by Jeremiah and his contemporaries were aimed at Judah's neighbors. Jeremiah, Ezekiel and Zephaniah prophesied against Philistia. The oracle of Jer. 47 is dated "before Pharaoh smote Gaza." It is historically vague, a general prophecy of doom. Ezek. 25:15-17 is likewise vague as is Zeph. 2:2-7. The Philistines did not join in Judah's revolt against Chaldea and may have joined the Chaldeans in attacking the Jews. This would account for Jeremiah and Ezekiel being hostile to them. As to why Zephaniah was foretelling their doom it is anyone's guess. In spite of the vagueness as to who would destroy the cities of Philistia, or perhaps even because of it, McDowell plays the prob-ability game once more with the destruction of the Philistine cities, giving the odds of mere humans predicting their fall as 1 in 12,000. Since none of the prophets foretold who was going to do the destroying, McDowell and the "experts" he cites say the prophecy of Ashkelon's fall was fulfilled when Sultan Baibars destroyed it in 1270 C.E. The two problems with this date as a fulfill-ment of prophecy are first, that all of the people who vexed the ancient Jews and their prophets were long dead by the time Baibars took Ashkelon. So who was God taking vengeance on? Does a transcendent, almighty God kill inno-cent people for what their ancestors, living 1800 years earlier did? The second problem is that, as I said in the last chapter, it would be remarkable if any city lying in the path of conquest (as those in Palestine do) were to have a history that was not filled with violence and destruction.

McDowell and his colleagues also point out that the Philistines were "cut off," i.e., leaving no descendants. And indeed, there are no Philistines alive today. There are also no Phoenicians, Chaldeans, Scythians, Picts, Gauls, Visigoths, Vandals, Iberians, or Huns alive today. In fact, of all the peoples of the ancient world living in reasonably well populated areas of Europe and the Near East, the only survivors are the Jews, the Armenians, Georgians,

Ossetians (Alans), Basques, Bretons (and other Celtic fringe populations), and the Albanians, who are the remnants of the Illyrians. Altogether, the territories of these peoples would not add up to a good-sized European state. Peoples are overwhelmed by invaders, lose their original languages and form new peoples and tongues over the period of centuries and millennia. But one would scarcely call that process the fulfillment of prophecy. For example, the Celtic-speaking peoples once controlled the British Isles, France, Switzerland, part of Spain, and the Rhine, Danube, and Po river valleys. Today, the only people who speak a Celtic tongue as their first language are the Bretons, who occupy the northwest corner of France. Prominent among the Celts were the Gauls. They were conquered by the Romans, eventually stopped speaking a Celtic language and instead spoke a local variant of Latin. After they were invaded by the Franks, a Germanic tribe, the two peoples merged to form the French by about 600 C.E. The fact that the Philistines, who occupied a small strip of coastline adjacent to Judah, are no longer with us after thousands of years is hardly evidence of divine wrath, or indeed anything out of the ordinary.

Another problem with the prophecies against the Philistines is that the post-exilic prophet Zechariah predicts that after God has chastised them a remnant of the Philistines will be restored and be converted to Judaism (Zech 9:5-8). If we look for long range fulfillment of these prophecies, then Zechariah must be factored in with the others. Yet if we do that the Philistines cannot be "cut off." In short, the Bible gives us two different contradictory prophecies of the fate of the Philistines. How do fundamentalists deal with such internal contradictions? Basically they deny their existence. Their attitude is summed up by CRI staffer Ron Rhodes (*Bible Answerman* show, December 23, 1992):

> If you've interpreted one Scripture in such a way that it's contradicted by another Scripture, your interpretation is wrong. Why? Because God does not contradict himself.

Other neighbors of Judah were also targets of prophetic wrath. Oracles against Moab are found in Jer. 48 and Ezek. 25:8-11. Those against Ammon are Jer 49:1-6 and Ezek. 25: 1-7. Zeph 2:8-11 is leveled at both Moab and Ammon. Edom is targeted in Jer 49:7-22, Ezek 25:2-14, Ezek. 35 and all of the short book of Obadiah. While most of these prophecies are the usual dire but historically vague pronouncements of doom and desolation, a few are notable either for the historic event that prompted them or for a reasonably historically verifiable prophecy. These are Ezekiel's prophecies in chapter 25 that the lands of Moab and Ammon would be taken by the "peoples of the east," generally thought to mean the Arabs; Jeremiah's rather mild oracle against Ammon in response to an Ammonite raid in 601; and the reason for the oracles against Edom. These are all somewhat tied together.

In 587, when Judah rebelled against the Chaldeans, Edom, and Philistia remained loyal to Nebuchadrezzar. The Edomites even took advantage of Judah's distress to invade the Negev. They may have been under some pressure from Arabs invading their homeland, since eventually they lost all of what had been Edom to the Arabs who founded the Nabatean kingdom. The eventual fate of the Edomites was that they became known as the Idumeans and were conquered by the Maccabees, who forcibly converted them to Judaism. Ezekiel prophesies that the Arabs will overrun Moab and Ammon, but does not mention such a fate for Edom. (For McDowell's probability tally on Edom, see the preceding chapter.) In response to an Ammonite raid, Jeremiah predicted that God would afflict the Ammonites, but would later restore their fortunes.

Let us see if these prophecies are true and if so to what degree by seeing how true or false Josh McDowell's supposed fulfillments are. The Arabs did eventually come to possess the lands of Moab and Ammon, but this did not occur until the seventh century C.E. when, fired by the new faith of Islam, the Arabs overran the Middle East, Persia, Asia Minor, Egypt, and North Africa. Again, this is a bit late for God to take vengeance on the Moabites and Ammonites of Ezekiel's day, who had been dead for 1200 years. Nevertheless, McDowell and company see this as fulfillment of a divine prophecy. They also see in the growth of Jordan's capital, Ammon, part of the fulfillment of Jeremiah's prophecy that God would restore Ammon's fortunes after a time, even though the Jordanians are Arabs rather than Ammonites. McDowell also sees in Jer. 48:47, which says that God will restore the fortunes of Moab in the latter days and Jer. 49:6 that Ammon's fortunes will be restored, the promise that the Ammonites and Moabites will one day be restored to their lands. This will certainly be a good trick, seeing that neither nationality exists any more than do the Philistines. (Of course, since they were probably absorbed by their Arab conquerors, the prophecy might even now be fulfilled!) The fact that its fulfillment is officially pending has not stopped McDowell from including it in his probability tally (p. 287), which he adds up as follows: the take-over by men of the east is 1 in 5; that the men of the east will make Ammon the site of their palaces (Ezek. 25:4) is 1 in 10, and the return of the Ammonites and Moabites is 1 in 20. Multiplying these together he gets a 1 in 1000 chance of the prophecy being other than divinely inspired. Even though this is a comparatively conservative number, McDowell is not even playing by his own rules when he adds in an unfulfilled prophecy. That he can so blithely do such a thing demonstrates that historical verification is quite dispensable in the fulfilled prophecy game should the prophecy not turn out to be true or even possible to fulfill.

Oracles Against Egypt

Jeremiah and Ezekiel also made dire prophecies concerning Egypt. McDowell uses the cities of Memphis and Thebes as examples of their fulfillment, as well as a prophecy concerning who would rule Egypt. The prophecies are in Ezek. 30: 13-15 and state that God will destroy the idols of Memphis, destroy Thebes, and end the rule of Pharaoh. McDowell lists their fulfillment as the decline of Memphis resulting from the building of nearby and competitive Cairo in the seventh century C.E., the destruction of Thebes by the Persian emperor Cambyses in 525 B.C.E., and, in that same year, the end of Egypt's independence, including the extermination of the pharonic line. All of these are true, but McDowell leaves out an important element of Ezekiel's prophecy. In chapter 30, the same one that contains the verses McDowell cites, verses 10-12 state:

> Thus says the Lord God: I will put an end to the wealth of Egypt by the hand of Nebuchadrezzar, king of Babylon. He and his people with him, the most terrible of nations, shall be brought in to destroy the land; and they shall draw their swords against Egypt, and fill the land with the slain. And I will dry up the Nile, and will sell the land into the hand of evil men; I will bring desolation upon the land and every thing in it, by the hand of foreigners. I, the Lord, have spoken.

Gleason Archer is a bit more honest when he claims that the prophecy that Nebuchadrezzar would conquer Egypt was fulfilled. Before we examine the validity of his assertion let's review the history of Nebuchadrezzar's struggles with Egypt and Egypt's internal affairs during this time. After trouncing the Egyptians at Carchemish in 605 and pursuing them nearly to their border, Nebuchadrezzar had to hurry back to Babylon to secure his accession to the throne after his father's death. Though his accession went smoothly, he was not able to take further action against Egypt until 601. At this point, however, he was defeated by Necho, and the boundaries between the two nations remained fixed for a time. In 588 Necho's grandson Hophra invaded Palestine and Syria, only to be driven back by Nebuchadrezzar in 587. After the Chaldeans razed Jerusalem there was a period of peace until 568.

In the intervening period Hophra, who like the preceding Saite kings had relied heavily on Greek mercenaries, had problems with conflicts between the Greeks and his native Egyptian troops. When he sent one of his generals, Amasis, to quell an uprising among the mercenaries, Amasis joined them and deposed Hophra in 569. Archer (pp. 277-278) claims that the funerary stela of Nes-Hor (now in the Louvre) an Egyptian commander during the reign of Hophra relates how an army of "northerners and Asiatics" penetrated nearly to the Ethiopian border. He takes this to be evidence that Nebuchadrezzar's assault on Egypt in 568 was an unqualified success. Archer's claim echoes that of George Rawlinson's two volume *History of Ancient Egypt* published in 1882. It was Rawlinson's contention that Nebuchadrezzar placed Amasis on the throne as a tributary king. However, both the *Encyclopeadia Britannica* and the 1988 *Atlas of Ancient Egypt* by John Baines and Jaromir Malek state that Nebuchadrezzar was attempting to put Hophra back on the throne, presumably as a puppet, but that the Chaldeans were held back by Amasis. Some histories of Egypt say that not only did Amasis crush the invaders but that Hophra was killed in the battle (see Trigger, 1983, pp. 339-340). Nicholas Grimal (*A History of Ancient Egypt,* 1988) also says that Amasis held back the Chaldeans, although he says that Amasis had already disposed of Hophra by that time. In his *Nebuchadrezzar and Babylon,* D. J. Wiseman says (1983, p. 30):

> The intention of Nebuchadrezzar's initiative was to take Egyptian pressure off the Babylonian garrisons in Syro-Palestine during a period of consolidation of control. There is no evidence to show that the aim was an invasion of Egypt so much as a curtailment of Egyptian influence on the cities of the via maris and hinterland.

Other authors see the events of 568 as a minor border skirmish, a full-scale battle ending in either a stalemate or another drubbing for the Egyptians, but not one that resulted in an invasion. Like Wiseman, they see Nebuchadrezzar's motives as being punitive rather than an attempt at conquest.

From all this it can be seen that the history of this period is a bit muddled. Nevertheless, the balance of scholarly opinion is that Nebuchadrezzar did not conquer Egypt. The only Chaldean record of the campaign is a cuneiform tablet dating Nebuchadrezzar's attack on Egypt as being in his 37th year (either 569 or 568). The tablet does not say what the outcome of the assault was, which also argues against a grand conquest, since the Chaldeans would certainly have bragged of it had they conquered or even badly savaged Egypt.

This leaves only Archer's claim concerning the funerary stela of Nes-Hor as evidence that Ezekiel's prediction that Nebuchadrezzar would conquer Egypt, or at least invade the land and "fill it with blood," was a true and fulfilled prophecy. Against all of the other dubious and inconclusive evidence, does the monument in question actually give some evidence that Egypt really suffered a massive Chaldean invasion as Archer claims? The answer is an unequivocal no. I wrote to the Louvre's Department of Egyptian Antiquities to find out exactly what Nes-Hor's monument did say. According to the Louvre, the statue (not stela) of Nes-Hor (Louvre A 90) bears a partially obliterated inscription recounting how, when Nes-Hor was governor at Elephantine, he defeated a mixed band of soldiers from the Aegean Isles (i.e. Greeks) and the Near East. Far from being even the vanguard of Nebuchadrezzar's army, these soldiers were deserters from Hophra's mercenary forces. They were apparently attempting to leave Egyptian territory in order to sell their services to the king of Cush. Nes-Hor's great contribution in defeating them was not that he repulsed the furthest thrust of a massive Chaldean invasion, but rather that he kept these formidable mercenaries from joining Egypt's enemies on its southern border. So, even the one slim piece of evidence supporting the fulfillment of Ezekiel's prophecy turns out to be yet another bit of poor scholarship, a chimera that evaporates once one takes the time to gather some reasonably detailed information. And the prophecies of Jeremiah and Ezekiel that Nebuchadrezzar would conquer Egypt in the midst of great carnage are shown to be simply untrue.

Prophecies Against Tyre and Babylon

I have saved two sets of historical prophecies for this chapter because they were (at least seemingly) foretold by prophets of both the Assyrian and Chaldean periods. They are also considered by fundamentalists to be among the most

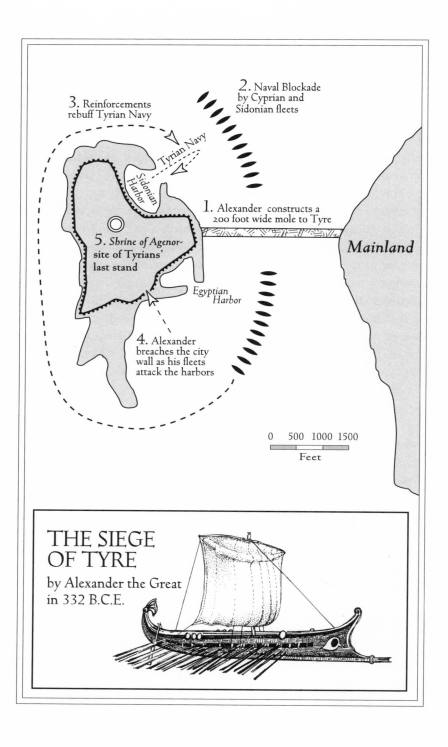

3. Reinforcements
rebuff Tyrian Navy

2. Naval Blockade
by Cyprian and
Sidonian fleets

Tyrian Navy

Sidonian Harbor

1. Alexander constructs a
200 foot wide mole to Tyre

Mainland

5. *Shrine of Agenor-
site of Tyrians'
last stand*

*Egyptian
Harbor*

4. Alexander
breaches the city
wall as his fleets
attack the harbors

0 500 1000 1500

Feet

THE SIEGE
OF TYRE

by Alexander the Great
in 332 B.C.E.

persuasive arguments for fulfilled prophecy, hence the validity of the Bible and the notion that God is working in the unfolding history of the world. This view must be wonderfully comforting. One can look back with complacency on such the horrors of history as the atrocities committed by the Assyrians, the Mongols, and by such men as Hitler and Stalin; the bloodshed in the name of religion in the Crusades, the Thirty Years War or by Muslim terrorists, Jewish fundamentalists, and the warring tribes of Northern Ireland; or even the long history of slavery, exploitation, and genocide, of which even our own nation has been guilty. One merely ascribes the horrors to satanic influences and accepts that God is ultimately in charge and that he will make it all come out right in the later days; that history's parade of empires is God allowing man some autonomy, then reining him in when his pride becomes overweening. Thus insulated against the past, one is protected from the present as well and need not be alarmed or sickened by what is happening today in places like Guatemala, Bosnia, the entire continent of Africa, and every regime on the face of the earth where men, women, and children are imprisoned, tortured, and murdered daily for merely being suspected of having democratic leanings.

At the risk of stripping away even a thin layer from this wondrous cloak of complacency, I must now demonstrate that the prophecies foretelling the fall of Tyre and Babylon are patently false.

Tyre

Josh McDowell's explanation of how Ezekiel's prophecy of the fall of Tyre was fulfilled by Alexander the Great (pp. 274-280) is commonly voiced by many other fundamentalists, including Gleason Archer (pp. 276-277) and Hank Hanegraaf. McDowell lays out the prophecy, made between 592 and 570 B.C.E., as containing seven specific predictions: (1) Nebuchadrezzar would destroy the mainland city, the main body of Tyre being on an island (26:8); (2) many nations would come against Tyre (26:3); (3) Tyre would be made like a bare, flat rock (26:4); (4) fishermen would spread their nets on the site (26:5;) (5) the debris of the city would be cast into the sea (26:12); (6) the city would never be rebuilt (26:14); and (7) none would be able to find Tyre ever again (26:21).

All of these predictions, says McDowell, were specifically fulfilled. Nebuchadrezzar did indeed destroy the mainland suburbs in the course of his 13 year siege of the city (586-573 B.C.E.). Then, almost two and a half centuries later, Alexander the Great besieged Tyre, again destroying the mainland suburbs. But this time Alexander's army used the debris of the destroyed mainland city to build a mole across the strait (i.e. threw the debris into the water) to sack the island city. So infuriated was the great conqueror by Tyre's obstinate resistance that he utterly demolished it. The island was made into a flat rock, the ideal place for fishermen to spread their nets. Though Tyre was rebuilt in time, it lost its former greatness. Nevertheless, its location was strategic enough that it was captured many times. Antigonus took it 18 years after Alexander sacked it, and the Moslems and Crusaders fought over it centuries later. Thus "many nations" came against Tyre. Crowning this edifice of cobbled history is McDowell's estimate via Peter Stoner that the chance that Ezekiel could have foretold all this through human wisdom alone is 1 in 75,000,000.

At first glance it might seem, particularly to a believer, as though Ezekiel had indeed predicted the future history of Tyre in some detail. But there are a number of problems with his interpretation. Notice that the prediction he lists as first—Nebuchadrezzar's destruction of the mainland suburbs—is out of order. Being verse 26:8, it should come after every prediction other than the two saying that Tyre would never be rebuilt or ever found again. What the prophecy actually states is that, presumably because Tyre failed to help its ally, Judah, against the Chaldeans, God will bring as many enemies against it as the sea has waves and that they will destroy Tyre and make it a barren rock where fishermen will spread their nets. All of this—verses 26:1-6—is a pretty general way of saying that Tyre would be utterly destroyed. It is more of a curse than a prophecy. The specific prophecy that Nebuchadrezzar would come against Tyre and destroy its mainland suburbs is not prophecy at all. The siege was from 586 to 573 B.C.E., and the prophecy dates between 592 and 570 B.C.E., making it quite possible that this part of the prophecy was either made after the fact or was a reasonable assumption on the part of Ezekiel of what was about to happen. The rest of the prophecy of Tyre's destruction makes it quite plain that Ezekiel is saying that Nebuchadrezzar would be the one to utterly destroy Tyre. History tells us that this prophecy is simply wrong. Tyre came to terms with Nebuchadrezzar and accepted Chaldean suzerainty in 573 B.C.E. That is why, in order to make the prophecy work, McDowell and other fundamentalists have to reach centuries into the future—long after everyone against whom Ezekiel and his God had a grudge had died—for its fulfillment in Alexander's time. As to the rest of the prophecy, Tyre's remains have not been lost to us, and there is a modern city of Tyre, though it is only a sleepy little fishing village. After thousands of years it is reasonable that any city would lose its greatness. This is hardly prophecy.

But there is yet another reason that even fundamentalists should *not* accept the conquest of Tyre as being fulfilled by Alexander the Great. Despite the fact that none of them mention it, there is another prophecy concerning the fall of Tyre in Is. 23 which specifically says that Tyre will be destroyed by the Chaldeans. Verse 13 says:

> Behold the land of the Chaldeans! This is the people; it was not Assyria. They destined Tyre for wild beasts. They erected their siege towers, they razed her palaces, they made her a ruin.

Isaiah's prophecy did not doom Tyre to oblivion, however. Once it has lain neglected for 70 years, it will live again, but God will turn Tyre's evil ways to good (Is 23:17-18):

> At the end of seventy years, the Lord will visit Tyre, and she will return to her hire, and will play the harlot with all the kingdoms of the world upon the face of the earth. Her merchandise and her hire will be dedicated to the Lord; it will not be stored or hoarded, but her merchandise will supply abundant food and fine clothing for those who dwell before the Lord.

"Those who dwell before the Lord" would have to be the Jews of the restoration. Thus, Isaiah predicts that the Chaldeans will destroy Tyre and that after 70 years it will be rebuilt and its profits will be turned over to the Jews. This prophecy presents fundamentalists with many problems. First of all their scenario of Ezekiel 26 being fulfilled by Alexander the Great cannot be true without making a liar of Isaiah. Second, Isaiah's prophecy is not true. The Chaldeans did not destroy Tyre and the city's profits did not benefit the returning Jews. Third, Tyre's 70-year period of desolation sounds suspiciously like that of Jerusalem predicted by Jeremiah. Thus, it could conceivably have been a prophecy of the Chaldean period that got tacked onto 1st Isaiah, either by error or deliberately as a way of enhancing the prophecy's validity. But if this is the case then all prophecies are suspect of being after the fact or at least a lot closer to it than they might seem. However it is taken Is. 23 brings McDowell's historical edifice down like a house of cards. Perhaps this is why fundamentalists prefer not to mention it.

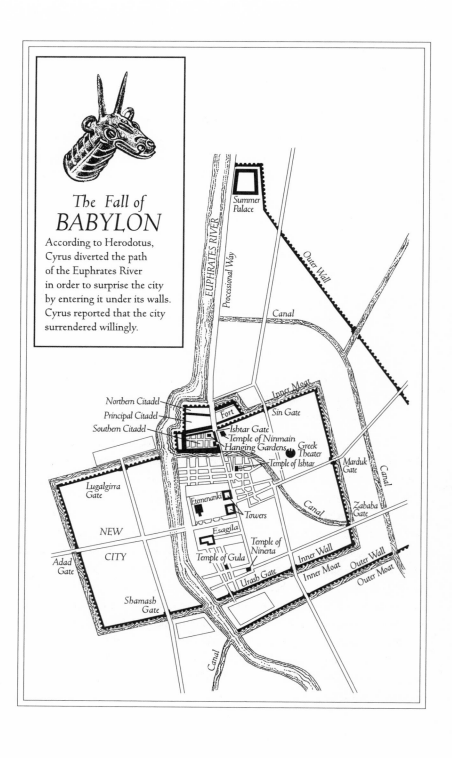

The Fall of
BABYLON

According to Herodotus,
Cyrus diverted the path
of the Euphrates River
in order to surprise the city
by entering it under its walls.
Cyrus reported that the city
surrendered willingly.

EUPHRATES RIVER

Summer
Palace

Processional Way

Outer Wall

Canal

Inner Moat

Northern Citadel
Principal Citadel
Southern Citadel

Fort

Sin Gate

Ishtar Gate
Temple of Ninmain
Hanging Gardens
Temple of Ishtar

Greek
Theater

Marduk
Gate

Canal

Lugalgirra
Gate

Etemenanki

Towers

Canal

Zababa
Gate

NEW

Esagila

Temple of
Ninerta

Inner Wall

Outer Wall

Adad
Gate

CITY

Temple of Gula

Urash Gate

Inner Moat

Outer Moat

Shamash
Gate

Canal

Babylon

Using selected prophecies from Isaiah 13 and 14, and Jeremiah 51, McDowell says of them that they predicted that: (1) Babylon would be like Sodom and Gomorrah (Is. 13: 19); (2) that it would never be inhabited again (Is. 13:20, Jer. 51:26); (3) that even Arabs would not camp there and nobody would even pasture sheep there (Is. 13:20); (4) that desert creatures will infest its ruins (Is. 13:21); (5) that its stones would not be removed for corner or foundation stones for other cities (Jer. 51:26); (6) that the site would not even be frequently visited (Jer. 51:43); and (7) that it would be covered by pools of water (Is. 14:23).

It seems reasonable to say of cities that are abandoned to ruin that they are like Sodom and Gomorrah, that few people will visit them, and that if they are in a desert region sheep will not be pastured there and they will be the haunt of wild animals. Considering that thousands of years of irrigation have greatly increased the salinity of Mesopotamian soil, it is also not unreasonable that the site of Babylon, originally a swampy area, would be part desert and part pools of brackish water. Finally, since Babylon's cornerstones and foundation stones were huge and heavy, it is unlikely they would be dragged away for other building projects. McDowell does admit (p. 307) that much of the city's brick was salvaged for use in nearby towns. Thus, these predictions could easily have been made without any divine inspiration. Nevertheless, McDowell again quotes Stoner's probability tally as follows: There is only a 1 in 10 chance that Babylon's destruction could be foretold by human insight; only 1 in 100 that it would never be inhabited again; 1 in 200 that Arabs would never camp there; 1 in 4 that sheep would not graze there; 1 in 5 that wild beasts would inhabit the ruins; 1 in 100 that Babylon's stones would not be taken to use in other building projects, and 1 in 10 that few people would visit the site. Completing the numerical alchemy by multiplying all these together, Stoner gets a 1 in 5,000,000,000 chance that predictions of Babylon's fall could be anything other than of divine origin.

McDowell cites as fulfillment of the prophecies of Isaiah and Jeremiah the decline and eventual abandonment of Babylon following the damage done to it during the struggles for succession between the generals of Alexander the Great following his death and says of Babylon (p. 305) that it died a slow death. Only by being extremely selective could McDowell and company see in such a fate the fulfillment of the prophecies in Isaiah and Jeremiah, and McDowell has been selective indeed. He has only used Is. 13:19, 20, 21, 23 and Jer. 51:26, 43. Yet in 1st Isaiah all of chapter 13 and part of chapter 21 are devoted to oracles against Babylon. Prophecies of Babylon's doom are salted through out chapters 50 and 51 of Jeremiah. In 2nd Isaiah all of chapter 47 and some verses of chapter 48 deal with the fall of Babylon while Cyrus of Persia is mentioned in Is. 44:28 and 45:1-13. Given all this material, why did McDowell restrict himself? Perhaps the reason is that a slow decline into oblivion is not what the prophets foretold. Consider the following from Isaiah 13:15-18 concerning Babylon's fall:

> Whoever is found will be thrust through, and whoever is caught will fall by the sword. Their infants will be dashed in pieces before their eyes; their houses will be plundered and their wives ravished. Behold, I am stirring up the Medes against them, who have no regard for silver and do not delight in gold. Their bows will slaughter the young men; they will have no mercy on the fruit of the womb; their eyes will not pity children.

Or consider these verses from Jeremiah 50 and 51:

> Jer. 50:10: Chaldea shall be plundered; all who plunder her shall be sated.

> Jer. 50:14-15: Set yourselves in array against Babylon round about, all you that bend the bow; shoot at her, spare no arrows, for she has sinned against the Lord. Raise a shout against her round about, she has surrendered; her bulwarks have fallen her walls are thrown down....

> Jer. 50:21:...Slay and utterly destroy after them, says the Lord....

> Jer. 50:29-30: Summon archers against Babylon, all those who bend the bow. Encamp round about her; let no one escape. Requite her according to all that she has done; for she has proudly defied the Lord, the Holy One of Israel. Therefore her young men shall fall in her squares, and all her soldiers shall be destroyed on that day, says the Lord.

> Jer. 51:3-4: Let not the archer bend his bow, and let him not stand up in his coat of mail. Spare not her young men; utterly destroy all her host. They shall fall down slain in the land of the Chaldeans.

> Jer. 51:11: Sharpen arrows! Take up shields! The Lord has stirred up the spirit of the kings of the Medes, because his purpose concerning Babylon is to destroy it,....

Added to these prophecies of doom is the prediction in 2nd Isaiah (47:11) that "ruin shall come on you suddenly." The picture given by these prophecies is one of sudden, violent destruction: the city plundered, its men slaughtered, its women raped, and its children dashed against walls. Clearly, this is in stark contrast to what McDowell sees as their fulfillment.

Oddly enough this picture is in keeping with the general fundamentalist view of the fall of Babylon, and many a pastor draws upon this supposed history to show the fate of decadent, blaspheming nations, usually with the insinuation that America is headed the way of Babylon.

With this prophetic background it is hardly surprising that fundamentalists, among others, regard as history the story of Belshazzar's feast in chapter 5 of the book of Daniel. Part of the story that is told of the fall of Babylon is the tale from Herodotus that Cyrus took the city by diverting the Euphrates river, which ran through the middle of the city, and stealing in under the walls via the dry river bed. Many fundamentalists cite this as a fulfillment of Jer 51:36, "...I will dry up her sea and make her fountain dry." All the while this is going on, the preachers tell their flocks, the decadent Babylonians are feasting and getting drunk, totally unaware of their impending doom. Even D. W. Griffith, who portrayed Belshazzar as a good guy, used such a scenario in his silent classic *Intolerance*. So well known is the story of Belshazzar's feast that, particularly if the hand writing on the wall is edited out, most people do not question its historicity. Of course it is a stirring story, something that makes ancient history palatable. Consider the pageantry of the tale, as it is often related by fundamentalist ministers. While the dissolute, besotted Belshazzar slurps wine from the pilfered sacred vessels, and his nobles revel in a drunken orgy thinking themselves secure behind their massive fortifications, retribution for their corrupt rule is coming on them. Grim and resolute, the noble Cyrus, his engineers having diverted the Euphrates, gives the signal. In near silence, the troops march in under the walls, where the river had only recently run. As they enter the doomed city, they hear the sounds of debauchery and drunkenness drifting from the palace. Then, suddenly, the city is in flames. The alarm is sounded, but it is too late, and before they even fully comprehend what is happening, the nobles are taken as the Medes and Persians storm through the palace. Belshazzar, pallid with fear, realizing too late the folly of his ways, is cut down with the goblet still in his hand. By dawn the city has been looted and burned, its population butchered or taken off into slavery. Thus ended the might and wealth that was Babylon. What drama! What pathos! What bunk!

In reality, about the only piece of truth in this florid tale is that Babylon changed hands from Chaldean to Persian rule. Fundamentalists are not entirely to blame for this scenario. To the degree that ancient history is taught at all in our schools it is taught badly. The popular rendering of the fall of the Chaldean empire is that it was hopelessly corrupt, and that Nabonidus and his son Belshazzar were a couple of incompetents. The father has often been represented as a doddering antiquarian—most happy when he was digging up the site of some Sumerian temple—who left the affairs of state in the hands of his playboy son. Belshazzar, we are often told, made a hopeless alliance against Persia with Lydia and Sparta. When Cyrus swept down upon them, they got their just deserts.

The facts are something else again. Nabu-na'id (Nabonidus) first came to prominence as an officer in service to Nebuchadrezzar when, in 585, he negotiated a treaty by which the boundary between the Median and Lydian empires was fixed at the river Halys and a bloody but indecisive war between the two empires was ended. This man of acute statesmanship was hardly the pottering old antiquarian as he has often been portrayed. When Nebuchadrezzar died in 562, he was succeeded by his son Amel-Marduk (Evil merodach in the Bible), who was murdered in a coup after only two years. His successor, Neriglissar, was Nebuchadrezzar's son-in-law. He died after an unsuccessful military campaign against the Medes in 556. When his son Labashi-Marduk tried to succeed him, he was murdered, and the nobility of Chaldea elected Nabonidus king.

Along with suffering a bad press, Nabonidus inherited an unfortunate and possibly untenable situation. Relations between the Chaldeans and the Medes had declined. The economics of the empire were seriously strained and it was riven by internal division. The wars and extensive building programs of Nebuchadrezzar and his successors had created inflation. From surviving Chaldean records we know that prices rose by 50% between 560 and 550, and by 200% between 560 and 485 B.C.E. (see Saggs 1992, pp. 147-8). Babylon's wealth was based on trade. The routes that fed into the city were from the Persian gulf, overland routes from Syria, and eastern trade routes that were now in the hands of the Medes. Of the three, one was in now hostile hands and the ports on the Persian gulf were silting up. Compare the ancient and present coast lines of the gulf and one can see that what were once ports are now far inland. Accordingly, Nabonidus looked to the west to rescue the economic situation. In his *The Greatness That Was Babylon,* H. W. F. Saggs says (1992, p. 148):

> Nabu-na'id's response to the situation in Babylonia was a remarkable attempt to move the centre of gravity of the empire westwards and secure the trade routes from south Arabia. Investing his son Bel-shar-usur (Belshazzar of Daniel...) as regent in Babylonia, he led an army through Syria to the oasis of Teima in northwest Arabia, where he executed the native king and made the town his base for the next ten years. During this period of residence in the west he pushed two hundred and fifty miles further southwards, through a number of places that can be identified, until he finally reached Yatrib [Muslim Medina...] on the Red Sea. Nabu-na'id specifically states that he established garrisons in and planted colonies around six oases which he names.

Another initiative undertaken by this surprisingly energetic ruler was a plot with Cyrus, king of Anshan, to overthrow the Medes. In 553 Cyrus led a revolt against his Median overlord, Astyages. At the same time Nabonidus attacked Harran and took it. Harran lay at the juncture of trade routes leading south to Babylon and west to Syria, Palestine and Egypt. And, with the success of the revolt, Nabonidus apparently thought that his new ally would open the eastern trade routes once again.

The taking of Harran is linked to the king's third initiative. Nabonidus was the son of a high priestess of the moon god Sin at the temple in Harran. He himself was a devotee of Sin, a deity that had analogues in the Aramean pantheon. It was apparently part of his westward shift that he elevated the worship of Sin over that of Marduk, whose analogues outside of Mesopotamia were less distinct than those of Sin, and who was in any case intimately associated with the city of Babylon. To this end he not only restored the temple of Sin in Harran, which the Medes had desecrated, but built a temple in Sippar intended to rival that of Marduk in Babylon.

So, the doddering antiquarian was in reality an energetic ruler doing his best to cope with a worsening political and economic situation. His 10-year absence from the capital was not due to madness or some eccentricity, as has been inferred in the past, and his investiture of his son Belshazzar as regent was not out of neglect for the empire. As to Belshazzar, he too seems the victim of a bad press. A look at a map of the day will show that his alliance with Lydia, Egypt and Sparta was not foolish. It was the only one possible. They were the only other great powers than Chaldea and Persia.

What happened to Nabonidus is that virtually everything he did backfired in ways that could not have been foreseen. As Ecclesiastes 9:11 says, "The race is not to the swift nor the battle to the strong…but time and chance happen to them all." The time and chance that happened to Nabonidus was twofold. His erstwhile ally Cyrus proved to be a worse foe than the Medes had ever been. When the Medes had been overthrown, the Lydians under Croesus had seized some of the western provinces of the empire, giving Cyrus a pretext for war. After an indecisive battle on the Halys, Croesus went into winter quarters, disbanding many of his troops as was the custom in those days. Wars were generally waged in the spring and summer, and battles were seldom fought in bad weather. Instead of following suit, Cyrus invaded Lydia and decisively defeated Croesus at Thymbra in 546. Nabonidus was now left to face Persia alone, with little hope that either the Spartans or the Egyptians could send effective help in case of an invasion.

Domestically, everything Nabonidus did antagonized the native Babylonians. It must be remembered that before the Chaldeans had led the revolt against Assyria they had been raiders and pirates, more of an aggravation to the Babylonians than anything else. In fact, in 731 B.C.E., the Assyrians, under Tiglath-pileser III drove the Chaldeans, who had usurped the native Babylonian prince, out of the city in response to the pleas of the Babylonians, just as Sennacherib would do in 703. Even as the new masters of the empire, they were merely tolerated by the older Babylonians. When Nabonidus not only absented himself from the city for a decade to center the empire further west and left it in the regency of his son, but also antagonized the priests of Marduk, the patron deity of Babylon, by devoting himself to the worship of the moon god, Sin, the disaffection of the Babylonians became acute. It must be remembered that throughout history, with the possible exception of our own noble experiment, religious acts have always been implicitly political. By snubbing the worship of Marduk, Nabonidus was relegating the city of Babylon to second-class status. Cyrus capitalized on this disaffection and seems to have fostered anti-Chaldean sentiment in the city. Inscriptions found in Babylon dating from the fall of the Chaldeans accused Nabonidus of being blasphemous, a heretic and demon possessed.

Militarily, the Chaldeans were not in a position to invade the much larger Persian empire and thus had to wait for the Persian attack. It began in 546 when the Persians threatened the coast from Elam and may have taken Uruk. For some time after that Cyrus seems to have been distracted by wars in the eastern part of his empire. In 539 the Persians forced a crossing of the Tigris river at Opis and marched on Sippar, just north of Babylon. It fell without a fight. Belshazzar may have fallen at the battle of Opis. Meanwhile, a revolt had broken out in Akkad. In October of 539 B.C.E., Gobryas, the Persian commander, entered Babylon virtually unopposed, for the simple reason that the Babylonians welcomed the Persians as liberators. The tale told by Herodotus of the diversion of the Euphrates may be true, but was not the major stratagem he would have us believe it was. In fact, according to the cylinder inscription of Cyrus dating from 538 B.C.E. he entered Babylon without a fight. In the words of Cyrus (in Matthews, 1991, p. 148):

> Thus, Marduk ordered Cyrus to march against his city of Babylon. He marched with Cyrus as a friend while the army strolled along without fear of attack. Marduk allowed Cyrus to enter Babylon without a battle....

In spite of all this, is it possible that the Persians betrayed the Babylonians, looted the city and left it desolate? Could they have posed as liberators then taken the Babylonians by surprise? That the city was not taken by surprise is attested to by the fact that a loyalist core held out in the city's citadel for a number of months. Cyrus, who had not even been present at the initial surrender, entered the city to view the taking of the citadel by storm, after which he observed the requisite pieties by participating in a sacrifice to Marduk. This is an interesting side note bearing on prophecy, since Jer. 50:2 prophesies concerning the fall of Babylon: "Bel is put to shame, Merodach [Marduk] is dismayed." This would indicate that the conquerors would sack the temples or at least hold the gods of Babylon in contempt. Again, history is quite different. Not only did Cyrus forbid any looting, but, according to the *Cambridge Ancient History* (Vol. 3 1990, p. 225):

> Cyrus, as a wise ruler, left the religious institutions of the people alone, and saw to it that this conquest should be attributed to the invitation of Marduk, the great god of Babylon.

Thus, there was no bloodbath. It was the Persians, not the Medes, who took the city. There was no humiliation of the native religion. The city was not taken by surprise while its rulers were feasting and drinking; Babylon fell at the end of a seven-year war. In short, the prophecies in Isaiah and Jeremiah were, quite simply, wrong, and the "history" related in Daniel 5 is pure fiction. Perhaps that is why McDowell failed to include them in his book. Were the prophecies of Babylon's fall in 1st Isaiah from Isaiah ben Amoz or were they inserted later? It scarcely matters since they were resoundingly wrong, but if God really did inspire the prophet, writing in the 700s to foretell the end of Babylon, why didn't he get it right?

One of the first things that should alert anyone that the story in Daniel and the biblical oracles predicting the fury of the Medes and Persians against Babylon simply are not true is that the city would be of far greater use to them intact than in ruins. Even when, in response to a revolt, Xerxes sacked the city in 482 B.C.E., destroyed its fortifications and melted down the golden statue of Marduk, he left Babylon functional as a commercial center. In 331 B.C.E., two centuries after the Persian conquest, Babylon was still important enough that Alexander the Great, to whom the city had just surrendered, confirmed its privileges and allowed it to issue its own coinage. The city began to decline only in 312 B.C.E., after it had been sacked by Demetrius, son of Antigonus, one of the *Diadochi* (successors to Alexander). Seleucus, who ultimately controlled the area, determined that it would be cheaper to build a new capital rather than repair the extensive damage in Babylon. To that end he transferred part of Babylon's population to the new city, Seleucia, on the west bank of the Tigris. After taking Mesopotamia from the Seleucids, the Parthians built their capitol, Ctesiphon, on the east bank of the Tigris opposite Seleucia. Trade was rerouted first through Seleucia, then through Ctesiphon, bypassing Babylon. Even then, the decline of Babylon was gradual. Jews, among them the rabbinical scholars editing the Talmud, were still living in Babylon in the second century C.E.

Despite the relative ease by which I was able to find the true history of the fall of Babylon in some detail in public libraries, fundamentalist ministers apparently have not availed themselves of the material. Here's the very popular Rev. Raul Ries of Calvary Chapel, Diamond Bar, on the subject (*Manna For Today*, KKLA, November 12, 1993):

> By the time Belshazzar was judged by God as the handwriting came on the wall, seventy years were used up and then...God judged Babylon by bringing Darius the king of Persia and the Medes and the Persians and sneaking in as the gates were left open just as God had said, as the guy that was watching the gates was drunk and fell asleep. They kind of cruised into the city and took over the city, and Belshazzar was killed that very night just as God had said in the book of Isaiah, chapter 5.

I should note that prophecies of the fall of both Nineveh and Babylon speak of God making the rulers of those cities drunk (Nahum 1:10 and Jer. 51:39). In fact the statement that God will "make them drunk" is used in prophecy over and over. Rather than treating it as a prophecy to be specifically fulfilled, it should be looked at in the same light as the Greek saying: "Whom the gods would destroy, they first make mad." In other words, whom God would destroy, he first makes drunk, i.e. destroys his reason.

Not all fundamentalists are either this blind to the discrepancy between the prophecies and history or are as willing to avoid the unpleasant facts as is McDowell. One line of millennial thinking sees the prophecies as yet unfulfilled. According their scenario, which I will explore in more detail in a later chapter, the Kurds are the modern day descendants of the Medes (not true) and will sack Babylon in the future, when it is the center of the empire of the Antichrist—who may just be Saddam Hussein!

Before we leave the discussion of the fall of Babylon let us consider the seeming prophecy in Isaiah that a future king named Cyrus would capture Babylon. Had it actually been made by Isaiah ben Amoz some two centuries before it happened it would be a prophecy indeed. Since, however, the mention of Cyrus is in Second Isaiah, at the time of Cyrus or after his reign, it is not a prophecy at all. This is particularly evident when we compare Isaiah 45:1 with the prophecy in 1 Kings 13:2 that a descendant of David named Josiah would burn the bones of Jeroboam's priests on the altar at Bethel. 1 Kings 13:2 says:

> And the man cried out against the altar by the word of the Lord: "Behold, a son *shall* be born to the house of David, Josiah by name; and he *shall* sacrifice upon you the priests of the high places who burn incense upon you, and men's bones *shall* be burned upon you" (emphasis added).

As I pointed out in an earlier chapter, this supposed prophecy was actually written down after the fact. Yet the use of the future tense suggests that it was intended to appear as a prophecy. This is not the case with either Isaiah 44:28 or 45:1:

> 44:28: [I am the Lord] who says of Cyrus, "He *is* my shepherd...(emphasis added)

45:1: Thus says the Lord to his anointed, to Cyrus, whose right hand I *have grasped*, to subdue nations before him and ungird the loins of kings to open doors before him that gates may not be closed (emphasis added).

That God says that Cyrus *is* his shepherd, and that he has *already* taken Cyrus by the hand, indicates that this was not even intended as a prophecy, but rather that it was a statement of God's favor toward Cyrus and that it was written by someone who was a contemporary of the Persian king. Had it been intended as a prophecy its wording would have mirrored that of 1 Kings 13:2. In succeeding verses of Isaiah 45 God addresses Cyrus directly (vs. 4: "I surname you, though you do not know me"; vs. 5: "I gird you, though you do not know me"), rather an odd way to act toward someone who is not yet alive. In 1 Kings 13 we do not hear God speaking *to* Josiah but rather about him.

⊰ 5 ⊱

"AND THE WORD BECAME FLESH AND DWELT AMONG US"

Do Old Testament Prophecies Foretell the Life of Jesus?

IN A CHAPTER ENTITLED "The Messianic Prophecies of the Old Testament Fulfilled in Jesus Christ," Josh McDowell lists a grand total of 61 Old Testament prophecies he claims were fulfilled in the life of Jesus. The first great problem with accepting these as valid proof is that there is no extra-biblical source of validation. True, the writers of the New Testament were separated by centuries from the writers of the Old Testament. However they held the same basic religious beliefs and were looking for Jesus to fulfill the messianic prophecies. Furthermore, the historicity of the details of the life of Jesus is not verified outside the New Testament, with the exception of the statement by Tacitus in the Annals of Imperial Rome that Jesus was crucified by Pilate for sedition and a reference in the writings of Flavius Josephus to James, the brother of Jesus. Thus, the validity of the gospels cannot be verified by external sources and must be taken somewhat on faith. As such, using them as fulfillment of Old Testament prophecy is likewise a matter of faith.

Upon examining McDowell's 61 prophecies, listed on pp. 144-166 of his book, I found that most of them could be easily disqualified. McDowell's errors fall into the eight following categories: (1) duplication, (2) statement too obvious to be a prophecy, (3) circular reasoning, (4) misinterpretation of the prophecy, (5) prophecy taken out of context, (6) translation errors, (7) interpretation of prophecies that stretch the definitions excessively, and (8) prophecies so vague as to be equally open to any number of interpretations. Of those that are left of the original 61, there are none that are obviously about Jesus to the exclusion of all other explanations. Let us consider each of these categories point by point.

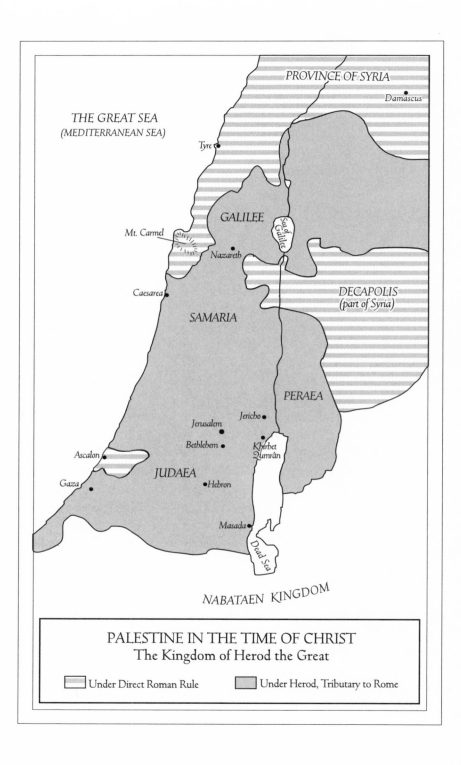

PROVINCE OF SYRIA

Damascus

THE GREAT SEA
(MEDITERRANEAN SEA)

Tyre

GALILEE

Sea of Galilee

Mt. Carmel

Nazareth

Caesarea

DECAPOLIS
(part of Syria)

SAMARIA

PERAEA

Jericho

Jerusalem

Bethlehem

Khirbet
Qumrân

Ascalon

JUDAEA

Gaza

Hebron

Masada

Dead Sea

NABATAEN KINGDOM

PALESTINE IN THE TIME OF CHRIST
The Kingdom of Herod the Great

Under Direct Roman Rule   Under Herod, Tributary to Rome

Easily Disqualified Prophecies

1. Duplication

McDowell has fudged his figures a bit by taking one incident and breaking it into two to get an extra prophecy or using one prophecy as the source of two separate fulfillments. These are as follows. The Immanuel sign of Isaiah 7 is used to foretell the virgin birth, said to be fulfilled in Mt. 1:18, 24, 25, and that the child would be called Immanuel, fulfilled in Mt. 1:23. Clearly, verse 23 from Matthew 1 is part of the same narrative as are verses 18, 24, and 25. These two prophecies are number 2 and 15 on McDowell's list. Numbers 8 and 9 on his list are that Jesus was a descendant of Jesse, fulfilling Is. 11:1 and that he was of the house of David, fulfilling Jer. 22:5. Since David was the son of Jesse, if Jesus were a descendant of David he would also be a descendant of Jesse. Thus, this should be one prophecy, not two. McDowell takes Jesus being betrayed for 30 pieces of silver and breaks it up into prophecies 34, 35, and 36—that Jesus would be sold for 30 pieces of silver, that the money would be thrown into the temple treasury, and that it would be the price of a potter's field. Not only has he expanded one fulfillment into three, he has used Zech. 11:12 for one and 11:13 for the other two. He also uses the story that Jesus was wounded and bruised, and smitten and spit upon, as two separate fulfillments (#40 and 41). Yet they are part of the same story. Finally, he divides Jesus' suffering thirst on the cross, and being given wine mixed with gall and myrrh, into two separate fulfillments (#53 and 54) of Psalm 69:21. When we trim the duplications from McDowell's list we remove six prophecies from the 61 total (#8, 15, 35, 36, 41, 54), leaving 55 prophecies.

2. Stating the Obvious

Prophecy numbers 4, 5, 6 and 7 are that the Messiah would be of the seed of Abraham, Isaac, Jacob, and of the tribe of Judah, respectively. The first three are saying that the Messiah would be a Jew, which is hardly prophetic. More than anything it is a tautology. Since the only two tribes left were the tiny tribe of Benjamin and that of Judah, which had virtually absorbed the former, and since the prophecy supposedly fulfilled is that the scepter would not depart from Judah (Gen. 49: 10, part of the J document), meaning more the kingdom than the tribe, this too is saying that the Messiah would be a Jew. That Jesus was a Jew can hardly be considered the fulfillment of divine, messianic prophecy.

Number 32 on the list has Ps. 110:1 as the prophecy and Heb. 1:3 the ful-fillment. In the psalm God tells the king to sit at his right hand, the place of honor. Hebrews says that after Jesus ascended he sat in that same place of honor. Of course, the claim in Hebrews that Jesus ascended and sits at the right hand of God the father is a statement of belief, unsupported by factual material, and thus not a solid fulfillment anyway. But seating Jesus as the son of God and king of kings in the place of honor hardly amounts to fulfilling a prophecy, just because a king is given the place of honor in a psalm. Trimming these five non-prophecies off the list we get 50.

3. Circular Arguments

Let us compare the prophecy and the fulfillment of number 17 on McDowell's list. First the prophecy, Psalm 110:4:

> The Lord has sworn and will not change his mind. "You are a priest for ever after the order of Melchizedek."

Now let us look at what McDowell considers the fulfillment, the epistle to the Hebrews 5:5-6:

> So also Christ did not exalt himself to be made a high priest, but was appoint-ed by him who said to him, "Thou art my Son, today I have begotten thee"; as he says also in another place, "Thou art a priest forever after the order of Melchizedek."

Clearly, the "fulfillment" is claiming Ps. 110:4 as validation of Jesus as a priest of the order of Melchizedek. But McDowell turns it around and makes Heb. 5:5,6 the validation of the psalm. Between them, the author of Hebrews and McDowell have argued in a circle, the author claiming Ps. 110:4 as sup-port for the position of Jesus and McDowell claiming that Heb. 5:5,6 fulfills and thus supports Ps. 110:4. I do not fault the author of the epistle, but I do fault McDowell. Prophecy number 14 is likewise circular. Ps. 110:1 has God telling the king, "Sit at my right hand, till I put thy enemies under thy feet." Jesus quotes this verse in Mt. 22:44 to make a point to the Pharisees. McDowell tries to make this a fulfillment of prophecy, which it is not. Again, Jesus is using the psalm to validate his point. To make his quotation a validation of the psalm, as though the psalm were a prophecy, not only stretches the definition of prophecy to absurd dimensions but argues in a circle as well.

Another case of circular argument is the claim (#22) that John the Baptist fulfilled the prophecy in Is. 40:3 of a voice "crying in the wilderness, 'Make straight the way of the Lord.'" This is indeed what the synoptic gospels claim. Yet in Jn. 1:23, the Baptist says of himself: "I am the voice of one crying in the wilderness, 'Make straight the way of the Lord,' as the prophet Isaiah said." Here John the Baptist is basing his validity on Isaiah. To make him the fulfillment of that prophecy, i e. its validation once again argues in a circle.

Likewise, 1 Peter 2:7 refers back to Ps. 118:22 to say that Jesus was "the stone which the builders rejected." The same is true of Jn. 15:25 and Ps. 69:4 where Jesus says he is hated without cause. These are numbers 28 and 48 respectively on the list. When Jesus was on the cross he said, according to Mt. 27:46, "My God, my God, why hast Thou forsaken me?" According to Lk. 23:46 he said, "Father into Thy hands I commit my spirit." In the first case, he was quoting Ps. 22:1; in the second he was quoting Ps. 31:5. McDowell tries to make the psalm verses quoted into prophecies (#55, 56), Jesus' words into fulfillments, and the reasoning is circular once again.

When Peter is preaching at Pentecost, he cites "a prophet" as foreseeing that Jesus' body would not be "abandoned to Hades, nor did his flesh see corruption." The "prophet" Peter cites is a psalmist and the line Peter quotes nearly verbatim is Ps. 16:10. McDowell uses Ps. 16:10 as the prophecy (#30) and Peter's words as a fulfillment for yet another circle. Trimming these eight from the list as invalid we are now down to 42.

4. Misinterpretations

One of the more common errors made by the over zealous is to interpret the Immanuel sign as a prophecy of the virgin birth of Jesus (#2). The King James Version renders Is. 7:14 as:

> Therefore the Lord himself shall give you a sign; Behold, a virgin shall conceive, and bear a son, and shall call his name Immanuel.

The same verse, as rendered in the Revised Standard Version, says that a "young woman" will conceive. The confusion came from the fact that the word used in the Hebrew, *almah*, meaning a young woman of marriageable age, was translated into Greek in the Septuagint as *parthenos* or "virgin." Had the Hebrew meant to say virgin it would have used *bethulah*, which means specifically a virgin. Thus, Is. 7: 14 was not a prophecy of anyone's virgin birth despite McDowell's attempts to reconcile *almah* with *parthenos* (pp. 145-6).

In any case, the child Immanuel was supposed to have been born in the first year of King Ahaz, 742 B.C.E., over 700 years before Jesus. How could this prophecy possibly refer to Jesus? Fundamentalists justify this through their doctrine of types. As Gleason Archer puts it (1982, p. 266):

> From the references that follow, it is quite apparent that there is to be a type of Immanuel who will be born in near future as proof that God is with his people to deliver them. Yet also an antitype will be born in the more remote future who will be both God and man, and He will deliver His people not only from human oppressors but also from sin and guilt.

There is absolutely nothing in Isaiah 7 that would lead anyone to conclude that Isaiah was speaking of anything but his own time. This is particularly true when we consider that Isaiah does speak of things which are plainly meant to be future events, such as in chapter 11. Often he prefaces such remarks with phrases such as "In that day." The doctrine of types is simply a way in which fundamentalists get to have their cake and eat it too.

As to Immanuel being a name that signifies its bearer is the messiah, Michael Arnheim points out in his book *Is Christianity True?* that Hebrew has no present tense for the verb *to be*. It is understood in sentences where it would occur in English. Thus, Hebrew sentences which translate literally as, "I lion" or "He hungry" actually mean "I am a lion" and "He is hungry." As such, Immanuel, rather than meaning "God with us," implying that the bearer is divine, is more correctly a complete sentence, "God (is) with us" (1984, pp. 118-119), just as the name of one of Isaiah's sons, Shear-jashub, is a complete sentence ("A remnant will return") and the name of another son, Mahar-sha-lal-hash-baz, is also a complete sentence: "The spoil speeds; the prey hastens." In fact, the English translation from the Masoretic text does render Immanuel as "God is with us." This actually fits Isaiah's prophecy as a sign to King Ahaz that he need not look to Assyria for help, since God will give him a sign; a child with the appropriate name of "God is with us" will soon be born, and before he knows good from evil, Judah's tormentors will be destroyed.

Another supposed prophecy that is plainly a misinterpretation is Jer. 31:15, which tells of Rachel weeping for her children, part of a prophecy of the restoration of the people of Israel to the land. McDowell has it fulfilled in

Herod's slaughter of all the male infants in Bethlehem (#12). This is simply manufactured evidence.

McDowell also uses Ps. 41:9, where the psalmist laments that even his best friend has "lifted his heel against me" as a prophecy of Jesus betrayed by Judas (#33). Not only is this a bit vague, but it may well be mistaking insult for assault. In the Middle East to show your heel or the underside of the shoe to someone is a serious insult. Thus Jesus tells his disciples if they are not well received in a town, shake the dust of its streets from their feet, i.e. leave them with a fitting insult. Trimming these three from the list we are left with 39.

5. Out of Context

When a number of McDowell's prophecies are restored to their original context it can be seen that they really have nothing to do with Jesus at all. For example, prophecy number 3 on McDowell's list is Ps. 2:7—to which he also adds 1 Chron. 17:11-14 and 2 Sam. 7: 12-16—that the Messiah will be the son of God. The fulfillment is in numerous affirmations in the gospels that Jesus was the son of God (Mt. 3:17, 16:16; Mk. 9:7; Lk 9:35, 22:7; Acts 13:30-33; Jn. 1:34, 49). The supposed prophetic verse in Ps. 2:7 is:

> I will tell of the decree of the Lord: He said to me, "You are my son, today I have begotten you."

On the face of it, this would seem to refer to a messianic king who is the literal son of God. However, there are problems with this view. God cannot be talking to the king if he had just that day begotten him, unless the king is a highly sentient zygote. Therefore, it would appear that the phrase, "today I have begotten you" is symbolic. It could well be a formula of adoption: God has chosen the Messiah as his son. In ancient times heroic figures were often referred to as a "son of God." But it is the context of the verse that makes it most unlikely that it was meant to refer to Jesus. Consider the verses that immediately follow Ps. 2:7:

> Ask of me, and I will make of the nations your heritage, and the ends of the earth your possession. You shall break them with a rod of iron, and dash them in pieces like a potter's vessel.

Somehow, the messianic king breaking the nations with a rod of iron and dashing them in pieces does not sound like the Prince of Peace.

Fundamentalists would probably counter that this is the Jesus of the second coming, the warrior-king and judge. Yet McDowell was using Ps. 2:7 as a prophecy of the life of Jesus in the first coming, i.e. the Prince of Peace. As to the supposed prophetic references in 2 Sam. 7:12-16 and 1 Chron. 17:11, the reference in Samuel is God telling David that after he is dead God will raise up his offspring and establish his kingdom for ever. Verse 14 says, "I will be his father and he will be my son." This could be argued either as a support for divine adoption of the Davidic kings or a prediction of Jesus as of that line and as the literal son of God. What proves that it could not possibly refer to Jesus is the second part of that same verse, where God says, "When he commits iniquity, I will chasten him with the rod of men, with stripes of the sons of men." Jesus as God incarnate obviously could not commit iniquity, ergo this passage in 2 Samuel cannot possibly refer to him. Since the passage in 1 Chronicles is an almost verbatim copy of the one in Samuel the same objection applies.

Is. 11:2 says of the Messiah that the spirit of the Lord will rest on him, along with wisdom, understanding, counsel, strength and knowledge. McDowell sees the fulfillment in the Holy Spirit in the form of a dove descending on Jesus at his baptism (#20). The spirit of the Lord resting on the Messiah is, however, quite different from the spirit descending on Jesus, which in Mark is the first sign we have of his divinity. The difference is highlighted when we put the verse in Isaiah back in context. After describing the attributes of the Messiah the next part of the chapter (Is. 11:6-9) describes his world. In it the wolf dwells in harmony with the lamb, the leopard with the kid, the lion with the calf, little children can put their hands in an adder's den without being bitten, and so on. This scarcely describes the time of Jesus. The root of Jesse in Isaiah 11, which Jesus is supposed to be, is spoken of in verse 14 as leading his people as they "swoop down on the shoulder of the Philistines in the west, and together they will plunder the people of the east." This does not sound much like Jesus either.

McDowell tries to make Ps. 69:9 as being a prophecy of Jesus scourging the money-changers from the Temple (#21). It reads: "For zeal of thy house has consumed me, and the insults of those who insult thee have fallen on me." Not only is the phrase way too vague to fit the specifics of Jesus' act, but if we put the verse back in context with those preceding and following it, even the angry mood of Jesus scourging the money-changers is lost. Instead, we see a mood of lamentation:

> For it is for thy sake that I have borne reproach, that shame has covered my face.
> I have become a stranger to my brethren, an alien to my mother's sons. For zeal
> for thy house has consumed me, and the insults of those who insult thee have
> fallen on me. When I humbled my soul with fasting, it became my reproach.
> When I made sackcloth my clothing, I became a byword to them. I am the talk
> of those who sit in the gate, and drunkards make songs about me.

In Is. 35:5-6a it says that the blind will see, the deaf will hear, the dumb will speak and the lame will leap. McDowell uses this as a prophecy of Jesus healing miraculously (#24). But if we put the verses back in context they are part of a general prophecy of the final restoration of Israel. Along with the healings mentioned there is a prophecy that streams will flow through the desert and "the burning sand shall become a pool" (Is. 35:7) This did not happen during the life of Jesus, and the prophecy has nothing to do with Jesus.

McDowell isolates a portion of a verse, Ps. 68:18a: "Thou hast ascended on high..." and tries to make it a prophecy of the ascension of Jesus in Acts 1:9 (#31). But the psalmist is addressing God as the Lord of Hosts, and the complete verse is (KJV):

> Thou hast ascended on high, thou hast led captivity captive: thou hast received
> gifts for men: yea for the rebellious also, that the Lord God might dwell among
> them.

If this phrasing is a bit hard to understand, consider the same verse in the Revised Standard Version:

> Thou didst ascend the high mount, leading captives in thy train, and receiving
> gifts among men, even among the rebellious, that the Lord God may dwell
> there.

Clearly, Jesus did not ascend leading captives in his train, and the portion of the verse McDowell uses can only work as even vaguely prophetic if the fragment is taken totally out of context. Once again McDowell uses a fragment of a verse as a supposed prophecy. One part of Zech. 13:7 says: "Strike the shepherd that the sheep may be scattered...." This is supposed to foretell the flight of Jesus' disciples at his arrest (#37). Yet the following verses, Zech 13:8-9 tell that after the shepherd is struck two thirds of the Jewish people will be destroyed, and the remaining third will be put through a refiner's fire and purified. Clearly, what Zechariah was talking about had nothing to do with the scattering of the eleven remaining disciples at the arrest of Jesus. In fact, fundamentalists use this prophecy from Zechariah as a specific prediction of the sufferings of the Jews at the hand of the Antichrist.

In Ps. 69:21 (prophecy #53) the psalmist laments: "They gave me also gall for my meat and in my thirst they gave me vinegar to drink." McDowell and other fundamentalists interpret this as a prediction of Jesus being given vinegar and gall (anything bitter, including bitter herbs) at the Crucifixion. There are a number of problems with this interpretation. First of all gall was not given to Jesus as "meat" or solid food as in the psalm. Second, both the RSV and at least one modern English rendering of the Masoretic text say nothing about gall. Rather it says, "Yea, they put poison into my food; and in my thirst they gave me vinegar to drink" (JPS, 1955). Another modern translation of the Tanakh does use the word gall instead of poison. But it is the context of the verse that makes it an unlikely prophecy of Jesus on the cross. Following his complaint the psalmist entreats God to blind his tormentors and afflict their loins (vs. 23), prays that their camp will be desolate (vs. 25), asks that they be shown no mercy (vs. 27), and that their names be blotted out from the book of life (vs. 28). This does not exactly square with the Crucifixion, when Jesus is supposed to have said, "Father, forgive them for they know not what they do" (Lk. 23:34). Only by being so selective as to destroy the context can fundamentalists make the psalmist's complaint fit the Crucifixion.

Ps. 34:20 says: "He keeps all his bones; not one of them is broken." Both Hugh Ross and McDowell use this as a prophecy that Jesus' legs would not be broken at the Crucifixion (#57). Not only is the verse a bit vague to be used in this way, it is totally out of context as well. In the psalm the Lord delivers the righteous from his afflictions and none of his bones are broken. Obviously Jesus was *not* delivered from his afflictions on the cross. Removing the prophecies taken out of context from the list, we are down to 31 from the original 61.

6. Faulty Translations

In at least five cases (#13, 23, 44, 59, 61) McDowell seems to be taking advantage of differences in translation to make his cited passages prophetic. In one case (#13) he translates Micah 5:2b as, "His goings forth are from long ago, from the days of eternity." He uses this as a prediction of Jesus' pre-existence as stated in Colossians 1:7. However, in the Masoretic text, Micah 5:2b is rendered, "whose origin is from old, from ancient days." This would more likely mean that the Messiah is descended from the Davidic line and is, of course, a descendant of Abraham as well.

In the second translation problem McDowell may not be too much at fault, since the RSV translates the verse as he does. In number 23 on his list he uses Is. 9:1 to foretell that Jesus would begin his ministry in Galilee. In Christian Bibles the verse reads:

> But there will be no more gloom for her that was in anguish; in earlier times he treated the land of Zebulun and the land of Naphtali with contempt, but later on he will make glorious the way of the sea, the land beyond Jordan, Galilee of the nations [Gentiles].

This verse corresponds to Is. 8:23 in the Hebrew text, which reads (JPS, 1955):

> For is there no gloom to her that was steadfast? Now the former hath lightly afflicted the land of Zebulun and the land of Naphtali, but the latter hath dealt a more grievous blow by the way of the sea, beyond the Jordan, in the district of the nations.

I have no idea why the text varies so between the Christian and Jewish versions. But in the Jewish text (of what, after all is a Jewish document) there is no indication that Galilee would be glorified in a later period. It is unclear in this translation whom the former and later refer to. Another modern translation of the Tanakh reads (JPS, 1988):

> For if there were to be any break of day for that [land] which is in straits, only the former [king] would have brought abasement to the land of Zebulun and the land of Naphtali—while the later one would have brought honor to the Way of the Sea, the other side of the Jordan and Galilee of the Nations.

So who are these former and later kings? The footnotes to this rendering admit that the meaning of the verse is uncertain, but make the assumption that the former king is Pekah and the second one is Hoshea. Pekah is the king who aligned Israel with Syria to revolt against Tiglath-pileser III. Hoshea led the second revolt against Assyria, which was crushed by Sargon II. Just how Hoshea would have brought honor to Galilee is hard to see, since his resistance against the Assyrians was just as futile as Pekah's. Regardless of that, however, neither of these translations gives any indication of Jesus glorifying Galilee through his presence. The third difference in translation (#44) is Ps. 22:16, where the psalmist, surrounded by enemies, laments:

> Yea, dogs are round about me; a company of evildoers encircle me; they have
> pierced my hands and feet…

At first this sounds a great deal like the crucifixion. However, the translation from the original Hebrew of the Masoretic text reads: "A company of evildoers encircle me, my hands and feet like a lion." This does not make much sense, but the translation from the Septuagint clears it up somewhat: "A company of evildoers encircle me; they dig into my hands and feet." It is possible that the source from which the Masoretic text was copied was corrupted, hence the odd reading. Modern English renderings of the text are: "like a lion they are at my hands and feet," and "like lions [they maul] my hands and feet." In both the Masoretic text and the Septuagint, once the word "pierced," which was not in the original Hebrew, is replaced by "dig into," "maul," or "they are at my hands and feet," the uncanny resemblance to the Crucifixion is lost.

Zech. 12:10 refers to the people looking "upon Me whom they have pierced," which McDowell uses as a prophecy that a Roman soldier would pierce Jesus with a spear (#59). The RSV rendering of the verse is similar to McDowell's, except that "Me" is replaced by "him." In both cases it would appear that the "they" who have done the piercing are the people. Yet in the Hebrew Bible, the pronoun refers to the Gentiles (JPS, 1955): "And they shall look unto Me because they [the Gentiles] have thrust him through." In another modern translation of the Tanakh the verse is rendered (JPS, 1988): "they shall lament to Me about those who are slain, wailing over them as over a favorite son and showing bitter grief over them as over a first-born." Thus, with proper translation, even the verse's tenuous similarity to the Crucifixion is lost

The fifth case where differences in translation change the meaning of the phrase is Is. 53:9, which in McDowell's book is rendered, "His grave was assigned to be with wicked men, Yet with a rich man in His death…" and which he says was fulfilled when Joseph of Arimathea put Jesus' body in his own tomb (#61). Both the RSV and the Masoretic rendering of the verse is: "And they made his grave with the wicked *and* with a rich man in his death…" (emphasis added). The notes in the *Oxford Annotated Bible* point out that some editors amended the last phrase from "with a rich man" to either "and his tomb with evil doers," or "with demons." Pivotal in how the translation reads is the word "yet" used by McDowell where the Masoretic text uses "and." If translated "*and* with a rich man," the rich man is viewed as akin to the wicked, which makes it impossible that it could refer to Joseph of Arimathea, whom all four gospels call a righteous man. Trimming the five translation errors from the list, we get 26 left.

7. Stretching It Too Far

Number 16 on McDowell's list has as its prophecy Deut. 18:18 where God says to Moses that he will raise up a prophet and put his word in the prophet's mouth. The verse is set in the context of Moses having just told the people to be wary of diviners and soothsayers, that God will raise up a prophet when one is needed. McDowell uses the crowd's acclamation of Jesus as a prophet (Mt. 21:11; Lk 7:16; Jn. 4:19, 6:14, 7:40) as fulfillment of this "prophecy." Quite frankly, the people calling Jesus a prophet simply has nothing to do with the verse from Deuteronomy. McDowell stretches it again when he tries to make Ps. 2:6, where God says he has installed his holy king in Zion, a prophecy fulfilled by the sign "Jesus of Nazareth, King of the Jews" being nailed on the cross over Jesus' head (#19).

In number 18 McDowell tries to stretch the statement in Is. 33:22 that the Lord is our judge, lawgiver, and king to foretell that Jesus would be a judge and uses Jn. 5:30 as the fulfillment. But in that verse Jesus says that he does nothing on his own initiative, but that his judgment is just because of "Him who sent me." In Ps. 109 the psalmist complains that his knees are weak from fasting. McDowell tries to stretch this to foretell the weakness of Jesus that made it necessary to force Simon the Cyrenian to carry the cross (#49). Isaiah 53:12 says of the suffering servant that he was "numbered among the transgressors." McDowell tries to stretch this to foretell that Jesus was crucified between two thieves (#45).

In Ps. 38:11 the psalmist complains that his friends and family are aloof and stand far off while he suffers. McDowell tries to stretch this to foretell that Jesus' friends and family were watching the Crucifixion from a distance (#43, Lk 23:49). Yet there is no indication in the gospels that these people were trying to avoid Jesus, rather that they witnessed what happened to him. In most cases these people were his faithful female followers. Continuing with the Crucifixion, McDowell tries to make Ps. 22:14b: "…my heart is like wax, it is melted within my breast;" a prophecy of blood and water pouring from Jesus' side when the soldier pierced it with a spear (#58). McDowell even says that Jesus' heart had literally burst. This is simply his own invention and is in no way biblical. Removing these seven stretched prophecies from the list leaves us with only 19.

8. Too Vague for Interpretation

The first prophecy on the list is both obvious and too vague to be a prophecy. In Gen. 3:15, God tells the serpent that he will put an enmity between the serpent's seed and the woman's and says that Eve's seed will bruise the serpent's head and the serpent will bruise his heel. McDowell uses this as a prophecy that Jesus as Messiah will be born of a woman. It is pretty obvious that the Messiah is a man, thus born of woman. But though Christians often read into Gen. 3:15 that the serpent is Satan and Eve's seed is Jesus there is no proof of it, and the validity of this interpretation remains a matter of faith. Another vague "prophecy" (#11) is Ps. 72:10:

> Let the kings of Tarshish and of the islands bring presents; The kings of Sheba and Seba offer gifts.

This is supposed to be a prophecy of the baby Jesus receiving the gifts of the Magi. Need I comment? Similarly, Malachi 3:1, that the Lord will come suddenly to his temple is too vague to be fulfilled by Jesus casting out the moneychangers (#26); the nations coming into Israel's light (Is, 60:3) is too vague to foretell Christianity being a light to the Gentiles (Acts 13:47-48a, #29); the psalmist complaining of malicious witnesses (Ps. 35:11) is too vague to foretell of Jesus accused by false witnesses at his trial (#38); another psalmist lamenting that his tormentors sneer at him is too general a description to fit Jesus being mocked before his Crucifixion (#42). Likewise two other psalmists, one protesting that people shake their heads at him and another complaining that people stare at him, are too vague to be prophecies of further sufferings of Jesus (#50, 51). Finally, Amos 8:9 speaking of darkness at noon in an apocalyptic vision really has nothing to do with the claim in Mt. 27:45 that darkness covered the land following the Crucifixion (#60).

Removing these nine vague prophecies trims the list from 19 to 10. By merely eliminating the gross errors I have already cut the list from its original impressive 61 to about one sixth of that number.

The (So-Far) Undisqualified Prophecies

The Nativity

Prophecies 9 and 10 on the list are that Jesus fulfilled prophecies in Jer 23:5 and Micah 5:2 that the Messiah would be of the line of David and that he would be born in Bethlehem, respectively. If we can believe the Nativity story, then these would indeed be fulfilled prophecies. However, the Christmas story has two basic problems. It runs counter to history and it involves two conflicting traditions. Before I elaborate on these points, let us consider what each of the four gospels has to say about the birth of Jesus:

The gospels of John and Mark do not touch on the Christmas story at all. Instead, they both begin with Jesus' meeting with John the Baptist. John alludes to Jesus' divine origin in Jn. 1:14 when he says, "And the Word became flesh and dwelt among us," but does not mention the virgin birth or any other part of the Christmas pageantry.

The traditional Christmas story we all grew up with, the subject of pageants and manger scenes, is pieced together from Matthew and Luke, but there are inconsistencies in Matthew, and Luke does not square with Roman history. Let us first consider Matthew. The gospel opens with (vs. 1): "The book of the genealogy of Jesus Christ, the son of David, the son of Abraham." Verses 2 through 17 give us a detailed genealogy for Joseph (and, so it seems, for Jesus as well). All of this is made pointless, however, in vs. 18, when the gospel tells us that Mary was with child by the Holy Spirit when she was betrothed to Joseph. We are then told that Joseph is considering divorce until an angel appears to him in a dream. In chapter 2 Jesus is born in Bethlehem, where Joseph and Mary already seem to be residing. No mention is made here of Caesar's decree, the story of there being no room at the inn, or the adoration of the shepherds. The stories of the gifts of the Magi, Herod's slaughter of the innocents, and the flight into Egypt are told. Chapter 3 opens with John the Baptist preaching in the wilderness.

Why, if Joseph is not the father of Jesus, does Matthew waste his time on a genealogy going back to David and Abraham, and why does he call Jesus the "son of David?" There was a tradition in the early Christian church, before the doctrine of the virgin birth became established orthodoxy, that Jesus was indeed part of the Davidic line of kings.

By far the most elaborate Christmas story comes from Luke. The virgin birth, only inserted in Matthew after the grand genealogy, is prepared for by the entirety of the first chapter, which begins with the miraculous conception of Elizabeth, mother of John the Baptist and Mary's kinswoman. None of the other gospels, by the way, give any indication that Jesus and John the Baptist are related. The story of Elizabeth's conception is followed by the Annunciation. No mention is made of Joseph's intent to divorce Mary. In fact, he has little more than a walk-on role here. With the exception of the brief mention in Matthew of Mary being with child by the Holy Spirit, the grand mythos of the virgin birth is the property of Luke alone. If it is so important, why do the other gospels not say more about this miracle? Also, why does Matthew not mention Luke's Roman census? The adoration of the shepherds finishes this quaint tale, but no mention is made of either the Magi, Herod's slaughter of the innocents, or the flight into Egypt. Why did not Luke, who gave such loving care to the virgin birth, even mention these important events?

And why did Matthew not say anything about Jesus being born in a manger? In Matthew, Joseph and Mary are already living in Bethlehem and only go to Nazareth after returning from Egypt out of fear of Archelaus, son of Herod. In Luke, Joseph and Mary are originally living in Nazareth and only go to Bethlehem for the sake of the Roman census. Even Gleason Archer notes that Matthew shows a bias toward the role of Jesus as fulfiller of Jewish prophecy. It was important to him that Jesus' origins be more identified with Bethlehem, home of the Davidic line of kings, rather than Nazareth in Galilee. Bethlehem, besides being the home of the Davidic line, is close to Jerusalem. Nazareth, on the other hand, and Galilee in general were in the extreme north on the edge of Syria. The area was originally divided between the tribes of Asher, Issachar, Naphtali, and Zebulun, and was lost when the Assyrians conquered Israel and took the 10 northern tribes off into captivity. While there seems to have been some Jewish presence in the land after that time, the main population consisted of Arameans. It was not reunited with the Jewish state until 104 B.C.E., when the Hasmoneans conquered it and forcibly converted its population to Judaism. A people who had been Jews for scarcely more than a century would not be a likely source from which the Messiah would spring. It is likely that Luke was a gentile convert to Christianity. Accordingly, it was of little concern to him that Joseph be so closely identified with Bethlehem. Nor is he as concerned as Matthew was with Joseph's ancestry. When Luke does get around to mentioning the genealogy (Luke 3:23-38) at the time of the baptism of Jesus, he traces Joseph's lineage through a son of David named Nathan, whereas Matthew's genealogy has Joseph descended from David's son Solomon. Gleason Archer's explanation (1982, p. 316) for this discrepancy is that Luke is not recording Joseph's line at all, but rather Mary's lineage, which, coincidentally, also goes back to David, though through his son Nathan rather than his better known son, Solomon. This is simply absurd and in no way biblical, since the Lucan genealogy works backward from Joseph, not Mary.

Given all these discrepancies between Matthew and Luke, and given that neither Mark nor John said anything about it, can we really believe that any of this Christmas pageantry is true? The fundamentalist explanation that the gospels were written from different points of view and that the authors stressed what was important to them just does not wash. It is one thing to either amplify or merely sketch an incident. It is quite another thing to leave it out of the narrative altogether, as Mark and John do with the Christmas story.

Before we deal with the prophecy that the Messiah would be born in Bethlehem, let us consider one last aspect of Luke's Christmas story, namely the decree from Caesar Augustus that all the people in the Roman empire were to go to their place of origin to be enrolled in a census. There really would be absolutely no point whatsoever in the Romans doing such a thing (one can imagine the unmanageable chaos such an act would throw the empire into), nor is there any historical evidence that Augustus or any other emperor ever undertook such a strange policy. History simply does not support the Gospel on this point. The decree in fact has no other purpose than to set Jesus up to be born in a manger, a curious situation if this is really Joseph's place of origin, where one would expect his extended family to be established and in a society where failure to extend hospitality to the wayfarer would be an unpardonable sin.

I should note, for the sake of honesty, that two friends of mine, both of whom are Christians (but not fundamentalists), have made a case for the possibility that the Romans might have insisted on enrollment at the place of origin because of birth records that might be kept there. They also point out that the Jews might have taken this so literally as to insist on going to their tribal place of origin. For that matter, the Romans could have been the ones insisting on the Jews going to such lengths to obey the imperial command, the whole thing being a local matter between the obstreperous Jews and the intransigent Romans governing the province. There was, after all, little love lost between the Jews and their Roman overlords. In any case, the lack of room at the inn and Jesus' birth in the manger would then make sense, since Joseph's family would no longer be living at their tribal place of origin. This is a reasonable enough argument, but we still have no evidence that Augustus gave such a decree. In any case, the Romans had already been taxing their provinces and did so, at least in the time of Augustus, with little order or consideration of a province's level of population or ability to pay. For example, the reason an incompetent general, P. Qunctillius Varus, was governing Germany and was led into a disastrous ambush, resulting in his own death and the massacre of two legions by the Germans in the Teutoberger forest in 7 C.E. (one of the greatest military disasters ever to befall Rome), was that the competent general who had been governing Germany, Tiberius, was putting down a revolt in Illyricum. The revolt occurred because the Roman army had been using Illyricum as its granary, and the empire had over-taxed the people of that province in grain to a point where they revolted out of desperation.

Another point against Luke's Roman census is that even had such a census been in effect Joseph and Mary would not have been part of it. At the time of the birth of Jesus both Nazareth and Bethlehem were part of the kingdom of Herod the Great. Though tributary to Rome, it was not under Roman administration. As such it would not have been part of the census.

As to Bethlehem as the site of Jesus' birth, Micah predicted about 700 B.C.E. that the Messiah would be born in that tiny village (Micah 5:2) Along with McDowell and other fundamentalists, Hugh Ross says that this prophecy was fulfilled by the birth of Jesus and sets the probability that it was a chance fulfillment at 1 in 100,000. Even if we could be sure that Jesus was really born in Bethlehem—and, as I have pointed out, where legend leaves off and history begins concerning the Nativity is impossible to tell—the prediction that the Messiah would be born in Bethlehem, home of the Davidic line of kings, is so mythically correct that it would have made it necessary to record that village as the Messiah's birth-place even if he had been born elsewhere. Indeed, it would appear as though both Matthew's and Luke's narratives were concocted to overcome the unfortunate fact that Jesus came from Galilee. Both gospels are trying to reconcile this with the requirement that the messiah be born in Bethlehem and be of the Davidic line of kings. Ultimately, whether one accepts or rejects the validity of this prophecy is a matter of faith, something the fundamentalists claim to have, but seem unwilling to base their belief on.

"That Scripture Might be Fulfilled"

A category of supposed prophecies where faith must be the final arbiter is when such a phrase as, "This was done so that scripture might be fulfilled," occurs, which appears in the fulfillments of three of the prophecies on the list (#25, 27, 52). In these supposed fulfillments either Jesus or the gospel writer refers directly back to the verse McDowell claims as the prophecy and says that this or that was done to fulfill it. This smacks of deliberate fulfillment. For example (#25), Ps. 78:2 says, "I will open my mouth in a parable; I will utter dark sayings of old...." McDowell uses Mt. 13:34, that Jesus spoke to the people only in parables, as fulfillment. But Mt. 13:34 says that Jesus did this to fulfill what was spoken by the prophet and quotes Ps. 78:2. Deliberate fulfillment could be done by the Messiah to tell the people that he was the one, or it could be done by either an impostor or someone who thought, erroneously, that he was the Messiah. Of course all of these possibilities assume that this was not a fiction added by the author of Matthew. The fulfillment of Zech. 9:9, that the Messiah will come riding on an ass, is seen in the entry of Jesus into Jerusalem on an ass (#27). But Mt. 21:4 says that this was done to fulfill Zech. 9:9, which again smacks of deliberate fulfillment.

In Ps. 22:18 the psalmist laments that his enemies are dividing up his garments and casting lots for his clothing. In all four gospels the soldiers cast lots to divide up Jesus' clothing. But only Jn. 19:23 says that this was done to fulfill scripture (#52). Was this done to fulfill a prophecy? Another question might well be, was Ps. 22, or any psalm for that matter, meant to be a prophecy? One's enemies dividing up one's clothes might well be coincidental.

Judas

There are now only 5 prophecies left out of the original 61. One of these is Zech 11:12-13. Hugh Ross also sees this as a prophecy that the Messiah will be betrayed for the price of a slave (30 pieces of silver) and that the money would be used to buy a burial ground for poor foreigners as is related in Matthew 27:3-10. Ross sets the probability of chance fulfillment at one in a hundred billion. In reality, the verses in question say nothing about the betrayal of the Messiah or the purchase of the potter's field in which to bury poor foreigners. The verses, told from the point of view of the "good shepherd," come after the point where he has given up trying to lead the sheep (the Jews after the exile).

Having broken his staff, indicating that the word of God is that the sheep are to be left prey to foreign powers, he asks for his wages, which come to 30 shekels. Then God tells the shepherd to cast his wages into the treasury. Since the verses do not say what Ross claims they say, his probability estimate is pointless.

Yet the use of 30 pieces of silver (or 30 shekels) and the casting of the money into the treasury has echoes in the story of Judas. If the story were free of internal contradictions then it would be easier to believe that the imagery of Zech. 11 was in some way predictive. But there are two stories of the death of Judas Iscariot. According to Matthew 27: 3-8, Judas, after having betrayed Jesus, repents, tries to give back the money he accepted from the priests, throws it down at their feet when they refuse to take it back, and runs out and hangs himself. The priests decide they cannot put blood money back into the treasury, so they use it to buy a potter's field in which to bury strangers. None of the other three gospels gives any account of Judas' death, but in Acts 1:18-19 (Acts was written by Luke) a quite different account is given. In this story, Judas does not repent, but buys the potter's field himself. As he is looking at his new acquisition, he falls forward, his guts burst open and his bowels gush out into the field.

How do inerrantists reconcile these two accounts? Gleason Archer states that the account in Acts of Judas acquiring a plot of ground was an ironic way of saying that the plot he acquired was his grave. But what about the two different ways he met his death? Archer, remarking on Judas falling headlong and bursting asunder, says (Archer, 1982, p. 344):

> This indicates that the tree from which Judas suspended himself overhung a precipice. If the branch from which he had hung himself was dead and dry—and there are many trees that match this description even to this day on the brink of the canyon that tradition identifies as the place where Judas died—it would take only one strong gust of wind to yank the heavy corpse and split the branch to which it was attached and plunge both with great force into the bottom of the canyon below.

Well, I suppose it could have happened that way, but in point of fact this scenario is nothing more than extrabiblical invention on Archer's part, something that is read into the text rather than being read out of it. How Judas met his death is of no importance to the Christian message, unless one insists on inerrancy. Then one is stuck with two contradictory stories and the curious silence of the gospels of Mark and John on the subject.

The Suffering Servant

The four remaining prophecies (#39, 40, 46 and 47) are based on the servant songs of 2nd Isaiah. Their interpretation as being fulfilled in the life of Jesus is largely a matter of faith. Was Jesus the "man of sorrows" spoken of in Is. 53:3? Possibly, but the suffering servant spoken of in Isaiah may not be a man at all. In Is. 42:18-24, 44:1-2 and 49:3 the servant is identified as the Jewish people.

Second Isaiah contains many allusions to Babylonian worship, contrasting the validity of Yahweh as the true god with the idols worshiped in Babylon. The prophet may well have been playing off the Babylonian Akitu festival in which a slave or convict was ritually made to bear the sins of the kingdom when he described the suffering servant in Is. 53 12 as being, "numbered with the transgressors; yet he bore the sin of many , and made intercession for the transgressors." Indeed, the idea of the scapegoat bearing the sins of the people is found in the Torah. So pervasive is the concept of an animal, person, or god who can expiate the sins of others that it is even found among the Mayans. One of their goddesses, Tlazoteotl, whose son was a maize god named Centeotl, was, like the Virgin Mary, called "the mother of God." Her name means "eater of dirt" because she could take upon herself the sins of her worshippers. The fact that the Mayan civilization developed in complete isolation from the cultures of the near east, and the striking parallels between Centeotl and Tlazoteotl on one hand and Jesus and Mary on the other indicate that similarities between Jesus and other "suffering servants" is more a matter of common mythic motifs than anything to do with predictive prophecy. In the end whether one decides that the servant songs refer to the Jewish people, to Jesus, or to some future Jewish messiah is a matter of faith.

PROPHETS OF THE PERSIAN EMPIRE

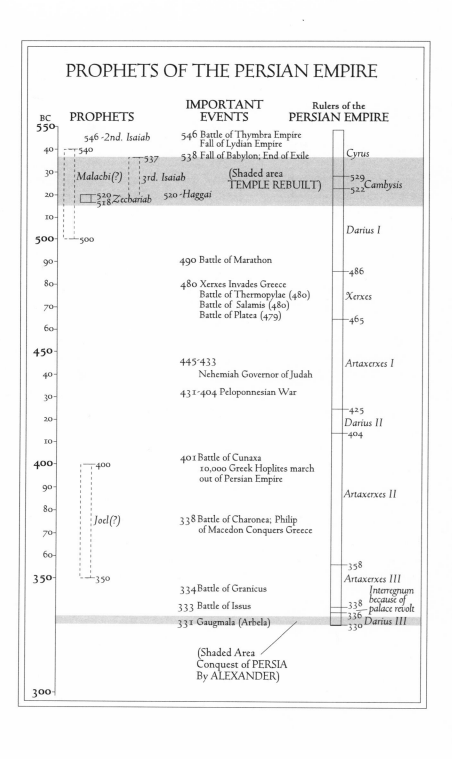

	PROPHETS	IMPORTANT EVENTS	Rulers of the PERSIAN EMPIRE
BC 550			
	546 -2nd. Isaiah	546 Battle of Thymbra Empire / Fall of Lydian Empire	
40	540	538 Fall of Babylon; End of Exile	Cyrus
30	537		529
	Malachi(?) 3rd. Isaiah	(Shaded area TEMPLE REBUILT)	Cambysis
20	520 / 518 Zechariah 520 -Haggai		522
10			
500	500		Darius I
90		490 Battle of Marathon	
80		480 Xerxes Invades Greece	486
		Battle of Thermopylae (480)	Xerxes
70		Battle of Salamis (480)	
60		Battle of Platea (479)	465
450			
40		445´433 Nehemiah Governor of Judah	Artaxerxes I
30		431´404 Peloponnesian War	
20			425
			Darius II
10			404
400	400	401 Battle of Cunaxa / 10,000 Greek Hoplites march out of Persian Empire	
90			Artaxerxes II
80			
	Joel(?)	338 Battle of Charonea; Philip of Macedon Conquers Greece	
70			
60			358
350	350		Artaxerxes III
		334 Battle of Granicus	Interregnum because of
		333 Battle of Issus	338 palace revolt
		331 Gaugmala (Arbela)	336 Darius III
			330
		(Shaded Area Conquest of PERSIA By ALEXANDER)	
300			

6

FROM PROPHECY TO CATASTROPHE

The Post-Exilic Prophets and the Growth of Apocalyptic Literature

THIS IS A PIVOTAL CHAPTER in which we will look into the shift from prophetic to apocalyptic writings. We will examine not only the prophets of the post-exilic period but the more apocalyptic oracles of prophets from earlier periods, which will shed light on the shift that occurred and how apocalyptic writings are related to prophecy. I use the term "apocalyptic" somewhat broadly to cover all descriptions of the "end-times." Actually, the proper classification for such literature is eschatology, the study of the end of things. Strictly speaking, apocalyptic literature deals with eschatology that is violent and cataclysmic. Since this type of eschatology characterizes Zoroastrianism, the increasingly apocalyptic nature of eschatological writings in the post-exilic period may well reflect a Zoroastrian influence. I have used the word apocalyptic to cover all eschatological predictions, even those from before the Exile, to stress that their use as a prop for the speculations of such fundamentalists as Hal Lindsey essentially transforms them into apocalyptic literature in the minds of fundamentalists.

The Historical Context of the Post-Exilic Period

After the return of the Jews from Babylon in 538 B.C.E., they began to feel that God's wrath against them, spoken of so fervently by the prophets, was at last appeased. Compared to the Assyrians and Chaldeans, the Persians were wise and compassionate rulers. Second Isaiah attributed the magnanimity of Cyrus to divine influence. Thus, a belief grew up among the Jews that their restoration was only the prelude to a time, not far off, when a descendant of David

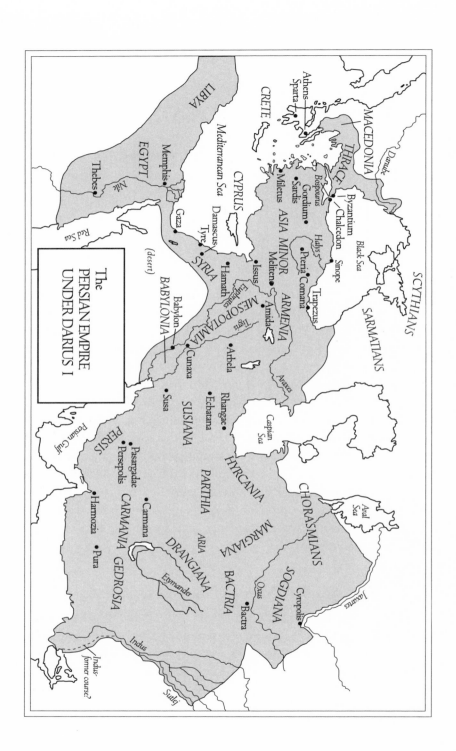

The
PERSIAN EMPIRE
UNDER DARIUS I

would rise and triumph over the nations, ushering in a utopian world in which all conflict would cease and all nations would follow Yahweh, heaping wealth upon Jerusalem in the process.

These messianic hopes rose to their peak in 520 B.C.E. with the proclamation by the prophet Haggai that the provincial governor, Zerubbabel, a descendant of David, was the long awaited Messiah (Haggai 2:20-23):

> The word of the Lord came a second time to Haggai on the twenty-fourth day of the month, "Speak to Zerubbabel, governor of Judah, saying, I am about to shake the heavens and the earth, and to overthrow the throne of kingdoms; I am about to destroy the strength of the kingdoms of the nations, and overthrow the chariots and their riders; and the horses and the riders shall go down, every one by the sword of his fellow. On that day, says the Lord of hosts, I will take you, O Zerubbabel my servant, the son of Shealtiel, says the Lord, and make you like a signet ring; for I have chosen you, says the Lord of hosts."

What prompted this bold proclamation was the unorthodox accession of Darius I to the throne of the Persian empire. Cyrus had been succeeded by his son Cambyses, who, before setting out to conquer Egypt, had his brother Bardiya murdered. Darius, only distantly related to the Persian royal line, had been an officer under Cambyses and was his son-in-law as well. When, on the way back from the conquest of Egypt, Cambyses died suddenly, a pretender named Gaumata seized power claiming that he was Bardiya and that he had escaped the intended murder. Gaumata seems to have actually been a Mede, rather than a member of the Persian royal house. However, for reasons of their own many of the nobles and governors of the empire went along with the fiction that Gaumata was Bardiya. Gaumata also won a great deal of popular support by decreeing a three year moratorium on tributary taxes and military service. Upon the pretender's demand that the army swear fealty to him, Darius swiftly returned to the capitol and, with the help of conspirators, murdered Gaumata. He then claimed the throne in 519, since Cambyses had died without leaving a male heir. However, since Darius was only distantly related to the ruling family into which he had married, his claim to the throne was tenuous at best. His accession provoked simultaneous revolts in many parts of the empire. Immediately upon having disposed of Gaumata, Darius hastened to put down a revolt in Babylon. While he was there, a Mede named Fravartish led a revolt in Media which was supported by a simultaneous revolt in

Armenia. Before he had fully put down these revolts Darius was faced with uprisings in Bactria and other eastern provinces and yet another false Bardiya, this time a Persian noble named Vahyazdata. The fragmentation of the Persian empire seemed imminent. Thus, it is not surprising that Haggai saw in this the hand of God overthrowing the "throne of kingdoms."

However, Darius prevailed, all revolts were crushed, and the Persian empire was stronger than ever. Zerubbabel vanishes from history at this point. Some historians speculate that he was quietly done away with by Persian agents. This would fit the subtlety of Persian rule. Rather than devastate Judah, they would simply remove the focus of the potential revolt. As oriental despots go, the Persians were remarkably tolerant and were happy to let the Jews rebuild their temple, but messiahs pushed the limits of even their enlightened tyranny. It is interesting to note, by the way, that despite the obvious falsehood of Haggai's prophecy, his book is considered canonical—thus inspired by God—by Jews, Catholics and Protestants alike. From this point on until the Hasmonean kings the Jews were ruled by high priests. If they did not have a messiah, the Jews at least enjoyed a period of relative peace from the fall of Babylon in 538 until Alexander the Great arrived in the Levant in 333, a period of 205 years.

The chronology of the post-exilic prophets is as follows. Second Isaiah is thought to have been written a little before the fall of Babylon in 539 or as early as 546. Third Isaiah was probably written during the rebuilding of the Temple. Both Haggai and Zechariah were written in 520 B.C.E., with Zechariah extending to 518. Malachi is hard to date, but it is thought to have been written between 540 and 500 B.C.E. Joel, likewise hard to date, is tentatively thought to have been written between 400-350. The fictional book of Jonah may date anywhere from the fourth to the third century B.C.E.

With the exception of 2nd Isaiah's prophecies about Cyrus, Haggai's failed prophecy that Zerubbabel was the Messiah, and the crowning of Joshua, the high priest, in Zechariah—which might actually have originally been the crowning of Zerubbabel—there is little in the post-exilic prophets that relates to historical events. Most of the prophecies are apocalyptic in nature. There are three basic prophecies involved in these early apocalypses. First, there would be terrible wars from which only a remnant of the Jews would be saved. Second, the Messiah would arise, vanquish Israel's enemies, and restore the kingdom. Finally, beginning with the return of all the Jews from every diaspora,

Jerusalem would become the center of a world empire, and all the nations would acknowledge Yahweh as the one true God. Though this belief in a future messiah dominated the Persian and later periods, its origin goes all the way back to 1st Isaiah.

Apocalyptic Writings Before the Exile

The earliest apocalyptic prophecy is in chapter 2 of Isaiah. We know that this refers to a time at the end of history because Is. 2:2 says: "It shall come to pass in the latter days that the mountain of the house of the Lord shall be established as the highest of the mountains...." In those latter days the nations will say to each other, "Come, let us go up to the mountain of the Lord...that he may teach us his ways..." (Is. 2:3). This prophecy of the triumph of Israel continues through verse 5. Verse 4 is the well known passage about men beating their swords into plowshares and their spears into pruning hooks, a verse which is copied verbatim in Micah 4:3. In Is. 9:6 we have the first messianic prophecy about the Prince of Peace:

> For unto us a child is born, to us a son is given; and the government will be upon his shoulder, and his name will be called "Wonderful, Counselor, Mighty God, Everlasting Father, Prince of Peace."

This would seem to foretell that the Messiah, being called "Mighty God," will be God incarnate. But this is not what the Jews had in mind. Their idea of the Messiah was a human king of the line of David. To understand what was actually meant we have to remember that in the original Hebrew there was no present tense for the verb "to be" and there also was not any punctuation. Just as Immanuel actually means "God *is* with us" rather than "God with us," so the seeming string of titles is actually a sentence. In the Jewish Scriptures this king is called *Pele-joez-el-gibbor-Abi-ad-sar-shalom*, which translates as "Wonderful in counsel [is] God the Mighty, the everlasting Father, the Ruler of Peace."

Micah tells us that the Messiah will be born at Bethlehem, home of the Davidic line of kings (Micah 5:2) and in Is. 11:6-9 we are told of what the world will be like under his rule. The wolf dwells with the lamb, the leopard with the kid, the calf with the lion, "and a little child shall lead them." The bear and the cow feed together and the lion will eat straw like the ox. Children will play with adders and not be bitten. This beatific picture sounds like it would have to be far in the future. But just when did Isaiah and Micah think this time would come? Isaiah 11 goes on to describe how the children of Israel will triumph in the latter days in verse 14:

> But they shall swoop down upon the shoulder of the Philistines in the west, and together they shall plunder the people of the east. They shall put forth their hand against Edom and Moab, and the Ammonites shall obey them.

So the same chapter that tells of the beasts living together in harmony still allows for the Jews to defeat and plunder their neighbors. Micah's Messiah born in Bethlehem (Micah 5:2) also operates in the world of that day. Micah 5:6 says that princes of Israel will rule the land of Assyria with a drawn sword, and verse 8 says that the remnant of Jacob will be like a lion among the nations. Clearly, the Messiah was to be a military leader like David, and his kingdom was to be established in the time of Assyria, the Philistines, Edom, Moab and Ammon. In other words the prophets saw the messianic kingdom as being established in the world of their day.

Isaiah 24 through 27 is a prophecy of universal judgment, in which God condemns all the nations of the earth. As in the story of Noah's flood, God condemns the earth as well as the nations in it (Is. 24:18b-20):

> For the windows of heaven are opened, and the foundations of the earth tremble. The earth is utterly broken, the earth is rent asunder, the earth is violently shaken. The earth staggers like a drunken man, it sways like a hut; its transgression lies heavy upon it, and it falls, and will not rise again.

The cosmic upheaval continues in verse 23: "Then the moon will be confounded and the sun ashamed." Where metaphor leaves off and literal fulfillment begins is hard to say. Obviously the earth has not transgressed God's law, and the sun, as an inanimate body, cannot be ashamed. Yet there probably was not a clear distinction in Isaiah's mind between the literal and the metaphoric. His age was not one of science, after all, and such modern western ideas as a strict separation between individuals and the group they belonged to, themselves and their property, or of a people and the land they inhabit, would have been foreign to Isaiah. Thus, in his oracle against Edom in chapter 34 the land is punished as well as the people (see Is. 34:9-10). This way of thinking is also seen in Joshua, which was largely written by the Deuteronomists. The children of Israel are instructed to utterly destroy

Jericho, kill all its inhabitants (except Rahab and her relatives) and put its silver and gold into the Lord's treasury. This is done, and God seems to be with his people. When Joshua's army attacks Ai, however, it is subjected to a humiliating defeat. The reason for this is given in Josh. 7:1:

> But the people of Israel broke faith in regard to the devoted things; for Achan
> the son of Carmi, son of Zabdi, son of Zerah, of the tribe of Judah, took some
> of the devoted things and the anger of the Lord burned against the people of
> Israel.

Notice that the verse says that Israel sinned, even though the crime was Achan's, and that God's anger is directed at all of Israel. When Achan's sin is discovered, not only is he put to death, but his sons and daughters and his livestock are as well. All of Achan's belongings are also destroyed. (Since Achan's wife is not mentioned perhaps she was saved by reverting back to being the property of her father.) After all this is done God's anger is appeased (Josh. 7:24-26). If we were to institute such a system of justice today we would not only give a man the death penalty but would shoot, gas, electrocute, or lethally inject his children as well (regardless of age), kill his pet cat and burn his house down. Though the absurdity and cruelty of such a system are self-evident, and though fundamentalists would be appalled at the suggestion that God approved of such acts, they still think that God did indeed demand such a price in Joshua's day. It is noteworthy that Gleason Archer makes no comment on this passage as a Bible difficulty. One reason fundamentalists can accept a supposedly unchanging god varying his punishments so greatly is a doctrine widely held among them called dispensationalism. I will discuss this concept at greater length in another chapter, since it is extremely important to apocalyptic scenarios. The relevance of dispensationalism to Achan's punishment is that, according to this doctrine, God dispenses covenants at various periods of history, each with its own set of rules and strictures. Thus, Achan's family was put to death under one dispensation, but modern families need not suffer such consequences. While this doctrine wreaks havoc with such concepts as justice, it does serve as a way to reconcile atrocities approved of by God with a commitment to ethics.

Since fundamentalists are not allowed to see God's wrath on Achan's family and indeed the whole nation of Israel for Achan's crime as being a product of that culture, but must actually accept that God really held nations responsible for the crimes of individuals, even holding children responsible for the acts of their parents, they also must see prophecies of punishing the earth in the same light. In other words, they cannot see these prophecies as the words of Isaiah, a man without scientific knowledge living over 2700 years ago. No, since the prophecies are given as the word of God, that means to them that God will indeed punish the earth. This idea does not lend itself well to an environmental consciousness.

In chapter 27 Isaiah says that "in that day" God will also punish Leviathan with his sword and that he will also slay the dragon of the sea. This is a bit curious, because in Job 41 God boasts of Leviathan as his creation. It is possible that Leviathan and the dragon of the sea represent Assyria and Egypt respectively. On the other hand, this may refer to Leviathan and Behemoth, which represent forces of chaos. The significance of the Lord punishing Leviathan in Isaiah is that it introduced the image of the dragon into apocalyptic literature. Originally, the myth of the triumph of the creator deity over the dragon of chaos, what is commonly referred to as the Combat Myth, was part of the Babylonian creation myth and had parallels in Baal's triumph over the dragon Lotan. That it was originally part of the Jewish creation myth is attested to by the fact that references to God having previously destroyed the dragon of the sea are salted through various psalms and prophetic books. Transferring the Combat Myth to the latter days was a way of saying that, after a climactic battle in which evil is extinguished, the world would be created anew.

Despite Isaiah's predictions, no messiah came to overthrow the Assyrians. The hope remained in the Chaldean period, however. Both Jeremiah and Zephaniah contain prophecies of universal judgment (Jer. 25:15-29; Zeph. 1:1-3). Jeremiah also predicts that the pagan nations will worship God (Jer 16:19-21) and that a descendant of David will reign over a restored Israel (Jer. 23:5-8). But the most specific prophecy dealing with the "latter days" is in Ezekiel 38-39. This is the Gog and Magog prophecy. Briefly, these chapters say that in the latter days, when Israel is dwelling in peace in unwalled cities, God will bring forth Gog, of the land of Magog, chief prince of Meshech and Tubal along with Gomer and all his hordes, Beth-togarmah from the uttermost parts of the north, as well as Persia, Cush and Put. They will attack Israel, but God will rain down fire upon them and destroy them utterly. I will deal with the Gog and Magog oracle in detail in a later chapter. For now let us consider who these nations are and when the latter days were in Ezekiel's mind. As I said in an earlier chapter, there is great uncertainty about who Gog prince of Magog is. However, Magog is mentioned along with Gomer, Tubal and Meshech as being sons of Japheth in the table of nations in Genesis 10. Togarmah is also mentioned as a son of Gomer. While we don't know precisely what nation is identified as Magog we do know that the sons of Japheth represent Indo-European-speaking peoples. More importantly, we know precisely who Gomer, Meshech, Tubal and Beth-togarmah are. Gomer is the biblical version of the *Gimmirai* of Assyrian records, whom the Greeks called the *Kimmerai*, which got latinized into the Cimmerians. As noted in earlier chapters, they were a barbaric tribe which invaded Asia Minor from the Caucusus mountains and raided both the Lydians and Assyrians. Meshech is the biblical term for the Mushki, a tribe allied with the Phrygians, who devastated the Hittite empire. Even into late Assyrian times they were a warlike people in western Asia Minor. Tubal is Tabal, a frontier state on the edge of the Assyrian empire, whose people, the Tibarani, were part of the flotsam cast up from the destruction of the Hittite empire, just as the Peoples of the Sea were the mixed remnant of the Mycenaean civilization. Tabal was the site of much struggle between the Assyrians and the invading peoples of Asia Minor who raided their western provinces. Beth-togarmah means "house of Togarmah." It is the biblical version of the city of Tilgarimmu, a strategic fortress in the northern corner of Tabal. Thus, all of these nations are from Asia Minor and all of them are from Ezekiel's time. Cush and Put are most likely Ethiopia and Libya, both of which had exercised power in Egypt. What all of this means is that, like Isaiah, Ezekiel saw the "latter days" when all the nations would attack Jerusalem as quite near his time.

The "enemy from the north" is another image that became a stock phrase in apocalyptic literature. On several occasions Jeremiah refers to evil looming out of the north or God bringing evil out of the north (Jer. 4:6; 6:1; 6:22-23). Does this mean Russia? Hardly. A glance at a map of the Middle East will show that of the north was the most likely invasion route into Israel in Jeremiah's time. The only notable invasion from the west, i.e. the sea, was that of the Philistines. Neither the Greeks nor the Romans invaded Israel from the sea. The only potential threat from the south would be Egypt. Yet in both the Assyrian and Chaldean periods the only attack from the south was Necho's ephemeral conquest from 609 to 605. Raiders came out of the desert on the

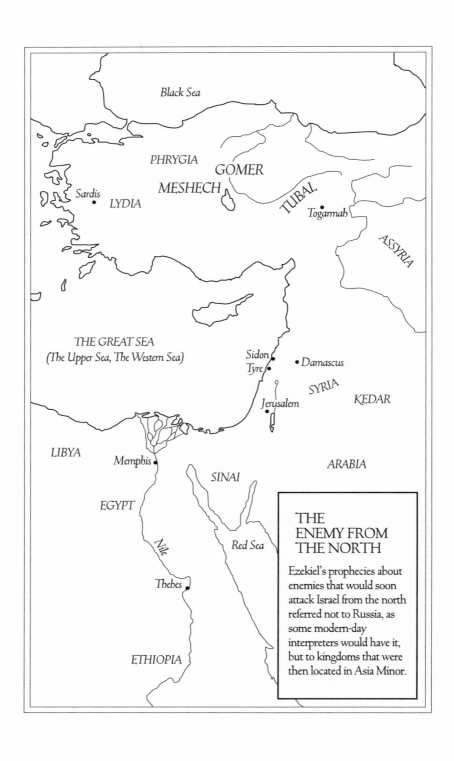

Black Sea

PHRYGIA

GOMER

MESHECH

TUBAL

Sardis

LYDIA

Togarmah

ASSYRIA

THE GREAT SEA
(The Upper Sea, The Western Sea)

Sidon

Tyre

Damascus

SYRIA

KEDAR

Jerusalem

LIBYA

Memphis

SINAI

ARABIA

EGYPT

Nile

Red Sea

Thebes

ETHIOPIA

THE ENEMY FROM THE NORTH

Ezekiel's prophecies about enemies that would soon attack Israel from the north referred not to Russia, as some modern-day interpreters would have it, but to kingdoms that were then located in Asia Minor.

east, but not conquering armies. But the invasion route of the Assyrians, Chaldeans, Persians, Alexander the Great, Antiochus Epiphanes and the Romans was from the north. And how far north was north? Ezekiel described Togarmah as being in the "uttermost parts of the north" (Ezek. 38:6). Yet that city lies well south of the Black Sea.

The Prophets of the Persian Period

Second Isaiah predicts that Cyrus will subdue the nations and deliver Israel. Assuming that this was a prophecy made by Isaiah ben Amoz at the time when the power of Assyria was at its height, Hugh Ross puts the probability of chance fulfillment of this prediction at one in a quadrillion (one followed by 15 zeroes). Since the material on Cyrus (Is. 44:27 through 45:13) is from just before (or possibly after) the likely event of his conquest of Babylon, the probability figure is nonsense. What is more important about Cyrus is that 2nd Isaiah calls him the Lord's anointed (Is. 45:1). This quite literally makes him the Messiah. The word messiah comes from the Hebrew *mashiah* which means anointed. Christ is derived from the corresponding Greek word. Both kings and high priests were anointed with oil as part of their inauguration ceremony as an indication of divine approval. After saying that Cyrus is God's chosen ruler and that he will build God's city (Jerusalem) and set his people free, chapter 45 continues with the prophecy that the nations will forsake idolatry and acknowledge that God is with the Jews, and that the wealth of Egypt, Ethiopia and the Sabeans will flow into Israel.

In chapter 65 a new world is described. God says he will create a new heaven and a new earth (Is. 65:17) and that the wolf and the lamb will feed together and the lion will eat straw like an ox (Is. 65:25).

Both Haggai and Zechariah saw the Lord's anointed as either Zerubbabel or the high priest, Joshua. Haggai's short book does not go further than that. But Zechariah contains a prophecy of the attack of the nations on Jerusalem (ch. 12), the death of the messiah on behalf of his people and the death of all but one third of the Jews (ch. 13) and the final destruction of the invading armies (ch. 14). This last event is foretold in lurid detail (Zech. 14: 12):

> And this shall be the plague with which the Lord will smite all the peoples which wage war against Jerusalem: their flesh shall rot while they are still on their feet, their eyes shall rot in their sockets, and their tongues shall rot in their mouths.

Zechariah also contains eight visions, much of whose imagery recurs in Revelation. In the first vision are four horsemen, two on red horses, one on a sorrel horse, and one on a white horse. They are angelic beings patrolling the earth. In the eighth vision there are four chariots drawn respectively by red, black, white, and dappled gray horses. These likewise patrol the earth. Both visions call to mind the four horsemen of the apocalypse. The woman representing sin, who is borne to Babylon in the seventh vision, is reminiscent of the representation of Babylon as a harlot in Revelation. Likewise, the imagery of the third vision, a man measuring the city of Jerusalem, and the fifth vision, the golden lampstands and olive trees, are repeated almost verbatim in Revelation.

Malachi added the divine messenger that will herald the coming of the last days, a final judgment based on the words and deeds of the people which are written in the book of remembrance and the prophecy that Elijah the prophet, who was taken up alive into heaven, will appear before the coming of the Messiah.

The book of Joel starts out with the description of a locust infestation, which the prophet considers God's judgment on the people. This becomes a prelude to the "day of the Lord" and the locusts become demonic, looking like war horses and devouring the land. Their assault becomes cosmic (Joel 2:10): "The earth quakes before them and the heavens tremble. The sun and moon are darkened, and the stars withdraw their shining." Joel calls the people to repent, and in answer to their prayers the day of the Lord is averted. In Joel 2:20 God says he will "remove the northerner far from you," and in verse 25 he says he will restore what the swarming locust has eaten. The locusts are described as "my great army, which I sent among you." The passage has a dreamlike quality. The locusts become an invading army from the north, the cosmos is shaken, then they are locusts again. Is the northerner a plague of locusts or Ezekiel's invading army? To attempt to answer that question would be to lose the poetry of the passage. Its main importance is that Joel's demonic locusts seem to be forerunners of those in Revelation. Other apocalyptic imagery is found in Joel 2: 30-31:

> "And I will give portents in the heavens and on the earth, blood and fire and columns of smoke. The sun shall be turned to darkness and the moon to blood before the great and terrible day of the Lord comes."

But God will protect his people. As a sign that he is with them, Joel 2:28

tells how their sons and daughters will prophesy and "your old men shall dream dreams and your young men shall see visions."

While there are condemnations of Tyre and the Philistines in Joel and Zechariah, the thrust of their prophecies has become, particularly in the case of Joel, increasingly cosmic, indefinite, and dreamlike. The struggling community of returned exiles had trouble even getting the resources to build the Temple, which still was not complete when Darius came to the throne. The petty squabbles with their neighboring peoples were muted by Persian suzerainty but taxing nonetheless. It would almost seem that the grandiosity of the visions increased in inverse proportion to the drabness of the people's lives. The long period of peace pushed the apocalyptic expectations ever further into the future as the relative stability of Persian rule deprived the Jews of both the invading armies of the last days and a messianic leader.

The original prophecies of imminent destruction uttered by Isaiah and Jeremiah echoed the very real threat of doom these men must have felt. Despite its fearsome imagery, Revelation could hardly produce a demonic army much worse than the Assyrians, who used terror as a tactic. While the Chaldeans were not so fearsome, their deportations could easily have spelled the doom of the Jewish people. The real terrors of the Assyrian and Chaldean periods gave the basic ingredients to the apocalyptic scenario, while the imagined terrors of the Persian years added many of the flourishes that would one day grace the apocalypse of John of Patmos.

The Book of Jonah

This last section is a bit of a departure from the latter days. Yet, since the predictions of the end of the world become ever more fanciful and less related to history, it is perhaps fitting that we end this chapter with a total fantasy. For the book of Jonah, while included among the prophets, is a work of fiction. I include it here for two reasons. First, Jonah was a post-exilic work. Second, an examination of the lengths fundamentalists will go to in order to justify its literal interpretation, even though their own hermeneutics allow for allegory, is instructive.

Though there was a historical Jonah, mentioned in 2 Kings 14:25 as a prophet to King Jeroboam II of Israel (786-746 B.C.E.), the story was written after the exile, probably in the fourth or third century B.C.E., possibly as an argument against the xenophobic policies of Ezra and Nehemiah. The book is written in a late form of Hebrew, which would fit that time period. The argument of the book is that God's grace extends to everyone, even the Assyrians—the Nazis of the ancient world—who not only carried off the northern tribes, but introduced the Samaritans into Israel as well and were thus responsible for planting strangers who practiced an impure form of Judaism in the midst of the returning Jews. Jonah's reluctance to go to Nineveh makes sense in post-exilic terms. If it were actually about the Jonah of Jeroboam's court, some 25 years before Assyria destroyed Israel, the wickedness of the Ninevites would not be any greater than that of any other idolatrous people. By making it clear that Jonah's disobedience to the Lord's call and his displeasure at the salvation of the people of Nineveh were in opposition to the expressed will of God, the writer of the Book of Jonah reprimanded those Jews who wanted to drive out anyone of mixed parentage by an appeal to God as being the god of all peoples—even the hated Assyrians. Here a work of great power is made absurd by the insistence that it must be literally true in the face of an historical record that shows no evidence to support Jonah's turning the Ninevites from their evil ways.

So adamant are fundamentalists that the tale be historically true that they even argue for its validity in scientific terms. Was Jonah indeed swallowed by a whale? Did he in fact live in its belly for three days? If one were to insist that the story be considered literally true, the logical interpretation of Jonah's stay in the belly of the whale (or great fish) would be that it was a supernatural occurrence, i.e. a miracle. Oddly enough, a number of fundamentalist ministers preaching on the subject have made a point of insisting that the story was not only literally true, but that it required no miracle, that indeed a man could survive three days inside a whale . Invariably, they cite the story of one James Bartley, a sailor on a whaling ship in the 1890s who was supposedly lost overboard while his ship was harpooning a sperm whale off the Falkland Islands. Thirty-six hours later as his shipmates were cutting the whale open, they discovered Bartley in the whale's belly, unconscious, his skin bleached by the whale's stomach acids, but alive. He was revived and suffered no lasting injury from having been gulped down by a sperm whale (even though the animal's digestive tract would have been a bit short of oxygen). The ministers who allude to this tale always claim that it is well documented. However, as is noted in a brief item on page 53 of the July 20, 1992, issue of *Christianity Today*, when Edward Davis, associate professor of science and history at Messiah College, investigated the story he found that it was simply not true. James Bartley was never lost overboard. The article quotes the wife of Bartley's captain as having said, "The sailor has told a great sea yarn."

One thing that is not readily clear is why fundamentalists would feel such a need to defend the story of Jonah being swallowed by a whale, even to the point of making a case for its being scientifically sound. The reason behind their dogmatic defense of the whale story in particular, as well as the whole book of Jonah in general as being actual history rather than allegory is supplied by Gleason Archer (1982, p. 301):

> ...according to Matthew 12:40, Jesus, the Son of God, believed that Jonah was completely historical. He showed this by stating, "For as Jonah was three days in the belly of a huge fish, so the Son of Man will be three days and three nights in the heart of the earth" (NIV).

Thus, it can be seen that fundamentalists are not really defending a minor book of the Old Testament when they insist that Jonah was a real person and that his story, including the whale, is history. Rather, they are defending the words of Jesus. Archer goes on to say that, as Jesus' resurrection was factual and served as an antitype of Jonah, the story of Jonah had to be factual as well, since a fictional past episode cannot serve as a prophetic source for a future literal fulfillment. What Archer does not consider is that if the story of Jonah were accepted as an important allegory by the people to whom Jesus spoke, then it would be logical for Jesus to use it as an allegory for death and resurrection. Jesus' allusion to the story does not require us to believe that he took it literally.

7

HEAD OF GOLD, FEET OF CLAY

The Book of Daniel

F UNDAMENTALISTS USE THE BOOK OF DANIEL as an example of both fulfilled prophecy and apocalyptic prediction, with the supposedly fulfilled prophecy validating their interpretation of the apocalyptic material. Along with the prophecies are a number of stories which purport to be historical. In point of fact the book is neither prophecy nor history, nor did its protagonist even exist. As corroborating proof that Daniel was a real person fundamentalists often cite Ezek. 14:14 and 28:3. In the first of these God tells Ezekiel that when a land sins against God even if Noah, Daniel, and Job were in that land their righteousness would not save any lives in it but their own. In Ezek. 28:3 God is sarcastically saying to the prince of Tyre how wise he is: "you are wiser than Daniel; no secret is hidden from you…" But the Daniel Ezekiel is referring to is not his fictional contemporary—who would have been in his teens at the time Ezekiel was preaching and thus hardly likely to have attained enough status to be on a footing with Noah and Job—but rather a legendary figure famed for his piety and wisdom, not only among the Jews, but even in the texts of ancient Ugarit.

As I pointed out earlier, Daniel, as apocalyptic literature, was not even included with the prophets in the Jewish canon, but is part of the Kethuvim or Writings. The book consists of a series of stories (chapters 1 through 6) followed by a series of apocalyptic visions (chapters 7 through 12). Had the visions really been given to a man living during the Exile some of them would indeed have been evidence of predictive prophecy. In fact, however, they were written after the fact and are not prophecies at all.

When Was Daniel Written?

How do we know that the Book of Daniel was written after the time of Alexander the Great? Is such a late date valid? Here is Rev. David Jeremiah's view of why biblical scholars have dated Daniel's prophecies after the fact (1982, broadcast on KKLA January 11, 1993):

> When the critics come to the Book of Daniel, they hate the ninth chapter. They hate it because it is pre-written history. Have you ever heard anyone talk about late-dating the Book of Daniel? Late-dating Daniel is a little game the critics play. It goes like this: "I don't believe in predictive prophecy. I don't think God could ever, or anyone could ever tell you what's going to happen before it happens. Here is a prophecy that seems to tell you what happens before it happens. So the only way to explain it is to assume that it was written after it happened." That's the little game they play: higher criticism.

After this accusation against the scholars of the Higher Criticism, Jeremiah goes on to relate an anecdote. Two American tourists in Jerusalem, Christians both, are looking at a model of the Second Temple of Jerusalem and speculating as to when the Temple will be rebuilt. A third man upon overhearing them introduces himself and explains that he is a New York rabbi. He asks them if they seriously believe that the Temple will ever be rebuilt. They respond, "Of course. Don't you read your own holy books, the Book of Ezekiel and the Book of Daniel?" The rabbi responds that he has in fact never read these books, saying that he was instructed at rabbinical school not to, and was particularly instructed not to read Daniel's prophecy of the 70 weeks of years.

Well, is that it? Do the biblical scholars who late-date Daniel know in their hearts that it is really fulfilled prophecy? Are they late-dating the book because of their blind intellectual pride? Are they rebelling against God? Do rabbinical colleges actually forbid their students to read Ezekiel and Daniel? As to the last, since David Jeremiah delivers this anecdote without reference or attribution, it is impossible to test its veracity. However, the three Jewish encyclopedias I consulted in writing this chapter, the work of rabbinical scholars, all have detailed analyses of both the Book of Ezekiel and the Book of Daniel. It would be unlikely that any rabbinical college would forbid their students access to material which I, a Gentile, freely read in a public library. In any case, such a prohibition would only provoke students, particularly the more curious and brighter ones, to violate it. Also, since Judaism lacks a central authority analogous to a pope, even if such books were declared off limits by one branch of the religion, another branch could freely violate such a taboo without being declared heretical.

And what about my used copy of the Jewish scriptures translated into English from the Masoretic text? From the inscription written at the front, it seems to have been given to a boy on his Bar Mitzvah. Yet it contains all of Ezekiel and all of Daniel. Are we to suppose that Jewish laity, even 13-year-old boys, are allowed to read what is forbidden to rabbinical students? As to the charge that biblical scholars are merely playing a sick game of intellectual snobbery in late-dating Daniel, there is ample evidence that the book was written well after the Exile. First of all, much of the book was written in Aramaic. If Daniel had really been written by a Jew of the Captivity, we would expect it to be written in Hebrew. Aramaic did not supplant Hebrew as the language commonly spoken by the Jews until well after the Exile. While Daniel starts out in Hebrew, it switches to Aramaic part way through chapter 2 and continues in Aramaic through chapter 7. Then it returns to Hebrew for the final five chapters. A fundamentalist could argue that the whole thing was originally written in Hebrew and only later partially translated into Aramaic. David Jeremiah says that since the sections written in Aramaic dealt with the Gentiles while those in Hebrew dealt with the Jews, Daniel wrote them in Aramaic because it was the *lingua franca* of both the Chaldean and Persian empires. This simply is not true. Chapter 8 deals with the struggles between Alexander the Great and the Persian empire. Yet, though it relates to the Gentiles, it is written in Hebrew. Regardless of what the prophecies deal with, however, the work was written for the Jews. There is no indication that the book was distributed to Gentiles of either empire. As to whether the work was originally in Hebrew or Aramaic, there are a number of reasons to believe that it was deliberately translated from Aramaic into Hebrew, since much of the Hebrew text follows the grammar of Aramaic rather than that of Hebrew. Further, there are a number of Greek and Persian words salted through the text that would not have been used until after the time of Hellenistic influence following Alexander the Great. Had the work been written in the Aramaic of the Chaldean court, it would have contained no Persian, and the Aramaic of the both the Chaldean and Persian courts would have contained no Greek. Therefore, the inclusion of Greek words invalidates Jeremiah's view. Of course, if it had been originally written in Hebrew, but translated into Aramaic in Hellenistic times, the inclusion of Greek words would be reasonable. However, the use of Aramaic grammar in the Hebrew sections of the book cannot be explained if the book was originally written in Hebrew. Also, the Hebrew that is used is a late form of the language. To understand the significance of this, consider the changes in usage in the English language over 300 years. If we found a manuscript purportedly written in 1690 that had phrasing and word usages common to the English of 1990, we would have a very strong clue that it was a fraud.

Furthermore, had Daniel actually been written prior to the Greek influence, the name of that greatest of Chaldean monarchs would have been rendered as Nebuchadrezzar. Yet, even in the Hebrew sections, the name is rendered Nebuchadnezzar. This is a much later rendering of the name. In Ezekiel and most of Jeremiah the name is written with an "r" after the syllable "chad." The exception in Jeremiah is in chapters 27-29. This is probably either an interpolation or a copyist's error, since the Babylonian rendering of the name is Nabu-kudurri-user. Thus, "chad-rezzar" would be the proper variant of the last part of the name, not "chad-nezzar," which derives from the Greek rendering of the monarch's name as "Nabuchodonosor." Had Daniel, supposedly a member of the Chaldean court and a confidant of its king, actually written the book, he would have used the proper spelling of the king's name. For that matter, the king himself, purported to be the author of chapter 4, would not have misspelled his own name.

Finally, there is the problem of faulty history. The opening verses of the book say that Nebuchadnezzar besieged Jerusalem in the third year of the reign of Jehoiakim, which would have been 606 B.C.E., and that he took the city, carried off some of the vessels from the temple and a number of hostages. In fact, the first siege of Jerusalem was in 595, and the temple would not have been looted until the city was sacked in 586. There was no deportation in 606. Chapter 4 is another historical fiction. Nebuchadrezzar did not go mad at any point in his reign. The supposed madness had originally been attributed to Nabonidus to explain his 10 year absence from Babylon. As I pointed out in the material concerning the fall of Babylon, his supposed madness was more likely to be Persian propaganda than historical fact.

At the end of chapter 5 Babylon is supposed to have fallen to "Darius the Mede." But there was no Darius the Mede. Babylon fell to Cyrus of Persia.

Both John MacArthur and Gleason Archer make the argument that "Darius" was a title rather than a name. The basis of MacArthur's argument is that, since a number of Persian kings were named Darius, that indicates that it was a title meaning king. Using MacArthur's logic we could say that since the names Edward, Henry, and George recur frequently in the list of kings of England they are titles in English meaning king. Archer's argument is a bit stronger. He points out that the Persian rendering of the name Darius (actually a Greek version of the original) is *Darayawush* which means "the royal one." Thus, "Darius the Mede" would have been a Mede with the title of viceroy. That's not a bad argument as far as it goes. However, the name Eric, held by at least one king of Norway is not a title, even though it means "prince." So, even with a name that means "the royal one," we have only a possibility that "Darius" was was a title. Archer identifies the holder of this title as Cyrus's general Gobryas, and says he only reigned a year or two as viceroy. Archer further asserts (1982, p. 288):

> It is clear from Daniel's failure to mention any date later than Darius's "first year" (9:1) that his reign must have been of very brief duration.

This is rather a thin argument, since all that is referred to in Dan. 9:1 regarding Darius the Mede is that Daniel had a vision in the first year of the king's reign. One could just as easily argue that if Darius only reigned one year there would be no point in speaking of the first year of his reign and that the reference to a first year indicates that there were other years during which Darius ruled, hence the first year had to be designated. If Darius only ruled for one year, Daniel's vision would have been related as having occurred in "the year Darius reigned." What is ultimately fatal to Archer's argument that Darius was a temporary viceroy over one province is the tale in chapter 6 of Daniel in the lion's den. There we are told that it pleased Darius to set 120 satraps over the kingdom (Dan 6:1). When his satraps come to him with the implausible plan that no one in the kingdom be allowed to pray to anyone but him, they say (Dan 6:6b-7):

> "O King Darius, live forever! All the presidents of the kingdom, the prefects and the satraps, the counselors and the governors are agreed that the king should establish an ordinance and enforce an interdict, that whoever makes petition to any god or man for thirty days, except to you, O king, shall be cast into the den of lions...."

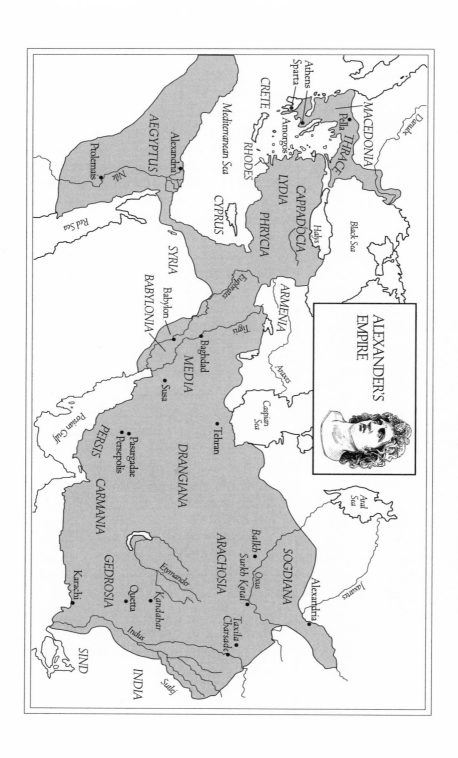

ALEXANDER'S
EMPIRE

MACEDONIA
THRACE
Pella
Athens
Sparta
Amorgos
CRETE
RHODES
AEGYPTUS
Alexandria
Ptolemais
Nile
Mediterranean Sea
CYPRUS
LYDIA
CAPPADOCIA
PHRYGIA
Halys
Black Sea
ARMENIA
Araxis
SYRIA
BABYLONIA
Babylon
Euphrates
Tigris
Baghdad
Caspian
Sea
MEDIA
Susa
Tehran
Red Sea
Persian Gulf
PERSIS
Pasargadae
Persepolis
DRANGIANA
CARMANIA
GEDROSIA
Karachi
Etymandro
Quetta
Kandahar
Indus
Sutlej
INDIA
SIND
ARACHOSIA
Balkh
Oxus
Surkh Kotal
SOGDIANA
Taxila
Charsada
Alexandria
Jaxartes
Aral
Sea
Danube

Daniel 6 invalidates Archer's argument for a number of reasons. First of all, how could a provincial governor appoint 120 satraps over the entire *kingdom?* If this is the work of Gobryas, acting governor of Babylon, then why use the word kingdom? If this really only meant the former kingdom of Babylon, we have an incredibly top-heavy bureaucracy. In reality there were only 20 satraps over the entire Persian empire. However, it is in the way Darius is addressed that we see that he could not possibly be Gobryas. "O king, live forever," was a common salutation in oriental despotism, but not one that anyone would have dared use while addressing a mere provincial governor. That the satraps call him "King Darius" is another blow to Archer's argument. If "Darius" is a title, the satraps are calling Gobryas "king the royal one" or perhaps "king viceroy," which is both redundant and nonsensical. Another historical error is that the Persians, particularly at the time of Cyrus, were noted for religious tolerance and would not have fomented rebellion in their newly conquered empire by making such an outrageous demand that no one dare pray to their own god for a month.

The Historical Context of the Book of Daniel

The destruction of the Persian empire by Alexander the Great, followed by his death before he could formalize the government and secure his succession, set in motion a series of wars and shifting alliances that went on intermittently for nearly 300 years, from Alexander's death in 323 B.C.E. until the defeat of Antony and Cleopatra VII at Actium in 31 B.C.E.

Immediately following Alexander's death it was decided that his generals, the Diadochi (i.e. "successors") would act as regents for his retarded half-brother Philip III and Alexander IV, his posthumous infant son by Roxanna, daughter of Darius III. The three leading generals were initially Antipater, viceroy of Europe, Perdiccas, viceroy of Asia, and Craterus, guardian of the kings. By 319 all three had perished. Roxanna and her son were murdered in 310 by order of Antipater's son Cassander, at which point all pretense of trying to maintain the unity of the empire was lost. Temporarily there were five successor states. Cassander ruled Macedonia and exerted varying degrees of control over the Greek city states; Lysimachus ruled Thrace; Antigonus controlled Asia Minor, Syria and the Levant; Ptolemy ruled Egypt; and Seleucus ruled Mesopotamia and Persia. By this time Alexander's Indian conquests had

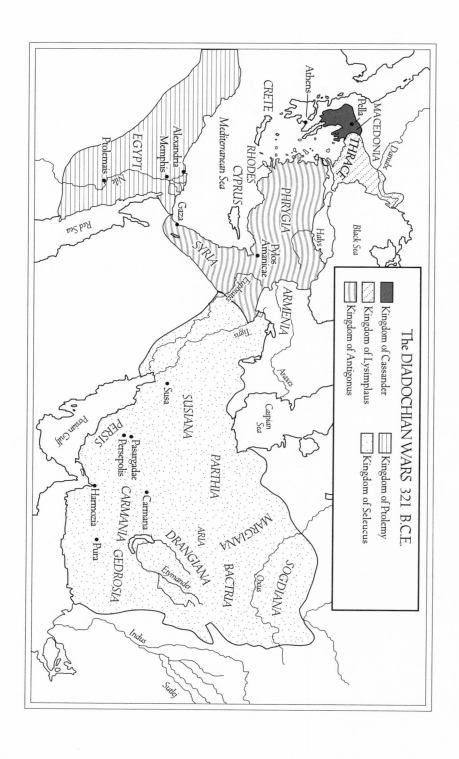

The DIADOCHIAN WARS 321 B.C.E.

Kingdom of Cassander
Kingdom of Lysimplaus
Kingdom of Antigonus
Kingdom of Ptolemy
Kingdom of Seleucus

been lost to the Indian emperor Chandragupta, and both Pontus and Armenia were independent. A final attempt to unify the empire by Antigonus and his son Demetrius ended when they were defeated by the combined forces of Seleucus and Lysimachus at the battle of Ipsus in 301. Antigonus was killed at the battle, and his kingdom was partitioned, with Ptolemy seizing the Levant and part of Syria, Seleucus taking the rest of Syria and part of Asia Minor, Lysimachus gaining some of western Asia Minor and other parts gaining their independence. There were now briefly four successor states. As the Diadochian wars continued, however, more of Alexander's empire was lost and Lysimachus fell in battle against Seleucus (281 B.C.E.). There were now three successor states. Most of Thrace was lost to invading Gauls, with a strip going to Seleucus, who also acquired more territory in Asia Minor.

The Diadochian wars were characterized by shifting alliances, betrayal, bribery, assassination, parricide, fratricide, and astounding reversals of fortune. The Diadochi were men of infinite ambition unfettered by even the slightest ethical restraint. A look at the career of Demetrius, son of Antigonus highlights the character of the men who were now masters of the part of the world to which the Jews belonged. Following the battle of Ipsus, Demetrius was in possession of only western Asia Minor, Cyprus, Cilicia in southeastern Asia Minor and the cities of Tyre and Sidon. He did, however, have the greatest fleet in the eastern Mediterranean. Lysimachus, Seleucus, and Ptolemy were all allied against Demetrius and quickly divided his kingdom between them. Lysimachus got western Asia Minor; Ptolemy took Cyprus, Lycia, Sidon and Tyre; and Seleucus took Cilicia (296 B.C.E.). It would have seemed that Demetrius was lost. However, in Macedonia Cassander had died in 297 and his eldest son Philip IV died in 294. Demetrius had gained power in Athens with an eye to invading Macedonia. With the death of Philip a power struggle ensued. Cassander's widow Thessalonice was ruling conjointly with her two remaining sons, Alexander and Antipater. When Antipater murdered her and seized the throne, Demetrius and King Pyrrhus of Epirus supported his brother Alexander. Demetrius arrived too late to be of any help, but Alexander, backed by Pyrrhus, drove his brother from the country. Antipater took refuge with Lysimachus.

When Demetrius arrived in 293, Alexander promptly escorted him back to his ships, reasonably deciding that Demetrius' real aim was to gain the kingdom for himself. However, one of Demetrius' guards murdered Alexander,

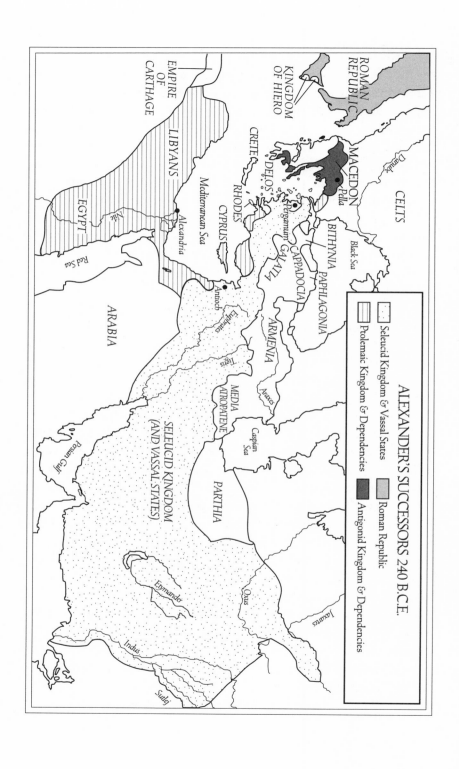

ALEXANDER'S SUCCESSORS 240 B.C.E.

and the Macedonian army elected Demetrius king. He aimed at reconquering the entire empire and assumed a double crown (standing for Europe and Asia) and a purple mantle depicting him as the sun. His accession in Macedonia was viewed with alarm by his neighbors, and in 288 both Pyrrhus and Lysimachus invaded. They succeeded in driving him out. Antipater was with Lysimachus and probably hoped to be reinstated as king. Instead, Lysimachus had him put to death and was himself elected king by the Macedonian army. Demetrius established his son Antigonus in Athens, then invaded Ionia in 287. He won an unbroken string of victories against Seleucus and invaded Syria in 286. However, his resources were dwindling and his army suffered heavy desertions. When the captain of his navy betrayed him, Ptolemy gained the fleet, and Demetrius was forced to surrender to Seleucus in 285. Seleucus kept Demetrius as a prisoner as a way to ensure good relations with Lysimachus. Should the latter have tried any treachery, Seleucus could always outfit Demetrius with an army and send him off to Thrace. But by 283 Demetrius had managed to drink himself to death.

Lysimachus was now ascendant. He controlled Macedonia, Thrace, and western Asia Minor. Only with the support of Pyrrhus was Demetrius' son Antigonus able to hold on to Athens. Nevertheless, after a series of political blunders and reversals, Lysimachus fell in battle against Seleucus at Koropedion in 281. Seleucus now looked to be the one to reunite the empire. But as he was entering Thrace, Keranous, the disinherited son of Ptolemy, who had taken refuge with Lysimachus, assassinated him. The Macedonian army elected Keranous king, and in 280 he defeated Antigonus at sea. It looked as if the Antigonid line would end in complete failure. However, Keranous fell fighting the invading Gauls in 279. Antiochus, son of Seleucus, had made common cause with Antigonus, who now landed in Macedonia. He defeated the Gauls in 277 and was made king by the Macedonian army. He wisely chose to eschew imperial ambitions, and the three successor states entered a period of relative stability.

This stability did not allow these states to remain great powers, however. Macedonia was embroiled in frustrating attempts to control the Greek city states, while the Seleucids and Ptolemies were intermittently at war over the control of Syria and Palestine. Faced with the rising power of such states as Pontus and Pergamum and rebellions in the east, the Seleucid empire was gradually eroded. The eastern half of Iran was lost to the Indo-Greek Bactrian kingdom, while Gedrosia, Media Atropatene and Parthia all gained their independence.

Fearing the rise of Rome, Macedonia gave aid to the Carthaginians in the Second Punic War. Once Carthage was defeated, Rome invaded Greece and defeated Philip V of Macedon at Cynocephalae in 197. The Seleucid Empire was undergoing a revival at this time under Antiochus III, called the Great. He had succeeded in recovering some of the Persian territory from the Parthians and had defeated the Ptolemies in 198, at which time Palestine passed to the Seleucids. His sister Cleopatra I was queen of Egypt and regent of the Ptolemaic Empire, making the later a virtual Seleucid fief. Following the defeat of Philip at Cynocephalae, Antiochus felt ready to challenge Rome's eastern expansion. Against the advice of Hannibal, to whom he had given refuge, he crossed the Aegean to Greece, where he was defeated by the Romans at Thermopylae in 191. Later that year his fleet was decisively defeated in two battles by the combined squadrons of Rome and Rhodes. The Rhodians again defeated him on the sea in 190. Finally, at Magnesia in Asia Minor his army was annihilated by the Romans under Lucius Scipio. He sued for peace and was forced to pay a heavy indemnity, reduce his forces, give up territory in Asia Minor and send his younger son Antiochus to Rome as a hostage.

Under Antiochus III's successor, Seleucus IV Philopater (187-175), the empire enjoyed a period of peace and reconstruction. This was brought to an end in a particularly Hellenistic fashion when Seleucus was assassinated by Heliodorus, one of his ministers. Seleucus had ransomed his brother from Rome by sending his own son Demetrius in his place. Antiochus put Heliodorus to death and assumed the title of regent on behalf of Seleucus's minor son, also named Antiochus. One of his men, a certain Andronicus, murdered the child in 171, possibly on the orders of the regent or perhaps merely in expectation of reward. Instead, Antiochus had him put to death. With Demetrius a hostage in Rome, the regent was now able to take the throne as Antiochus IV Epiphanes, a name infamous in history, though in fact he was merely a typical Hellenistic monarch.

Cleopatra I had died in Egypt in 172, leaving her two sons in the charge of incompetent ministers who plotted an attack on Antiochus in order to regain Palestine. Antiochus anticipated their plans, however, foiled their attack on Palestine in 170 and invaded Egypt in 169. Rome was at the time involved in a second Macedonian war and could not intervene on Egypt's behalf. Easily defeating his surprised enemies, Antiochus captured Memphis and the king, Ptolemy VI Philometor. Alexandria held out against him and put the second of Cleopatra's sons, Ptolemy VII Euergetes, on the throne. This allowed Antiochus to pose as the champion of the rightful king against a usurper.

Meanwhile problems had been brewing in Judah. The high priest Honya III (known in Greek as Onias III) had been deposed by his brother Jason, who was a Hellenized Jew. There was a great deal of strife between more traditional Jews and those who embraced the Greek culture. One of the sore points between the two groups was, for example, that young Hellenized Jews practiced athletics in the nude at the gymnasium within sight of the Temple. Jason was himself overthrown by another Hellenized Jew named Menelaus. Onias had fled to Antioch, where he took sanctuary in the precinct of Apollo. He was lured out of sanctuary under a ruse and murdered by Andronicus in 171, at about the same time that same officer did away with Antiochus Epiphanes' nephew. While Antiochus was in Egypt it was rumored that he was dead. Acting on this false belief Jason overthrew Menelaus, and Jerusalem rose in revolt against Menelaus' faction. This strife appears to have been a matter of local politics. However, it alarmed Antiochus, who seems to have taken it as a general revolt.

Having installed Ptolemy VI Philometor as king in Memphis, Antiochus returned from Egypt, put down the revolt and horrified the Jews by entering the holiest of holies and taking gold from the temple to pay for his Egyptian campaign. He also reinstated Hellenized Jews in places of power. That might have been the end of his problems had his Egyptian policy worked as he intended. He had hoped that the rival kings in Memphis and Alexandria would keep each other from threatening Palestine. But in 168 the two Ptolemies joined forces against him. He invaded a second time and was on the verge of conquering Egypt when he was confronted by the Roman envoy Gaius Popillius Laenas. Rome had just defeated Perseus of Macedon, bringing the second Macedonian war to a successful conclusion. Thus the Romans were now able to intervene in Egypt. When Popillius Laenas confronted Antiochus in the street in Alexandria demanding that he quit Egypt or face war with Rome, Antiochus, not feeling strong enough yet to face Rome, temporized and said that he would have to give the envoy his official response later, whereupon the Roman drew a circle in the dirt around the king and demanded his answer before he stepped out of it. Totally humiliated, the

Seleucid king was forced to quit Egypt.

Antiochus saw in the revolt of Jerusalem a potential threat to his empire. He assumed, probably with some reason, that the Jews would readily aid the Ptolemies in the event of a future war. Here we see the old pattern of the Assyrian and Chaldean periods emerging once again, wherein Egypt would use Judah as a cat's-paw against a more powerful neighboring empire. Rather than deporting the Jews, Antiochus decided to forcibly integrate them by virtually putting an end to Judaism. In 167 he declared that Yahweh was to be identified with Dionysus and his worship integrated into the that of the Greek pantheon. To that end he made it against the law under penalty of death to circumcise children or to refuse to eat pork. On December 25, 167 B.C.E., the pagan festival of lights celebrating the rebirth of the sun after the winter solstice was held in Jerusalem, and the temple was rededicated to Zeus Olympios, a statue of whom was put up inside the Temple. The statue seems to have borne a remarkable resemblance to Antiochus himself.

This policy was enforced brutally and eventually provoked a revolt. Mattathias of the family of Hashmon (the Hasmoneans) and his sons, most notably Judas Maccabeus (Judas "the hammer"), waged guerrilla warfare against the imperial forces. While this was never a serious threat to the empire, it was a constant drain. When in 164 Antiochus Epiphanes died campaigning in Persia, Lysias, guardian of his son Antiochus V Eupator, then only nine years old, agreed to discontinue the policy of forced Hellenization, perceiving that it was having the exact opposite of its intended effect. Thus, on the 25th of December 164 the Temple was purified and rededicated to the worship of Yahweh. However, this was not the end of the struggle by any means. Starting with the return from Rome of Demetrius, Antiochus Epiphanes' nephew, the Hasmoneans were able to play various pretenders off against each other, offering their aid at the price of ever greater autonomy, eventually winning complete independence, conquering most of the areas of the kingdom of David and forcibly converting their inhabitants to Judaism.

Some notes on religion are of importance before we leave the discussion of the historical context of the Book of Daniel. First of all, Antiochus Epiphanes has always been held up as the ultimate in arrogance. The name Epiphanes meaning "(god) manifest" would seem to bear this out. Yet other Hellenistic rulers also affected such titles. The epithet Epiphanes was also used by Ptolemy V (203-181). Antiochus II (261-247) was surnamed Theos, meaning god, and a later Seleucid queen named Cleopatra (not to be confused with the famous Cleopatra VII of Egypt) was surnamed Thea or goddess. Soter, meaning savior, was a surname used by Ptolemy I and VIII of the Ptolemaic line; Antiochus I, Seleucus II and Demetrius I of the Seleucid line; and Attalus I and Eumenes II of the Attalid rulers of Pergamum. The precedent of emperor worship was originally set by Alexander the Great, who decided after reaching Egypt that he was the personification of Zeus-Ammon.

The other point, which is rather peripheral to this book but which should not be passed over, is the date of the pagan festival of lights. December 25 is, of course, Christmas. Most Christians understand that the date was rather arbitrarily assigned as the birthday of Jesus. That it coincides with the Jewish holiday of Chanukah (also called the festival of lights) is because both are tied to the original pagan festival of lights. December 25 is also the birthday of Sol Invictus (Unconquered Sun), a Mithraic deity who died and was reborn. There are a number of Roman mosaics depicting Jesus as Sol Invictus and Apollo, and Roman coins from the time of Constantine, that first "Christian" emperor, variously depict him with Sol Invictus and next to both the Christian Chi-Rho symbol and a horse's head, representing the chariot of the sun god (see Wilson 1988, pp. 161-163). The Christian mythos of death and resurrection was present in many of Christianity's rivals and could easily have originated with them.

The Stories of Daniel

The book opens with Daniel and three of his friends, Hananiah, Mishael, and Azariah taken hostage by Nebuchadnezzar along with other young men of the Judean nobility. They are given Babylonian names by the chief eunuch. Daniel is called Belteshazzar, and the other three are called Shadrach, Meshach and Abednego. In the first chapter they are distinguished by refusing to "defile" themselves with the king's food, with the result that they are healthier and more alert than the other young men of the court. Chapter 2 concerns Nebuchadnezzar's dream of the idol, which I shall deal with later. In chapter 3 Nebuchadnezzar makes a golden idol and insists that all must worship it. Daniel is not mentioned in this story, but Shadrach, Meshach, and Abednego are. When they refuse to worship the idol the king has them thrown into a fiery furnace. Looking into the furnace, he sees them walking about with an angel, unscathed. The king calls to them to come out and decrees that anyone who speaks ill of the God of the Jews will be executed. The story in chapter 1 is not the material of history, so there is no way to verify it. As to the story in chapter 3, had Nebuchadnezzar been so impressed with the God of the Jews, we would have expected either conversion on his part, or at least inclusion of the worship of Yahweh into the Babylonian pantheon. Of course, neither of these things seems to have occurred. In chapter 4, the narrative switches from third person to first person, and the speaker is Nebuchadnezzar, who tells how God humbled his pride by striking him mad for seven years. After that time, Nebuchadnezzar's madness left him and his authority was returned to him. Not only is it highly likely that the grasping, fratricidal princes of Chaldea would have put Nebuchadnezzar to death had he shown any sign of weakness—the Chaldean succession following him was marred and confused by acts of familial assassination—but there simply is no evidence that the king suffered any episode of madness whatsoever. One possible source for a legend of kingly madness among the Chaldeans is in the perceived eccentricities of Nabonidus, father of Belshazzar. In fact among the Dead Sea Scrolls found at Qumran there is a manuscript called the Dream of Nabonidus, in which that king is the Chaldean monarch humbled by God It would appear that the alleged foibles of Nabonidus were later transferred to Nebuchadnezzar to make this most powerful of the Chaldean kings a foil for the demonstration of God's power. I have dealt with chapter 5, Belshazzar's feast, in the material on the fall of Babylon. Chapter 6, where Daniel is thrown into the lion's den for praying to God, involves the mythical King Darius the Mede and is, like all the other tales, fiction.

Viewed in the historical context of the struggle against Antiochus Epiphanes, these stories reveal a common thread. In all of them the foreign king along with his court is either arrogant, corrupt, or merely foolish. Daniel and his friends triumph by adhering to the strictures and tenets of their faith in spite of being threatened with torture and death. Idolatry is lampooned. All of this fits well as a veiled attack on Antiochus Epiphanes.

In the first chapter, the young men are taken into the world system (i.e. Nebuchadnezzar's court). Fundamentalists see a parallel in this to the corrupting influence of secular education. Speaking on Daniel 1, David Jeremiah said (*The Turning Point*, KKLA October 20, 1992):

It's not unlike a young person today who's a Christian going off to a secular university, studying all these things, these secular things. There's not anything wrong with that, by the way, if that young person's got his head on straight, he's got good teaching at home and he can separate the trash from the good information...[Nebuchadnezzar] wanted to brainwash them into thinking like a Babylonian. He wanted them to walk around looking like Jews on the outside, but being Babylonian on the inside. And, my friends, that is exactly the purpose most secular universities have if they don't know Christ. They don't care if you walk around looking like a Christian on the outside if they just teach you how to think like a humanist on the inside.

Jeremiah is not alone in his opinion that secular universities are modern versions of the Babylonian system. Here are two selections from Rev. John MacArthur on Daniel 1 (*Grace to You* KKLA October 23, 1992):

This was a brainwashing process. You know something? It's not unlike what universities and colleges are set to do to young people today: take away their faith; rob their heritage; reform them with the godless, atheistic, humanistic, socialistic information that so fills their books and the minds of their teachers. Sending your young person today to a college or university is not always doing him a favor at all, but exposing him to a brainwashing process. Sadly, even the seminaries in our country, that once held up the word of God, who have now abandoned it as the authority, are brainwashing people to believe that human answers tell us that we can't trust God; His word is not true—another brainwashing process.

[The Chaldeans] wanted them to forget God, forget the truth of God, wipe out everything of the past. Believe me, people, this is the effort of modern education. From the time your child goes off to school, except for God-fearing teachers and people that love Christ that intersect with your children, they will get a humanistic, godless, atheistic system of values that is geared by Satan to whitewash God out of the picture and to render those minds brainwashed to serve Satan. That's the plot.

It is interesting to consider that Rev. Mr. MacArthur, as president of the Master's College, and David Jeremiah, president of Christian Heritage College, both small religious universities, each have a vested interest in turning the young of their respective flocks away from secular colleges. However, they are not the only ones to see a threat of brainwashing indoctrination in the secular education system. Here is Rev. Raul Ries on the same parallel argument (*Manna for Today* KKLA, October 13, 1993):

> Isn't that what our public schools are trying to do to our children? Isn't that what society's trying to do with us? They're trying to push the church out and bring in humanism and bring in New Age.

The fears of the fundamentalists are to some degree justified in that their world view does not hold up too well when exposed to outside criticism. In fact, guests on Dr. James Dobson's *Focus on the Family* program (January 16, 1996) said that of Christian youth going to secular colleges, 80% fall away from the faith. Of these, 60% never return, meaning that roughly half of the Christian youth attending secular colleges are permanently lost to the faith. Fundamentalist fears are greatly exaggerated, however. There is no systematic plot to destroy the faith of their young people. The fears of the Jews at the time of Antiochus Epiphanes were *not* exaggerated. The Hellenizers did indeed want to seduce their young men away from Judaism. Daniel 1 is a call to Jewish youth not to be taken in by the worldly system. By refusing the king's food and drink, a parallel to refusing to eat pork, the young men turn out to be superior to the other youths at court.

The impotence of the world system is attacked in Dan. 2 when none of the king's soothsayers or "Chaldeans" can tell him the meaning of his dream. The list of the types of soothsayers in Nebuchadnezzar's court as "the magicians, the enchanters, the sorcerers and the Chaldeans" (Dan 2:2) is another clue to the dating of the book. If it had been written at the time of the Chaldean empire, "Chaldean" would have referred to a nationality. It was only centuries after that time that the word Chaldean became synonymous with astrologer.

In chapters 3 and 6 we have parallel stories. In the first, Daniel's three friends are thrown into a furnace because they refuse to bow down to the idol Nebuchadnezzar has made. In the second, Daniel is thrown into a lion's den when he continues to pray to Yahweh despite the ordinance against praying to anyone but the king. In both cases the Jews come out unscathed. Again, the reference is to Antiochus Epiphanes.

Likewise, the madness of Nebuchadnezzar in chapter 4 and the drunken revels at Belshazzar's feast in chapter 5 refer very specifically to Antiochus IV. The Jews regarded him as a madman and a blasphemer, even parodying his name by referring to him as Antiochus Epimenes (i.e. "the mad"). Belshazzar's profaning the Temple vessels by using them in a feast parallels Antiochus stripping the Temple of its gold. Belshazzar also fits the character of Antiochus in his drunkenness. Common to many of the prophets are oracles that God will make the offending nation drunk. This is probably synonymous with the Greek saying that "Whom the gods would destroy they first make mad."

The Parade of Empires

Now let us consider the prophecies of Daniel, which fundamentalists view as predicting both history and "end-times." In chapter 2, Nebuchadnezzar has a dream of a great idol, the head of which is gold, the breast and arms of silver, the belly and thighs of brass and the legs of iron, with the feet being a mix of iron and clay. The symbolism of Nebuchadnezzar's dream is mirrored in Daniel's dream, in chapter 7, of four beasts coming out of the sea. The first is a winged lion; the second a bear with three ribs in its mouth; the third a four-headed leopard; and the fourth an indescribable beast with ten horns. Another horn grows up in the midst of these horns. Three of the previous horns are torn out by the roots by its eruption. The little horn has eyes and a mouth and speaks great things.

The fundamentalist reading of the symbolism of these apocalyptic dreams is that the head of gold and the winged lion represent Babylon. The idol's arms and breast of silver and the bear with the three ribs in its mouth represent the succession of the Medo-Persian empire. The three ribs in the bear's mouth represent the major conquests of Persia, namely the Lydian empire in Asia Minor, the Chaldean Empire and Egypt. The belly and thighs of brass and the four-headed leopard represent the empire of Alexander the Great. The four heads stand for Alexander's four generals, who divided his empire between them after his death. They are Ptolemy, Seleucus, Cassander and Lysimachus.

Up to this point, biblical scholars, regardless of their views on inerrancy, will either agree with this interpretation of the symbols, or hold the view expressed by Herbert G. May, Old Testament editor of the OAV, that the Medes and Persians should be separated in the prophecies, making the fourth beast and the legs of iron Alexander's empire. Though this separate succession goes against history, it is somewhat more compatible with the book of Daniel in that the successor to the Chaldeans represented there is the mythical Darius the Mede. Thus, Daniel seems to imply that the Medes succeeded the

Chaldeans, and that the Persians supplanted them after the fall of Babylon. Therefore, the Medes could be represented as the bear with three ribs in its mouth, since the Book of Daniel's interpretation of history would be that imperial conquests took place while the Medes were still in charge. Regardless of which view of the Medes and Persians is accepted, the point where fundamentalists and biblical scholars part company is on the interpretation of the legs of iron and feet of clay of the first vision, and the fourth beast with its 10 horns in the second. The fundamentalist view is that these symbols represent the Roman Empire and its aftermath, and that the 10 toes of the idol correspond to the 10 horns of the beast. But what do the fundamentalists make of the significance of the 10 horns? David Jeremiah gives us a popular fundamentalist interpretation (1982, broadcast on KKLA December 3, 1992):

> (Y)ou come to verse 7 of Daniel, chapter 7, and you're reading through the verse and you read about the Roman Empire and you read that the beast...had ten horns. And you stop and you say, "Now wait a minute. The Roman Empire never had ten horns." There's no evidence in history that there ever was a ten-part Roman Empire. So between the last phrase of Daniel 7:7 and the phrase that goes before it, there's a mark. And we're moving, as we move to that last phrase, clear ahead to those events which are going to take place when the Lord comes back the second time...and all of this about the king and about the Antichrist and about the Son of Man is removed from the first part of Daniel 7:7 by over 2,000 years.

But if there is over 2000 years between the beast that is the Roman Empire and the 10 horns on the beast's head, how can they be part of each other? What about all of the other nations that have risen and fallen since Rome ceased to be? Jeremiah's explanation involves a rather odd reading of history (1982, KKLA December 7, 1992):

> Though it has been dispossessed of its authority and dominion, the Roman kingdom is still alive. It has never been taken over by a greater kingdom. And the Bible teaches us that when Christ comes back, it will be this final form of the Roman kingdom over which he is victorious.

In other parts of his study on the Book of Daniel, Jeremiah says that the modern nations of Europe are all part of Rome. He points out how Charlemagne had himself crowned emperor of Rome and how the German emperors called their state the Holy Roman Empire. Jeremiah's education seems to have missed Voltaire's pithy analysis of the Holy Roman Empire, to wit that it was not holy, was not Roman, and was not an empire.

It is another contention of David Jeremiah's that there has been no other world empire since Rome. The many states of Europe, along with the United States, in his view, constitute the idol's feet of iron mixed with clay—a broken and impure residue of the Roman state. I do not know what constitutes a world empire in this man's eyes, but apparently the empire built up by Jenghis Khan and his successors, which under Kublai Khan, by 1260 C.E., ruled the Asian steppe, China, Siberia, Russia, and Persia, does not count. Perhaps by the world, Jeremiah means the Mediterranean world or the Near East. If so, he seems to have missed such entities as the Umayyad Caliphate, which extended from Spain to the Indus river in 717 C.E., or its successor as the prime Moslem state, the Abbasid Caliphate which in 749 C.E. extended from Morocco to the Indus. By 1071 the Seljuk Sultanate held an empire roughly equivalent in size and synonymous in territory to ancient Persia, which was after all one of the world empires of Daniel's vision. Perhaps Jeremiah would insist that the territories would have to be synonymous with those of Rome. Yet, if Vladimir's marriage into the Eastern Roman royal house gave him inclusion into the Roman system, then the territories of the Byzantine Empire would have to constitute Roman territory. It was that very empire that the Ottoman Sultanate had conquered, including most of the Balkans by 1453 C.E.

Ignoring this extraneous parade of empires that I have just listed, Jeremiah interprets all history following the empire of Alexander the Great as Rome and sees the symbolism of the boulder smashing the idol, or the angel slaying the fourth beast, as the triumph of Jesus over the world empire at the end-time.

Since most Americans have only a foggy view of history, particularly ancient history, it is easy to sell the idea that Rome is the last of the four empires symbolized in Daniel. In a public school education—where U. S. history is taught in the fourth, eighth and 11th grades, while world history is taught only in the 10th grade—ancient history usually jumps from Alexander's empire to the Roman Republic with only a few paragraphs on the Hellenistic world and absolutely nothing about the power struggles between the Seleucids and the Ptolemies. In fact, the fourth beast, or the legs of iron represents either the Seleucid Empire or the empire of Alexander the Great, depending on whether or not one separates the Medes and the Persians. The last of the beast's 10 horns, called the little horn, is Antiochus IV Epiphanes. He was the seventh Seleucid king. Add to that Ptolemy I, Lysimachus and Cassander, the other co-inheritors of Alexander's realm along with Seleucus I, and you have 10 kings, symbolized by 10 horns. That the last little horn uproots three horns by its eruption also fits Antiochus Epiphanes, whom the Jews would naturally see implicated in the assassinations of his brother, Seleucus Philopater, and his nephew Antiochus. That he benefited from his other nephew, Demetrius, being held hostage in Rome could also be laid at his door. Thus, the little horn pushed out three others. There is corroboration for the view that the little horn is Antiochus Epiphanes in the vision of the ram and the he-goat in Daniel 8. In this vision, Daniel sees a ram charging north, south and west. No other beast can stand before him. Then a he-goat with one horn between his eyes comes from the west and overcomes the ram. In the midst of the goat's glory, his one horn breaks and four horns spring up from its base. Out of one of these horns grows a little horn that grows great and overthrows God's sanctuary. The angel Gabriel explains to Daniel that the ram represents Persia, while the goat represents the king of Greece, i.e. Alexander the Great. Gabriel goes on to say that the four horns represent four kingdoms that will rise out of the goat's empire. Out of one of these kingdoms rises the little horn. Thus, the little horn is not the Antichrist as fundamentalists would have us believe, nor does it come out of Rome. It is instead Antiochus Epiphanes. David Jeremiah's interpretation of the visions is that the little horn is Antiochus in this vision but the Antichrist in the vision of the four beasts. Making use of the doctrine of types he sees Antiochus Epiphanes as a fore-runner to the Antichrist. Oddly enough, since his interpretation of the "notable horn" of the he-goat is that it also is an Antichrist prototype, that makes Alexander the Great another forerunner. Apparently, Jeremiah's view is that the career of each and every world conqueror, from Alexander to Napoleon to Hitler and Stalin, is a trial run for the events leading up to Armageddon and the final confrontation between Christ and Antichrist.

In Daniel 11 there is a prophecy of a war between the king of the south and the king of the north. Though Hal Lindsey has woven this into his end of the world scenario, with the king of the south representing the Moslems and the king of the north representing Russia, the prophecy clearly states that the king-doms involved rise out of the division of Alexander's empire. After giving details on the war, which is between the Ptolemies and the Seleucids, the prophecy tells of the "contemptible person" who will gain the kingdom of the north by guile. He deceives, plunders and blasphemes until he is overthrown. Again, the one being spoken of is Antiochus Epiphanes, not the Antichrist.

The book of Daniel is actually looking back at past empires that had fallen and predicts that Antiochus Epiphanes will suffer their fate. His kingdom is derisively represented as an unstable mix of iron and clay in the prophecy of the idol. In the prophecy of the four beasts, Antiochus is not even a fearsome animal, but rather a little horn growing on one of the beasts. He is also the little horn on the he-goat.

The Seventy Weeks

Now let us compare modern biblical scholarship with that of the fundamentalists by examining the prophecy of the 70 weeks of years. In Daniel 9, the prophet is praying to God for enlightenment concerning Jeremiah's prophecy that the Jews would be in captivity for 70 years. Gabriel appears to him and says that the proper interpretation of the prophecy is "70 weeks [or sabbaths] of years," i.e. 7 x 70 = 490 years. Gabriel goes on to say that from the time of the command allowing Jerusalem to be rebuilt to the point when an anointed one (*messiah* in Hebrew) will be killed is sixty-nine weeks of years, or 7 x 69 = 483 years. Then the "people of the prince to come" will destroy Jerusalem after making a covenant with many for a week (7 years) which he will violate in the middle of the week (3 1/2 years). At that point, he will cause the observance of the sacrifice to cease and will cause abominations and desolations until he is defeated at the end of the 490 years. The fundamentalist interpretation of this prophecy is that the first 483 years end with the crucifixion of Jesus, after which there is a pause in the prophecy, the church age. The final seven years, they say, is the tribulation period at the end of the world that Jesus speaks of in the Olivet discourse and which John of Patmos speaks of in the Book of Revelation.

Let us examine the fundamentalist reasoning behind this interpretation and compare it to history and to scholarly views of the prophecy. In 537 B.C.E., Cyrus gave the order allowing the Jews to return to Judah and rebuild their temple. Since 537 - 483 = 54 B.C.E., the question arises as to how this can be construed to jibe with the Crucifixion, which should be either 32 or 33 C.E. We seem to be off by 87 years. However, the fundamentalist view is that the command in Cyrus' time only allowed the rebuilding of the temple, not the city. That was not allowed, according to the Book of Nehemiah, until the 20th year of the reign of Artaxerxes, or 445 B.C.E., which means 445-483 = 38 C.E. While that is close, it's still off by five to six years, and the fundamentalists claim that the prophecy is exact. At this point they come up with a bit of creative dating by insisting that, since the Jewish lunar calendar only had 360 days as opposed to our 365-day year, the calculation must be done as follows: 360 x 483 = 173,880 days. Divide that by 365 to get the number of our years and you get 476.38 years. Subtract that from 445 B.C.E. and you end up in April, 32 C.E., just at the right time for the Crucifixion.

This sounds quite impressive at first glance, and Hugh Ross gives the probability of chance fulfillment as 1 in 10,000. However, there is a slight hitch that completely unravels this supposedly exact prophecy. Considering that many Jewish holidays are seasonal and tied to a solar calendar of solstices and equinoxes, a lunar calendar of twelve 30-day months, or 360 days, will run afoul of such seasonally calculated festivals as Passover, which starts on the first full moon after the vernal equinox, if the festivals are placed in any month of that lunar calendar. The five-day discrepancy between the solar and lunar year will cause the month to cycle around through various seasons, while Passover is still bound to the vernal equinox. Accordingly, the Jewish calendar had a rather complicated system of leap years to compensate for the difference. In a cycle of 19 years, the third, sixth, eighth, 11th, 14th, 17th, and 19th years had an extra month added.

To understand this system fully we must dispense with the initial fiction of 360-day years with twelve 30-day months. Actually, the Jewish calendar has five "full" or 30 day months (Tishri, Shevat, Nisan, Sivan and Av), five "defective" or 29-day months (Tevet, Adar, Iyyar, Tammuz, Elul) and two months whose days varied between 29 and 30 days (Heshvan, Kislev). Thus, the regular Jewish year was and is 353, 354 or 355 days long. During leap years the month of Adar goes from 29 to 30 days and is called Adar I, followed by the extra month of Adar II, which is 29 days long. Thus leap years are either 383, 384, or 385 days long. In a cycle of 19 years there would be seven leap years of 384 days and 12 regular years of 354 days. Thus, 7 x 384 = 2688 days, and 12 x 354 = 4248 days. Therefore, 19 years would be 2688 + 4248 = 6936 days. Nineteen 365 day years equals 6935 days (19 x 365 = 6935). So, at the end of 19 years the Jewish lunar years would be roughly equal in length to the same number of 365 day solar years. Thus, the use of the 360-day year to compute the prophecy of the 70 weeks of years is totally invalid.

In any case, the extra-canonical Book of Enoch, written at about the time of the Second Temple, describes a Jewish calendar that is obviously solar. Thus, by the time the 490 years were starting to unfold, there was at least one other system of 365-day years. Also, for various political reasons, some of the kings of Israel, such as Jeroboam I, modified the calendar. At certain points in Jewish history there were rival calendars.

However, fundamentalists could argue that Daniel speaks of seven or three and one half year periods based on a 360-day calendar. Since leap years were every third year or every other year, the fundamentalists might argue that these calendars were not based on the mix of 354-day and 384-day years. Perhaps these were symbolic years. If so, then the original arithmetic holds, and the fundamentalist interpretation of the 70 weeks of years is correct. Or is it? Remember that their assertion is that 173,880 days (483 x 360 = 173,880) divided by 365 = 476.38, which subtracted from 445 B.C.E. = April of the year 32 C.E. Actually, when we divide 173,880 by 365 we get 476 years and 138.7 days. This puts us into May rather than April of the year 32. The situation gets a bit worse when we consider that the solar year is actually 365 1/4 days long, necessitating an extra day every four years in the Julian calendar, our own system of leap years. If we divide 173,880 by 365.25, we end up with 476.06 years or 476 years and 21.9 days or 21 days and 21.6 hours, putting the Crucifixion on January 21 sometime after 9:00 P.M. We might even have to further alter the date if we add the reforms of the Gregorian calendar.

In any case the validity of the fundamentalist time scale that fits the prediction of the Crucifixion in the Book of Daniel assumes not only that we start from 445 B.C.E. rather than 537 B.C.E., and not only that we must be calculating Daniel's years as being 360 days rather than 365 days; it also assumes that we accept that Jesus was 30 when he began to preach and 32 when he was crucified and that he was born at the junction of 1 B.C.E. and 1 C.E. Actually, not one of these dates can be verified. The only Roman record we have of Jesus is in the *Annals* by Tacitus, in which it is said that he was crucified by Pilatus (Pontius Pilate). We do not really know that the year of the Crucifixion was 32 C.E. In fact we do not really even know that Jesus was born at the beginning of what is variously called the Christian or Common Era. Nor are the biblical accounts of his birth of much help. After saying that the births of John the

Baptist and Jesus were in the time of Herod the Great (Lk. 1:5)—who died in 4 B.C.E.—Luke says that the Roman census took place when Quirinius was governor of Syria (Lk. 2:2). While there was a census of the Jews under Quirinius, it took place in C.E. 6. Matthew also says that Jesus was born during the time of Herod the Great (Mt. 2:1) and that the holy family returned from Egypt after Herod had died (Mt. 2:19). So, taking the accounts in Luke and Matthew together, Jesus could have been born any time from 4 B.C.E. to 6 C.E., a period of 10 years. Clearly, with conflicting dates as to the time of Jesus' birth and no solid date for his death, the fundamentalist attempt to make the first 69 of Daniel's 70 weeks of years culminate at the Crucifixion is simply ludicrous.

Not only have the fundamentalists failed to reckon the Jewish calendar correctly, they have also come up with some strange reasons for separating the last seven years from the rest of the prophecy and some ideas on the time periods involved that are so mystical in their ideas of numerical symmetry as to fit nicely into the so-called "psychic sciences." As an example of the later consider the following quote from David Jeremiah (1982, broadcast on KKLA January 12, 1993):

> There were 490 years before the captivity if the Israelites that are very significant, because for those 490 years the Jews violated their sabbath year. It was that 490 years, or their 70 of sabbaths, that caused God to finally take the Jews into captivity. So in the middle there's the 70 years of captivity, and God is now saying to Daniel…."Just as the 490 years of the past when you violated the sabbath consummated in this time of captivity, there's going to be another 490 years in the future."

Leaving aside for the moment the fact that there is no Biblical record as to whether or not the Jews obeyed the Levitical command to let their fields lie fallow every seventh year—a command whose origin may well have been post-exilic in any case—Jeremiah's assumption that the captivity actually did last 70 years is, as I pointed out earlier, at variance with historical reality. The Jewish captivity was closer to 49 years. This is not the only time the good pastor alludes to the captivity as being 70 years. He does it repeatedly in his study of the Book of Daniel. This is particularly curious, since he also lists the year of Cyrus' proclamation allowing the Jews to return to Judah as 536 B.C.E., the fall of Jerusalem to the Chaldeans as in 586 B.C.E., giving the length of captivity, by Pastor Jeremiah's own figures as being 50 years.

In his study of the Book of Daniel, Jeremiah also alludes to the pause in the prophecy that separates the last seven years from the first 483, or 69 weeks of years. He calls this period the parenthesis (1982, broadcast on KKLA January 11, 1993):

> You see, God operates this way as far as the Jewish people are concerned. Whenever he's not dealing with them, he stops his clock...So this 490 years are only 490 years of God's actual dealing with the Jews, Where are we today? Well, we're right in the parenthesis. In the middle right now, there's a stopping-off place, if you will. When Israel rejected Jesus as their Messiah, He turned to the Gentiles and He put aside his plan for the Jews. All of the 69 of the 70 weeks have been fulfilled. I believe we're right at the end of the parenthetical section. And pretty soon the Rapture is going to come and then the great tribulation that we know as the 70th week of Daniel will be ushered in. It can't be long before Jesus comes back. That's the scope of prophecy, 490 years of God's dealing with the Jewish people.

How do fundamentalists justify their contention that there is a 2,000-or more, year gap between the first 483 years and the last seven? There are two basic reasons. First, in Matthew 24, Jesus alludes to the coming tribulation as the time spoken of in Daniel. Interestingly enough, the other two synoptic gospels (Mark and Luke) do not mention Daniel in their versions of this teaching of Jesus, called the Olivet discourse. The second reason is that, since they consider the "anointed one who is cut off" (see Daniel 9:26) to be Jesus, and since the "prince who is to come" makes a seven-year covenant with the Jews after that time, and since no one has made such a seven-year agreement, then violated it half-way through, the prophecy has yet to be fulfilled. Its failure to be fulfilled on the heels of the Crucifixion should tell anyone reading the book that it was not meant to apply to Jesus. But the fundamentalists "know" that it was Jesus because the prophecy of an anointed one (messiah) being cut off must refer to Jesus. The reasoning gets a bit circular, but that rarely deters fundamentalists.

In sharp contrast to fundamentalist scholarship that fails to note the disparity between the 70 years of prophesied captivity and the historical record of a 49 years, the interpretation in the Jewish Encyclopedia is not only congruent with history, but manages to be that way without fudging the calendar. In order to understand the interpretation, let us first look at specifics of the prophecy itself in Daniel 9:25-27:

> Know therefore and understand that from the going forth of the word to
> restore and build Jerusalem to the coming of an anointed one, a prince, there
> shall be seven weeks. Then for sixty-two weeks it shall be built again with
> squares and a moat, but in a troubled time. And after the sixty-two weeks, an
> anointed one shall be cut off, and shall have nothing; and the people of the
> prince who is to come shall destroy the city and the sanctuary. Its end shall
> come with a flood and to the end there shall be war; desolations are decreed.
> And he shall make a strong covenant with many for one week; and for half of
> the week he shall cause sacrifice and offering to cease; and upon the wing of
> abominations shall come one who makes desolate, until the decreed end is
> poured out on the desolator.

One thing I have noticed that is lacking in fundamentalist interpretations
of the prophecy is the setting apart of the first seven weeks of years. This is
interesting, since these seven weeks of years are mentioned as coming before
the appearance of an anointed one, but after the going out of the word to
rebuild Jerusalem. This anointed one is sometimes thought of as Zerubbabel,
who was the first leader among the returning Jews and who, as a scion of the
House of David, could be considered an anointed one. The problem with this
view is that, since seven weeks of years, or 7 x 7 years = 49 years, come between
the going out of the word to rebuild the city and the coming of an anointed
one, and since Zerubbabel led the first contingent of returning Jews back
shortly after Cyrus gave the decree allowing the return, he could not have
been the anointed one who came 49 years after the going out of the word. In
fact even if we date the going out of the word to rebuild the city as being in
the 20th year of the reign of Artaxerxes, which would put the appearance of
this first anointed one at 445 B.C.E. - 49 years = 396 B.C.E., there is nobody
in either the Bible or history who would fill the bill as a notable anointed one.
The *Jewish Encyclopedia* solves the problem by pointing out the following
(Vol. 4, p. 433):

> The context demands, furthermore that the origin of the prediction concern-
> ing the rebuilding of Jerusalem be sought in Jer. XXV 11-13 and the parallel
> passage, ib. XXIX. 10. The "anointed," the "prince," mentioned after the first
> seven times seven units, must be Cyrus, who is called the anointed of the Lord
> in Isa. LV 1 also. He concluded the seven weeks of years by issuing the decree

of liberation, and the time that elapsed between the Chaldean destruction of Jerusalem (586) and the year 538 was just about forty-nine years.

So the time of the "going forth of the word" to rebuild Jerusalem, in this interpretation, is the prophecy in Jeremiah, and the first 49 years constitutes the captivity. The next period is 62 weeks or 7 x 62 = 434 years. By subtracting that from the date of Cyrus' decree (538 - 434 = 107) we get the year 107 B.C.E., which is off somewhat from 171 B.C.E., the year Antiochus Epiphanes possibly had the high priest Onias III killed. The *Jewish Encyclopedia* acknowledges this, but points out that the chronology of the time was quite inexact. This would fit the ignorance of history shown in the Book of Daniel with respect to Nebuchadnezzar's madness and the non-existent Darius the Mede. If we accept this explanation, then we come to the last seven years of the prophecy, which the *Jewish Encyclopedia* sets at 171-164 B.C.E. This would begin with the murder of Onias III, followed by an agreement between Antiochus and the Hellenized Jews, which is violated after three and a half years (in 167) by the desecration of the Temple.

This is by no means the only scholarly interpretation of the 70 weeks of years. Both the *Abingdon Bible Commentary* and the notes in the OAV state that the phrase "going forth of the word to restore and build Jerusalem" is open to too many interpretations to be pinned down to a certain date. As far as I know, however, no biblical scholar who is not a fundamentalist finds any basis for separating the last seven years of the prophecy from the first 483. Thus, since no destruction or desecration of the temple took place seven years after the Crucifixion, the 70 weeks of years cannot refer to Jesus.

One reason fundamentalists cannot accept these events as having to do with past history is that Daniel also predicts the end of the world just following the overthrow of Antiochus Epiphanes. However, just as in Isaiah and Ezekiel, the latter days were likely perceived by the author of Daniel as being in the near future. We must always bear in mind that to Isaiah seeing the Assyrian onslaught, to Ezekiel experiencing the Exile, and to the author of Daniel witnessing the attempted destruction of his people's identity, the end of the world seemed to be unfolding before their very eyes.

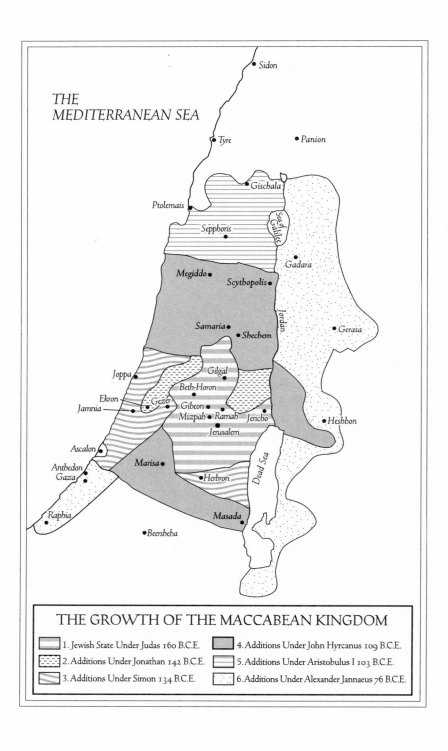

THE
MEDITERRANEAN SEA

• Sidon

• Panion

• Tyre

Ptolemais •

Gischala •

Sea of Galilee

Sepphoris •

Megiddo •

Scythopolis •

Gadara •

Samaria •
• Shechem

Gerasa •

Jordan

Joppa •

Gilgal •

Beth-Horon •

Ekron •
Jamnia —
Gezer •

Gibeon •

Mizpah • Ramah •

Jericho •

Heshbon •

Jerusalem •

Ascalon •

Marisa •

Dead Sea

Anthedon •
Gaza •

• Hebron

Raphia •

Masada •

• Beersheba

THE GROWTH OF THE MACCABEAN KINGDOM

1. Jewish State Under Judas 160 B.C.E.		4. Additions Under John Hyrcanus 109 B.C.E.
2. Additions Under Jonathan 142 B.C.E.		5. Additions Under Aristobulus I 103 B.C.E.
3. Additions Under Simon 134 B.C.E.		6. Additions Under Alexander Jannaeus 76 B.C.E.

8

THE LAST DAYS

Apocalyptic Writings of the New Testament

WHILE BY FAR THE GREATEST APOCALYPTIC WORK in the New Testament is the Revelation of John, there are important passages in the Gospels and epistles which supply part of the doctrine of premillennialism. It is obvious if one reads these passages without presuppositions that their literal interpretation would be that they refer to the second coming of Christ as taking place in within the lifetime of the authors. While this is vigorously disputed by fundamentalists, it is in keeping with what we have seen with respect to the apocalyptic passages in the Nevi'im. Also, as with the Book of Daniel, the historical context is crucial to understanding the thinking of the writers of the New Testament.

The Historical Context of the New Testament

After the Temple was cleansed and rededicated to Yahweh in 164 B.C.E. some of the Jews were content to remain under Seleucid rule. However, the Hasmoneans and their supporters continued the war. After Judas Maccabeus fell in battle in 160, his brother Jonathan assumed leadership. He was able to exploit dissensions between rival branches of the Seleucids, allying himself to one side and then to the other, extracting ever greater autonomy as the price of his allegiance. By the time he died in 142 B.C.E. Judah had won its independence. The rule of the new state passed to his brother Simon and then to Simon's son John Hyrcanus I, who conquered Galilee, Idumea, and other areas adjacent to Judah.

The rising power of the Hasmoneans was aided by an alliance with Rome and by the decline of the Seleucids. Ravaged by intermittent civil war the

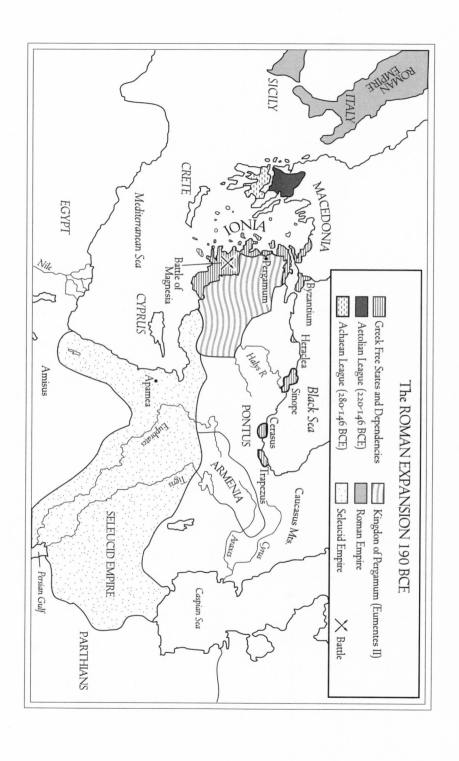

The ROMAN EXPANSION 190 BCE

Greek Free States and Dependencies

Aetolian League (220-146 BCE)

Achaean League (280-146 BCE)

Kingdom of Pergamum (Eumenes II)

Roman Empire

Seleucid Empire

✕ Battle

ROMAN EMPIRE

SICILY

ITALY

CRETE

MACEDONIA

IONIA

Battle of Magnesia

Pergamum

Byzantium

Heraclea

Sinope

Black Sea

Cerasus

Trapezus

EGYPT

Nile

Mediterranean Sea

CYPRUS

Amisus

Apamea

Halys R.

PONTUS

Euphrates

ARMENIA

Caucasus Mts.

Tigris

Araxes

Cyrus

Caspian Sea

SELEUCID EMPIRE

Persian Gulf

PARTHIANS

Seleucids lost territory to the Parthians, who by 124 held all of Mesopotamia. Of the once great Seleucid realm only Syria now remained. By 62 B.C.E. Syria was a Roman province.

Friendship with Rome, originally a benefit, proved fatal to Jewish independence in the long run. Roman policy was to exploit the dissensions within a region, aiding the weaker side, then utilizing its help while at the same time becoming indispensable to their ally, gaining some internal control and ultimately dispensing with any pretense of equality. By that time there was usually a violent reaction among the more patriotic forces of the erstwhile ally, giving the Romans justification to invade. Thus it was that Rome made use of the fleet of Rhodes and an alliance with Pergamum during the First Macedonian War and the struggle with Antiochus III in 190. After the decisive defeat of Perseus at the battle of Pydna in 168, which ended the Second Macedonian War and the independence of Macedonia, the Greek city states that had been allied with Rome found themselves reduced to Roman protectorates. By 89 B.C.E. the Greek mainland, Rhodes, and Pergamum were all Roman provinces, and most of the rest of Asia Minor was made up of Roman protectorates.

Judah went from ally to protectorate as the result of a civil war which broke out in 67 B.C.E. between King Hyrcanus II and his more vigorous brother, Aristobulus II. Each side sought Roman support. Pompey was in Damascus in 63 B.C.E. and intervened on the side of Hyrcanus, the weaker of the two. Despite the overwhelming superiority of Roman arms it took eight years to completely subjugate Judah, and resistance flared up again when the Parthians invaded Syria and set the son of Aristobulus, Antigonus Mattathias, on the throne. The Romans eventually reconquered the eastern provinces and drove out the Parthians. When Mark Antony had Antigonus beheaded in 37 B.C.E. Hasmonean resistance to Roman rule was broken.

During the civil war a certain Idumean (Edomite) officer named Antipater had aided the Romans as part of his own design to gain control of the kingdom. Under the Roman protectorate he was the real ruler of Judea. His descendant Herod the Great married Mariamne, niece of Antigonus and granddaughter of Hyrcanus II. This gave the Herodean line a claim to be the rightful rulers of Israel, although their power derived from Rome.

While the Romans instituted a system of emperor worship as a sort of loyalty oath, it was not intended to displace any other religion and, respecting tradition, they exempted the Jews from the requirement of a yearly token

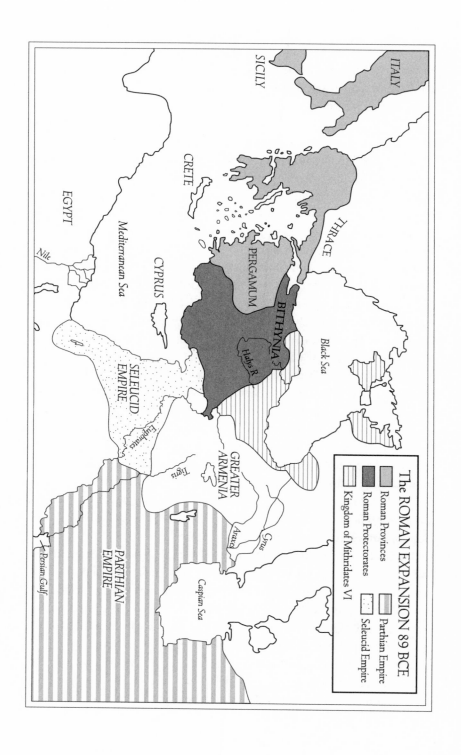

The ROMAN EXPANSION 89 BCE

Roman Provinces
Roman Protectorates
Kingdom of Mithridates VI
Parthian Empire
Seleucid Empire

ITALY

SICILY

CRETE

EGYPT

Nile

Mediterranean Sea

CYPRUS

PERGAMUM

BITHYNIA

Halys R.

THRACE

Black Sea

SELEUCID
EMPIRE

Euphrates

Tigris

GREATER
ARMENIA

Araxes

Cyrus

Caspian Sea

PARTHIAN
EMPIRE

Persian Gulf

sacrifice. Nevertheless, the Jews resented Roman rule and rose in revolt in 66 C.E. The revolt was eventually crushed by Titus, who took Jerusalem and destroyed the second Temple in 70. In spite of this crushing loss, followed by mass deportations, the Jews revolted again in 132, this time led by Simon Bar Kochba, who was thought to be the Messiah. The Romans crushed this revolt in 134, built a Roman city on the site of Jerusalem called Colonia Aelia Capitolina, and built a shrine to Zeus on the Temple mount. Thus, during the time of Jesus and the early Christian church, the Jews and newly converted Christians lived in a world which seemed to them ruled by injustice and one that was alive with messianic expectations.

The Olivet Discourse: Jesus Describes the Last Days

Common to Matthew 24, Mark 13, and Luke 21 is the Olivet Discourse, a description of the last days given to his disciples by Jesus on the Mount of Olives. He tells them that the end-times will be preceded by earthquakes, famine and war. While much of the imagery is suitably vague and poetic, and Jesus does say that no one knows the day or hour of his coming, he also states (Mt. 24:34): "Truly I say to you, this generation will not pass away till all these things take place."

Despite their dogma that the Bible should be interpreted literally except when it obviously uses symbolism or allegory, fundamentalists readily violate their own hermeneutics, going to great lengths to explain away the fact that Jesus was telling his apostles that the world would end in the lifetime of their generation. The possibilities that Jesus could have been wrong, that he might never have said these words, or that they were meant to convey something other than the literal end of the world are not considered. Typical of fundamentalist reasoning are the following statements by Gleason L. Archer (1982, p. 338):

> Obviously these apocalyptic scenes and earth-shaking events did not take place within the generation of those who heard the Olivet discourse. Therefore Jesus could not have been referring to His immediate audience when He made His prediction concerning "this [generation]."

Archer goes on to say that possibly the word for generation, *genea,* was used as a synonym for *genos,* meaning race. Thus the Jewish race would not pass away before the end-times. Alternatively, he says that the generation spo-

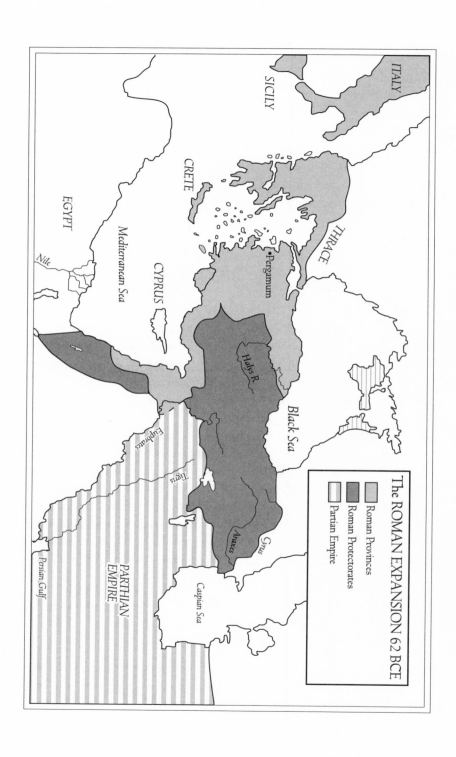

The ROMAN EXPANSION 62 BCE

Roman Provinces
Roman Protectorates
Parian Empire

ITALY

SICILY

CRETE

EGYPT

Nile

Mediteranean Sea

CYPRUS

THRACE

Pergamum

Halys R.

Black Sea

Euphrates

Tigris

Araxes

Cyrus

Caspian Sea

PARTHIAN EMPIRE

Persian Gulf

ken of could mean the generation of the last days. It will not pass away until everything He predicts takes place. Neither of these rationalizations stands up to those rules of hermeneutics to which fundamentalists themselves claim to adhere. For example, a universal hermeneutic is that a verse is to be interpreted in the context from which it is taken. Generation cannot stand for race, because the context in which Jesus is speaking is one of time, not nationality. Nor can the generation referred to be some future generation. Throughout the Olivet discourse Jesus refers to the events as happening in the time of his disciples. Consider the exhortations he gives them in the following verses from Matthew 24:

> vs. 9 Then they will deliver *you* up to tribulation....
>
> vs. 15 So when *you* see the desolating sacrilege....
>
> vs. 20 Pray that *your* flight may not be in winter....
>
> vs. 33 So also, when *you* see all these things [the signs of the end] *you* know that he is near, at the very gates (emphasis added).

Archer's final words in defense of the possible substitution of genos (race) for genea (generation) is that the Aramaic word that Jesus used could logically be translated into either of the Greek words. But if Archer is right, then we can never know for sure if any doctrine, prophecy or statement by Jesus has been rendered correctly, regardless of how scrupulously the original autographs of the gospels were copied or how well the Greek has been translated into English. If the Greek itself is wrong then the whole New Testament is unreliable. This flies in the face of Archer's own assertion that God protected the human authors of the Bible from error. Also, the argument that the message of the Bible has been hopelessly garbled in the translation is vigorously opposed by fundamentalists. Yet here is Archer trying to use such an argument to defend the Bible. Therefore, his argument is invalid. You cannot have it both ways. Either there exists great doubt as to what Jesus actually said or the word "generation" is correct, and a literal interpretation of the Olivet discourse makes a liar out of Jesus.

Another common argument concerning the Olivet discourse is that the pronoun "you" was meant in a generic sense and that Jesus was addressing Christians in general. That is, of course, a possibility. However, there is no way one can stretch Jesus' words in Mark 8:38 and 9:1 (parallel verses Lk. 9:26-27; Mt. 16:27-28) to cover anything other than the generation of his day:

"For whoever is ashamed of me and my words in this adulterous and sinful generation, of him will the Son of Man also be ashamed, when he comes in the glory of his father with the holy angels." (Mk. 8:38)

And he said to them, "Truly, I say to you, there are some standing here who will not taste death before they see the kingdom of God come with power." (Mk. 9:1)

The only way to interpret this other than as a prediction that Jesus would return in that very generation is to assume that the kingdom of God coming in power would mean the establishment of the Christian church. This interpretation fails, however, since in the lifetime of that generation, the founding and spread of the church was hardly "with power." Furthermore, this coming with power is in the context of the preceding verse, which speaks of Jesus coming in the glory of God the Father and "with the holy angels." I do not see how that can be interpreted in any other way than Jesus's return in the second coming at the end of the world.

Gleason Archer's defense is that the phrase referring to Jesus coming in his kingdom could refer either to the Transfiguration or to the miracle of Pentecost. Of the two he favors the latter. Leaving aside for the moment that the miracle at Pentecost cannot be historically verified, let us concentrate on whether it fits Jesus's words. Using Archer's own dictum that different accounts of the same event should be harmonized—a dictum that may be valid in this case since the varying accounts do not greatly contradict each other—let us compare the wording of Mark 8:38-9:1, Matthew 16:27-28 and Luke 9:26-27:

"For whoever is ashamed of me and my words in this adulterous and sinful generation, of him will the Son of man also be ashamed, when he comes in the glory of his Father with the holy angels." And he said to them, "Truly, I say to you, there are some standing here who will not taste death before they see the kingdom of God come with power" (Mk. 8:38-9:1).

"For the Son of man is to come with his angels in the glory of his Father, and then he will repay every man for what he has done. Truly I say to you, there are some standing here who will not taste death before they see the Son of man coming in his kingdom" (Mt. 16:27-28).

"For whoever is ashamed of me and of my words, of him will the Son of man be ashamed when he comes in his glory and the glory of the Father and of the holy angels. But I tell you truly, there are some standing here who will not taste death before they see the kingdom of God" (Lk. 9:26-27).

If we harmonize in Matthew's statement that Jesus will repay everyone for what he has done, we have a description of Jesus returning to judge the world. This hardly fits Pentecost. If we harmonize the three versions of what those who haven't tasted death will see, we have "the kingdom of God come with power" (Mk.), "the Son of Man coming in his kingdom" (Mt.), and "the kingdom of God" (Lk.). We can perhaps stretch Luke's "kingdom of God" to fit the establishment of the Christian church, or perhaps Mark's kingdom of God coming "with power" to fit Pentecost. But, in the terms of the trinitarian doctrine Archer himself professes to believe, we cannot possibly make Matthew's statement that some of those standing before Jesus would see "the Son of man coming in his kingdom" in any way fit Pentecost. The reason for this is that, according to Acts 2:4, at Pentecost the disciples were filled with the *Holy Spirit.* The doctrine of the Trinity is adamant on this point: While the Father, the Son, and the Holy Spirit are all part of the Godhead, they are separate entities and are *not* part of each other. Assuming as fundamentalists do that Matthew accepted the doctrine of the trinity, we must believe that when he says that those standing before Jesus would see the Son of Man, i.e. Jesus, the *Son* as opposed to the Holy Spirit, he is quoting Jesus as saying in Mt. 16:28 that some of those hearing his words will be alive at the second coming. This obviously did not happen. Therefore, either Jesus was wrong and cannot be God incarnate or he did not say these words, which makes the gospels wrong, or he meant them in some symbolic sense that cannot be made to fit Pentecost unless one is ready to throw out the doctrine of the Trinity.

Even if we could overlook the problem of the wording of Mt. 16:28, Archer's argument that the words of Jesus—which sound very much like a prediction that the world would end in the generation of those hearing them—were not meant to be taken in the literal sense creates more problems than it solves. If a fundamentalist argues against a literal interpretation of a seemingly apocalyptic prophecy in the Bible, how can he then defend the idea that Daniel, the Olivet discourse, Paul's reference to the rapture or even the Book of Revelation are meant to be interpreted in the literal sense? Archer's argument that Jesus was referring to Pentecost when he spoke of the kingdom of God is the first misstep on a slippery slope that ultimately undoes biblical inerrancy and with it fundamentalism.

Finally, there is the problem that the one specific thing Jesus predicts is the destruction of the Temple. Many fundamentalists assert that this was indeed a prophecy that was fulfilled in 70 C.E. If Jesus spoke these words it was a prophecy made before the fact. However, since the earliest gospel, that of Mark, was probably written after 70 C.E. these words could have been put in Jesus' mouth by the author. Ironically, the situation is not made any easier for fundamentalists if Jesus actually was foretelling the destruction of the Temple in C.E. 70, since the prophecy that not one stone will be left standing on another is part of the events that the rest of the Olivet discourse places in the last days. At this point some fundamentalists argue that when Jesus referred to "the end of the age" in the Olivet discourse what he meant was not the end of the world, but rather the end of the age of temple sacrifices, which did indeed end with the destruction of the Temple in 70 C.E. However, as can be seen from the quotations from Matthew 24 below (which are paralleled in Mark and Luke), the events being described go far beyond the Roman sack of Jerusalem:

> vs. 14: And this gospel of the kingdom will be preached throughout the whole world, as a testimony to all nations; and then the end will come.
>
> vs. 21-22: For then there will be great tribulation, such as has not been from the beginning of the world until now, no, and never will be. And if those days had not been shortened, no human being would be saved; but for the sake of the elect those days will be shortened.
>
> vs. 29-31: Immediately after the tribulation of those days the sun will be darkened and the moon will not give its light, and the stars will fall from heaven and the powers of heaven will be shaken; then will appear the sign of the Son of man in heaven, and then all the tribes of the earth will mourn, and they will see the Son of man coming on the clouds of heaven with power and great glory and he will send his angels with a loud trumpet call and they will gather his elect from the four winds, from one end of heaven to the other.

Obviously, the gospel had not been preached to the entire world by 70 C.E., even if we interpret the whole world as being nothing more than the Roman Empire. Further, despite the ferocity with which the Romans crushed the Jewish revolt, there is no way one could construe such purely human actions to assert that they would result in the end of the human race if not checked. That this tribulation marks the end of the world and not merely the end of the Jewish state is made explicit when verse 21 says that such tribulation is greater not only than any that has been: "until now, no, and *never will be.*" Since this tribulation is not to be surpassed by any in the future it must refer to the end of the world. Finally, verses 29-31 list specific events that likewise can only relate to the end of the world. Here the sun and moon are darkened; the stars fall from the the sky; the peoples of the earth are in terror, for they see the sign of Jesus returning in the clouds. The angels sound the last trump and gather the elect. Thus if Jesus really believed that the Temple would be destroyed less than half a century after his death, he had to also believe the generation of the end-times was that of his time. If "this generation" did not mean that of his disciples, then the prediction of the destruction of the Temple can't have been meant for that generation either.

Apocalyptic Passages in the Epistles

It is clear that Paul also saw the end as being within his generation. In 1 Thessalonians 4:13 through 5:11 he tells of Christ's return. He says that first those who have died in the faith will rise. Then he says (vs. 17-18):

> then *we* who are alive, who are left, shall be caught up together with them in the clouds to meet the Lord in the air; and so *we* shall always be with the Lord. Therefore comfort one another with these words (emphasis added).

This brief passage is one of two sources of the fundamentalist doctrine of the Rapture. The other is found in Matthew's rendering of the Olivet discourse in Mt. 24:40-41:

> Then two men will be in the field; one is taken and one is left. Two women will be grinding at the mill; one is taken and one is left.

The word rapture derives from the Latin verb *rapere* meaning to seize or snatch away. Ironically, *rapere* is also the root word for rape. While modern millenarians hope for the Rapture in their lifetimes, Paul was probably telling the Thessalonians that the end would come in their time. This view is corroborated in 1 Corinthians 15:51, where Paul says "We shall not all sleep (i.e. die)," before the return of Christ. Earlier in the same epistle he urges the Corinthians to avoid marriage if they possibly can, the reason given is in 1 Cor. 7:29: "I mean, brethren, the appointed time has grown very short; from now on let those who have wives live as though they had none." Paul is saying here that the time is so short to the end of the world that even married couples should prepare for it by practicing celibacy. It is interesting to me that Paul's writings are considered divinely inspired even though he was obviously wrong about how soon the world would end.

Paul was not alone in this belief. The anonymous author of the epistle to the Hebrews, which seems to have been written before 70 C.E., exhorts believers to meet together and encourage each other, "all the more as *you* see the Day [the Second Coming] drawing near" (Heb. 10:25, emphasis added). Also, the epistle 1 John, which may indeed have been the work of the author of the gospel of John and was probably written near the end of the first century, says, "Children, it is the last hour," (1 John 2:18).

Fundamentalists may claim that the pronouns "you" and "we" were meant in a generic sense for Christians of all ages and even argue that John's reference to "the last hour" could encompass all time since Jesus walked the earth as the last days, but, as in the Olivet discourse, the more generic the time frame becomes the less literal the prophecy becomes, thus vitiating the arguments of dispensational premillennialists.

The Authorship and Historical Context of the Book of Revelation

The Book of Revelation, also called the Apocalypse of John, is the second great pillar of fundamentalist "end-time" scenarios, the first being Daniel. The word apocalypse is derived from a Greek verb for "to uncover" or reveal what was hidden—in this case the ultimate future of the world. At first glance, many bewildered readers delving into John's vision will see nothing but a chaotic mix of weird monsters, dire prophecies and odd numbers. They may well conclude that what was hidden still is. Yet the book does have a very intricate structure. Upon dissection and with considerable simplification, we see that the main parts are as follows:

1) The prologue on earth, messages to the seven churches in Asia Minor and the prologue in heaven.

2) Three series of seven judgments: the seven seals, the seven trumpets and the seven bowls. Between each series of judgments are various parentheses which include lesser visions, many of which are derived from Zechariah.

3) Various visions of the rise and fall of the kingdom of the Antichrist: The woman and child pursued by the dragon, the vision of the Antichrist and the false prophet as two beasts, the great whore of Babylon.

4) The return of Jesus as a warrior king, the battle of Armageddon, the establishment of the millennial kingdom, the binding, loosing, and final defeat of Satan, and the Last Judgment.

According to the early second century Christian apologist Irenaeus, the book of Revelation was written during the time of Emperor Domitian (89-96). Since certain passages in the book refer to the Temple in Jerusalem, it has been suggested that they were written before C.E. 70, but that the book was not put into its final form until late in the reign of Domitian. There is no indication, however, of multiple authorship. The author, John of Patmos, does not claim to be the apostle John, and his writing style seems different from those of either the Gospel or Epistles of John. However, from his use of Greek words with Aramaic grammar, it would appear that he too was a Jewish Christian rather than a Gentile convert.

Patmos is a rocky island in the Aegean roughly five by 10 miles in area that was used as a penal colony in Roman times. John states that he was exiled there for his Christian beliefs (Rev. 1:9). Under Domitian emperor worship was promulgated to a far greater degree than it had been before. Persecution of Christians, who refused to perform the token sacrifice, was also intensified. Nero had brutally persecuted the Christians of Rome, using them as scapegoats for a fire that devastated the city in C.E. 64, but his atrocities had not spread much beyond the capital. Just as Domitian spread emperor worship, which the Romans used as something of a loyalty oath, far and wide, so too did he extend the empire's attacks on Christians. This enforced idolatry and sharply increasing persecution naturally caused Christians, already looking for the imminent return of Jesus, to see their world in increasingly apocalyptic terms.

The Prologues and the Letters

John opens his book by saying that he saw a vision on the Lord's day of Jesus

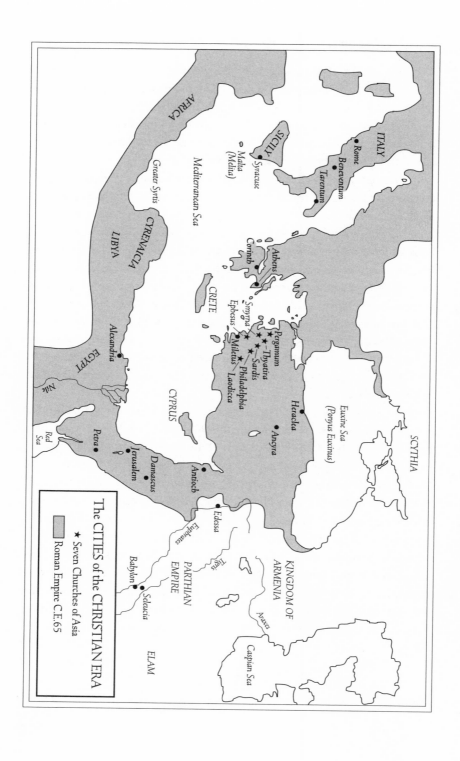

The CITIES of the CHRISTIAN ERA

★ Seven Churches of Asia
▨ Roman Empire C.E.65

telling him to write to the seven churches in the Roman province of Asia. These churches were located in the cities of Ephesus, Smyrna, Pergamum, Thyatira, Sardis, Philadelphia, and Laodicea. The reason for choosing seven particular churches would likely have to do with the mystical significance of the number seven, which was the number of completion, as in the seven-day creation.

Many fundamentalists see them as symbolizing seven ages of the Christian church, taking John's criticism or praise of the congregation as an indication of the state of the church in any given time period. While interpretations may vary, the following is a fair indication of the fundamentalist view of church history as prophetically revealed in chapters 2 and 3 of the Apocalypse of John. The first age is represented by Ephesus. The church is growing and full of vigor, but John chides it for losing its first bloom of love. The second age is represented by the long suffering church in Smyrna. This would be the church of John's own day and afterward, suffering martyrdom at the hands of the Romans. Pergamum is warned to be watchful and not compromise with the world. This is often taken to represent the church growing in power and influence in the later empire and being corrupted by it. The corruption becomes worse in the age typified by Thyatira, where the church has tolerated the teachings of a Jezebel, a false prophetess. Verse 2:22 refers to the fate of "those who commit adultery with her." This is symbolic of those who commit adultery with Rome, personified later in the book as the Great Whore of Babylon. Thus, this refers to the corruption of the church by Rome at the hands of Constantine. By accepting the status of Rome's official religion, the church committed adultery with the empire. John tells the church of Sardis that it is dead, merely going through the motions of Christian worship. The fundamentalist interpretation is that this is the Catholic church of the Middle Ages. By contrast, the Church of Philadelphia is the church of the open door and represents the Protestant Reformation. Laodicea, the church that is lukewarm, represents the mainline churches of the 20th century. Evangelicals, of course, have regained the vitality of the church in Philadelphia.

In order to make this scheme work, fundamentalist ministers often have to take a rather odd view of history. For example, in relating how dead the medieval church was, David Jeremiah relates an anecdote about how one of his teachers at seminary said that he could cover the evangelical activities of the middle ages in one sentence. Then he smiled and said there was not any evangelism is the Middle Ages. History gives a rather different reading. At the beginning of the Middle Ages, about 450 C.E., the Eastern Roman Empire was Christian. The empire had ceased to exist in the west, but the peoples of Italy, Spain, the Romanized Celts of Gaul and Britain, as well as the Irish, were Christians and some of the invading Germanic tribes were at least nominally so. This had only a slight effect on their behavior. For example, the Christian Visigoths sacked Rome three years in a row. They did refrain from looting Christian churches, however. The Vandals, still being pagans, gave Rome a more businesslike looting when their turn came, hence the word "vandalism." As for the rest of Europe, most of the Teutonic peoples, including the Anglo-Saxons, the Saxons of Germany and the Scandinavians, were pagans, as were all of the Slavs, the Baltic peoples, the Finns and the Magyars. Despite losing Egypt, the Middle East and North Africa to Islam by military conquest, the church did indeed evangelize, so much so in fact that all of Europe was Christian by the end of the Middle Ages, *circa* 1450. Some of the conversion was by force as when Charlemagne conquered the Saxons and Frisians or when Olav Tryggvason used an army to superficially Christianize Norway. And, on occasion, invading peoples or habitual raiders were defeated and forced to accept Christianity as part of the terms of peace, as in the case of both the Magyars (Hungarians) and the Danes. However, the Slavs, Balts, Anglo-Saxons, various German tribes, Swedes and Finns were converted largely without resorting to force. In the case of the Slavic peoples, the brothers Cyril and Methodius even made up an alphabet tailored to the Slavic languages (the Cyrillic alphabet) so that the Bible could be translated into them effectively. Thus, Pastor Jeremiah's teacher either knew nothing of the history of the church over the one thousand year period called the Middle Ages or he was merely indulging in a bit of anti-Catholic propaganda.

Once John has written the seven churches, he is taken up to heaven where 24 elders and four beasts minister to God. The elders represent the 12 patriarchs of the Old Testament and the 12 apostles of New Testament. The beasts are reminiscent of the vision of the angelic beings in Ezekiel 1.

The Judgments

After the prologue in heaven, the Lamb of God (Jesus) opens the seven seals revealing the first set of judgments on the world. The first four of these are the four horsemen of the Apocalypse. They are usually seen as Conquest (on a white horse), War (red horse), Famine (black horse), and Death or Pestilence (pale horse). The imagery of the differently colored horses clearly derives from Zechariah, chapters 1 and 6, but rather than being angels patrolling the earth, these are sent out to scourge it. Many fundamentalist interpreters consider the first horseman to be Jesus, who appears later riding on a white horse. However, as F. Bertram Clogg points out in his article in the *Abingdon Bible Commentary*, Christ is already represented as the Lamb who is opening the seals. Noting that the rider on the white horse is given a crown and carries a bow, and further noting that conquest and war as two separate horsemen are redundant, Clogg sees the rider on the white horse as symbolizing the Parthians and invasion from without, while the red horseman represents civil war. Not only was the bow the favorite weapon of the Parthians, but their empire, which bordered that of Rome on the Euphrates, was of nearly equal power. Furthermore, the Romans had something of a terror of Parthian horsemen, who in 53 B.C.E. had annihilated a Roman army under Crassus at the Battle of Carrhae. Mark Antony had invaded Parthia in C.E. 36, failed to take the city of Phraaspa in Media and had lost 30,000 men in his retreat back to Roman territory.

Peace had finally been arranged in Nero's time by which Armenia became a buffer state between the two empires. But they still bordered each other on the Euphrates and there was intermittent war between them for centuries. Taking Clogg's interpretation then, the four horsemen represent a Parthian invasion followed by civil war, famine and plague. It is a fitting opening for the destruction of the world since it involves purely human actions and their consequences. The fifth seal continues the human actions precipitating the end-times and symbolizes persecution by showing the souls of those martyred for the faith crying out for vengeance. It is with the sixth seal that more cosmic events begin. There is an earthquake, the sun turns black, the moon turns blood red, the stars fall from the sky, and the heavens are rolled up like a scroll, imagery that was probably borrowed from Is 34:4, Amos 8:9, and Joel 2:30-31. Stated briefly, the first six judgments are that the Roman Empire would be invaded, civil order would break down resulting in famine and pestilence, the faithful would be persecuted, and the cosmos would be overturned. In other words, the end-times would open with the world in chaos.

At this point there is a pause between the sixth and seventh seal, the first

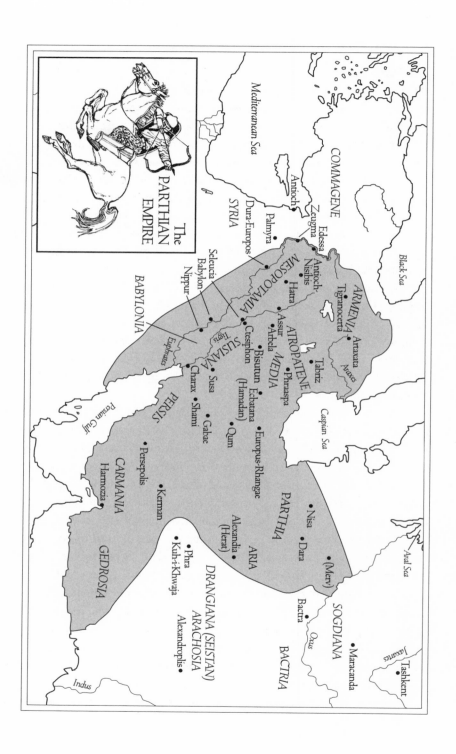

The
PARTHIAN
EMPIRE

Mediterranean Sea

Black Sea

Caspian Sea

Aral Sea

Persian Gulf

COMMAGENE

SYRIA

Antioch
Zeugma
Edessa
Dura-Europos
Palmyra
Antioch
Nisibis
MESOPOTAMIA
Hatra
Assur
Arbela
Ctesiphon
Seleucia
Babylon
Nippur
Euphrates
Tigris
SUSIANA
Charax
Susa
Shami
Gabae
BABYLONIA

ARMENIA
Tigranocerta
Artaxata
Araxes
Tabriz
ATROPATENE
Phraaspa
MEDIA
Bisutun
Ecbatana
(Hamadan)
Europus-Rhangae
Qum

PERSIS
Persepolis
Kerman
CARMANIA
Harmozia
GEDROSIA

Indus

PARTHIA
Nisa
Dara
Alexandria
(Herat)
ARIA
Phra
Kuh-i-Khwaja
DRANGIANA (SEISTAN)
ARACHOSIA
Alexandropolis

(Merv)

SOGDIANA
Maracanda
Oxus
Bactra
BACTRIA

Jaxartes
Tashkent

parenthesis, during which God puts his seal on 144,000 of the faithful. They are represented as the perfection of Israel, i.e. the Christian church, and the number is symbolic of that perfection, being the 12 tribes squared and multiplied by 1,000.

When the Lamb opens the seventh seal, seven angels appear, who are each given trumpets. As each angel blows his trumpet a new judgment is unleashed. This second set of judgments is very much like the third set, in which seven angels pour plagues upon the earth from seven bowls. Between the trumpets and the seven bowls are visions relating to the rise of the Antichrist or The Beast, as he is called in Revelation.

The judgments of the bowls are intensifications of the judgments of the trumpets. So let us consider them together. The first trumpet causes hail, fire and blood to fall from heaven. One third of the world is scorched. This is related to the plague of the fourth bowl which causes the sun to scorch the earth. The catastrophes the second and third trumpets bring are related. At the second trumpet a fiery mountain is thrown into the sea, poisoning one third of it, while at the third trumpet, the star Wormwood falls to earth and poisons one third of all fresh water. Likewise, the second and third bowls cause *all* the sea and fresh water to turn to blood. Everything living in the sea dies. The fourth trumpet causes the sun, moon and stars to lose one third of their light. It is paralleled and intensified by the *fifth* bowl which plunges the kingdom of the Beast into darkness. The fifth trumpet and the first bowl are related. At the fifth trumpet a plague of demonic locusts with tails like scorpions (among other things) torment all those who don't have the seal of God on their foreheads. The imagery of the locusts is probably derived from Joel, although it is greatly intensified in Revelation. In contrast, the first bowl causes all those who bear the mark of the Beast, the opposite of the seal of God, to break out in sores.

The sixth trumpet and the sixth bowl are matched and also probably relate back to the first horseman. At the sixth trumpet four angels bound at the Euphrates are released and lead an army of 200,000,000 horsemen to kill one third of the human race. At the sixth bowl the Euphrates is dried up to prepare the way for the "kings of the east." What lay east of the Euphrates was the Parthian empire. Clogg points out that there was a popular Roman superstition that the emperor Nero had escaped assassination in 68 C.E. and had fled to the east, or had risen from the dead and appeared in the east as *Nero redi-*

vivus. Between 69 and 88 C.E. three different pretenders claiming to be Nero appeared and tried to claim the imperial throne. The popular fear was that a vengeful Nero would lead the Parthians to invade Rome. In response to the invasion from the east, the Antichrist gathers his forces and assembles them at Armageddon. The plain of Megiddo had been the site of many battles in the ancient world. The name Har-Megiddo, or Armageddon, means "hill of Megiddo."

Finally, the seventh trumpet and seventh bowl are in marked contrast to each other. At the seventh trumpet, John sees a vision of the ark of the covenant in Heaven amidst an earthquake, thunder, lightning, and hail. When the seventh bowl is poured out Rome—referred to here as Babylon—is destroyed by an earthquake and huge hailstones.

Between the sixth and seventh trumpets (the demonic locusts and the vision of the ark in heaven) is the second parenthesis. In this interlude an angel gives John a little scroll, which he is instructed to eat. The same incident is found in Ezekiel 2:8, from which this scene is obviously borrowed. Following this John is given a measuring rod and told to measure the Temple. This image is borrowed from Zech. 2: 1-2. Two witnesses then come forth and prophesy for 1,260 days, i.e. three and one half lunar (360 day) years. This is the same time period so often referred to in Daniel. The witnesses are symbolically described as two olive trees and two lampstands. Again, the imagery is derived from Zechariah's fifth vision (Zech. 4: 1-14) The witnesses are killed by the Beast and left unburied in the street in Jerusalem. Then three and a half days later they are resurrected and taken up into heaven in a cloud. At that point Jerusalem is shaken by an earthquake which kills 7,000 people. The witnesses may be Moses and Elijah, standing for the law and the prophets. Some commentators think that it was part of an earlier work by John, which he incorporated here as an introduction to the visions of divine conflict.

The Final Conflict

Between the judgments of the trumpets and the bowls is the story, told in a series of visions, of the rise of the Beast. The first of these is of a woman about to give birth, who is pursued by a red dragon. The woman is described as being "clothed with the sun, with the moon under her feet, and on her head a crown of 12 stars" (Rev. 12:1). She is generally considered to represent God's people as Israel (hence the crown of 12 stars), since she is about to give birth, and Jesus was born from Israel. As she is about to give birth, the dragon appears and waits by her to devour her child as it is born. The dragon is described as having seven heads and 10 horns. His 10 horns are reminiscent of the fourth beast from the sea in Daniel 7. However, he is identified later in this vision as the Devil. As the child, who is described as "one who is to rule the nations with a rod of iron" (Rev 12:5) is born it is caught up to God. The woman flees to a place in the wilderness prepared as a refuge for her and is nourished for 1,260 days or 42 thirty-day months or 3.5 years. This again is an allusion to Daniel 9:27, where the last week of the 70 weeks of years, that is seven years, is the climactic time. During the second half of that week of years, i.e. three and one-half years, the contemptible person causes the sacrifice to cease in the temple. Thus, the 3.5 years the woman—variously interpreted as Israel and the Christian Church—is hiding is the second half of the period of tribulation referred to in the Olivet discourse. This vision changes without preamble into the story of how the dragon, Satan, fell from heaven:

> Now there was war in heaven, Michael and his angels fighting against the dragon; and the dragon and his angels fought, but they were defeated and there was no longer any place for them in heaven. And the great dragon was thrown down, that ancient serpent, who is called the Devil and Satan, the deceiver of the whole world—he was thrown down to the earth, and his angels were thrown with him.

Once he has been thrown down Satan attempts to kill the woman, but she is kept safe. It should be noted that the imagery of war in heaven, the defeat of the dragon by God and his angels, and the beasts that rise from the sea—both in Daniel and Revelation—derives ultimately from the myth of the primeval combat between Marduk and Ti'amat in the Babylonian epic *Enuma elish*.

Next, John sees a vision of a beast rising from the sea. It has seven heads, 10 horns, 10 diadems on its horns and a blasphemous name upon its heads. It also has the form of a leopard, feet like a bear's and a lion's mouth. Thus, the Beast has attributes of all four of the beasts from the sea in Daniel, as well as those of the Dragon, who gives the Beast his power. One of the Beast's heads seems to have a mortal wound, from which it revives. In Rev. 13:5 the Beast is given a mouth "uttering haughty and blasphemous words." This hearkens back to Daniel 7:8, where the little horn has a "mouth speaking great things." The Beast holds sway over the earth for 42 months (3.5 years). Another beast rises out of the earth. This one looks like a lamb, but speaks like a dragon. It works wonders and deceives people into worshipping the first beast. It also causes all those who worship the beast to be marked in the right hand or on the forehead with the mark of the Beast, which is a number representing the name of the Beast. That number is 666. To buy or sell one must bear the mark of the Beast. This is effectively a boycott against those sealed with the mark of God. In contrast to this is a vision of the Lamb (Jesus) on Mount Zion with the 144,000 sealed with the mark of God and a prediction of the fall of Babylon.

The Beast represents both Rome and the Antichrist. The second beast is referred to as the False Prophet. The healing of the mortal wound, along with the worship of the Beast and the number 666, all point to the Nero redivivus legend. Nero as the resurrected and worshiped emperor brings to mind emperor worship, which particularly offended early Christians, and a blasphemous parody of Jesus. The number 666 can be understood a number of ways. The letters of the Greek and Hebrew alphabets had numerical equivalents. If the name *Neron Caesar* is written in Hebrew letters, their sum is 666. If the name is written as Nero, rather than Neron, the sum is 616, which appears in place of 666 in some ancient manuscripts. Another interpretation of the number of the Beast is that man, created on the sixth day of creation, is symbolized by the number 6, which also stands for imperfection. The reason for this is that 6 falls just short of 7, the number of completion, and because of the fall of man. Thus, 666 represents human pride and failing multiplied. Christ in this symbology is represented by the number 888. The eighth day being the perfection of the universe at the end of the millennial kingdom. Following the visions of the rise of the Antichrist are the judgments of the seven bowls. Then comes a vision of the great harlot sitting on the scarlet beast with seven heads and 10 horns. She is richly dressed, and on her forehead is written "Mystery, Babylon the Great, Mother of Harlots and Abominations of the Earth" (Rev. 17:5 KJV). An angel explains to John that the beast's seven heads are seven hills upon which she is seated and the 10 horns are for 10 kings who will reign with the Beast. Of course, the city on seven hills is Rome, its identification with Babylon relating to the legendary wealth, power and wickedness of that city in Old Testament writings. The 10 kings could stand for Parthian satraps who will reign with the returning Nero or they could stand for 10 emperors who had ruled in Rome at the time Revelation was written. These are Augustus, Tiberius, Caligula, Claudius, Nero, Galba, Otho, Vitellius, Vespasian and Titus. On the other hand, the seven hills are also spoken of as seven kings. If Galba, Otho and Vitellius, all of whom together only reigned one year, are omitted, we have the seven emperors.

As can be seen by the description of Rome above and by the interchangeable nature of the beast, which is variously Satan, the Antichrist, and the Roman empire, the symbolism of the book is both tantalizing and somewhat confusing at points. For example, Nero can be seen as the Antichrist ruling the Roman empire or as the leader of the Parthian hosts intent on destroying it. Although fundamentalists represent the battle of Armageddon as being at least initially between Rome and the kings of the east, i.e. the western and eastern nations of the world, the only battle that takes place there in Revelation is between the forces of Christ and those of Satan. Conceivably, Nero's invasion from Parthia could be viewed as setting him up as the Beast.

Christ is represented as riding a white horse and dressed in a white robe that is dipped in blood. After the battle of Armageddon, Satan is bound for 1,000 years. This is the millennium. Though it is a glorious time, it is not the final end of history. After the millennium Satan is loosed, deceives many and gathers an army from the four corners of the earth, specifically from Gog and Magog (of which we will speak later). He attacks Jerusalem, is defeated and thrown into the lake of fire along with the Beast and the False Prophet. Then comes the Last Judgment and the creation of a new heaven and earth.

Because of the vagueness of some of the symbolism, the difficulty of determining where symbolism leaves off and specific reality begins, and because of the dream-like nature of the vision, different writers from different ages have been able to place the end in any number of centuries. Along with the postmillennial and premillennial views, there is within orthodox Christianity an amillennial view that sees the vision as highly symbolic and as already fulfilled in the fall of Rome and the triumph of Christianity. Much time and worry wasted in speculating on the end of the world could have been avoided if this view had been more popular in the Christian religion.

⊰ 9 ⊱

THE END OF THE WORLD

The Rapture and the Second Coming

F UNDAMENTALISM BEGAN AS A REACTION to the drift of most main line denominations toward modern ideas such as the acceptance of evolution and the idea that the Bible was not inspired in all its parts, as well as what they saw as increasing worldliness in the church. Implicit in the fundamentalist world view is the feeling that their beliefs are ridiculed and spurned by the world. As such it is not surprising that they have something of a siege mentality and that they see the world as a cosmic battleground between the forces of good and evil. The focus of their hopes and fears is the final showdown between Christ and Satan at the "end-time." In this chapter I shall give a brief history of millenarianism and critique the premillennial scenario, particularly as popularized by Hal Lindsey in *The Late Great Planet Earth* and its latest update, *Planet Earth 2000 A.D.*

End-Times Past

This is not the first century in which the world was supposed to end. As we have seen from the Olivet discourse and references to the end in the epistles of Paul and John, the earliest view of the church was that the end of the world was imminent. When Christ did not come in power in that generation, and the world failed to end in the first century, explanations were sought. In 2 Peter, which despite being attributed to the apostle was probably written early in the second century, chapter 3 refers to scoffers who will come in the last days pointing out that the world has not ended yet. To counter them, the author says in verse 3:8 that with God one day is a thousand years. Though this would seem to put the end off indefinitely, Christians continued to look for signs of the last days. In 156 C.E., Montanus of the Phrygian city of Pepuza preached that the end was near and that Christ would first appear at Pepuza. One of the great early Christian thinkers, Tertullian, joined the Montanist movement in 207, but despite its many adherents Pope Zephyrinus (d. 217) declared Montanism heretical. In 364 Hilary of Poiters preached that the Antichrist was soon to be born. Many Christians already felt that Emperor Julian the Apostate, who in 362 reinstated paganism as the official religion (Christianity had virtually become the state religion in 337) was the Antichrist. However, Julian fell in battle in 364, and the empire was once again Christian.

In 378, however, the Visigoths, whom the Romans had allowed to settle within the empire when they were fleeing the Huns, revolted and annihilated the Roman army at Adrianople. Ambrose (340?-397) decided that this defeat signaled the beginning of the end. With respect to the Roman Empire, he was quite right. Without a Roman army to hold them in check, the barbarians would destroy the world. He decided that the Goths were Gog, and the Huns, since they came from a land formerly occupied by the Massagetae, a Sarmatian tribe, were Magog. When in 395 the Huns invaded the eastern provinces, Jerome (340-420), who up until then had dismissed millenarian prophecies, also decided that the Huns were Magog. As the depredations of the Huns and the Germanic tribes increased, a wave of millenarianism swept the empire in the last decade of the fifth century. The western empire fell in 476, and it looked as if the world, which for Christians of that day did not extend far beyond the Roman Empire, was definitely beginning to unravel.

Augustine (354-430), however, believed that the millennium had begun with the nativity of Jesus. In his scenario all time was encompassed within a period of 7,000 years, each millennium corresponding to a day in the week in which the world was created. Six thousand years had passed by the time of the Nativity, and 1,000 years from that time Jesus would return and the world would end. The failure of the world to end under the blows of the Goths and Huns, along with the conversion of the former and the demise of the later, caused many Christian thinkers to adopt Augustine's timetable. As the year 1000 C.E. approached, a wave of panic swept over Europe (at least among those who both could read and agreed with Augustine), followed by a sense of profound relief when the year came and went with no more than the usual round of mayhem, misery, and malnutrition common to that time and place. One of the reasons that the year 2000 C.E. has attained such eschatological status is that the survivors of the non-apocalypse of 1000 C.E. decided that divine mercy had intervened to allow Christians another thousand years in which to convert the world.

In spite of the revised timetable, however, millenarian movements continued to flare up at times of catastrophe or social upheaval. Tanchelm of Antwerp (d. 1115) claimed to be the second incarnation of Christ, as did Budo de Stella in Brittany one generation later. Both men ran afoul of the Church, declared the Pope the Antichrist, and managed to wreak havoc in their countries until their movements were crushed and they were executed. Joachim of Fiore (d. 1201), whose writings influenced both the early Dominicans and the Franciscans, declared that the millennium would begin in 1260. Also, the flagellant sects that rose during the Black Death of 1348-49 preached self-mortification of the flesh as a means of preparing for the end-times, which the plague no doubt presaged.

Toward the end of the Middle Ages, various utopian movements sprang up that resulted in peasant uprisings. These had in common to some degree the belief that the Church and the nobility were oppressing the people, that the Pope was the Antichrist, and that if those in power who had become corrupted by greed were annihilated, then the poor would inherit the earth and the millennial kingdom would begin. Among these uprisings were the 1381 Peasants' Revolt in England, the 1358 Jacquerie uprising in France, and that of the Taborites, a branch of the Hussites of Czechoslovakia. The Hussites were followers of John Huss, one of the first Protestant reformers (burned at the stake 1414), and the utopian/millenarian movements gradually merged into the Protestant Reformation, finally flaring up again in the Peasants' War in Germany in 1525. Luther repudiated the revolt and called for the nobility to crush it. The alignment of Lutherans and, to an even greater degree, Calvinists, with propertied interests and against millenarian extremes quite possibly saved Protestantism from the fate suffered by earlier movements. However, the Calvinists did retain apocalyptic imagery when referring to the religious warfare of the time, indicating that on at least a subliminal level they saw the events of their day as leading to Armageddon. For example, Oliver Cromwell referred to the Irish Catholics as being a part of the Antichrist. This view was wonderfully liberating in that it streamlined and simplified the logistics of dealing with defeated populations, as evidenced by the massacres at Drogheda and Wexford.

After the religious wars of the 17th century subsided and were replaced by the Age of Enlightenment, millenarianism died down, although millenarian views were held by the Independents in England and the Pietists in Germany. In America, the most spectacular millenarian movement was launched by William Miller (1782-1849), who predicted the Second Coming would take place on March 21, 1843. When that date came and went, Miller shifted the prediction to July 10, 1843, then to March 21, 1844. Christ having failed to oblige him three times in a row, Miller recalculated the date to be October 22, 1844. Though their founder was discredited by the failure of the world to end on cue—a non-event they called "the Great Disappointment"—the Millerites continued as a sect and eventually became known as the Seventh Day Adventists. They stand near the end of an almost 2,000-year tradition of failed prophecies steeped in unreason and often used as a cover for barbarous acts. Why this history of failure, including that of their founder, has not shaken their faith or the faith of other premillennialists lies not in knowledge but in ignorance, not in reason but in reaction, the same sort of reaction that gave rise to Protestant fundamentalism early in this century.

The catalyst for the reaction that was to generate fundamentalism was the American Civil War. The religious tone of America at the time the Civil War started combined the common sense outlook of Newtonian science with an evangelical world view that saw God working in history, with the United States in the role of a new Israel. That America would span the continent was seen as manifest destiny, a destiny that included an obligation to Christianize the world and, eventually, in the North, to free the slaves. A post-millennial view of the future, i.e. that the Second Coming of Christ would occur *after* the millennial kingdom had been established and purged the world of its ills, prevailed. It dovetailed nicely with the basic optimism that has always characterized Americans and it was part of a Christianized version of the myth of progress. Thus, the Civil War was seen in the apocalyptic terms expressed in "The Battle Hymn of the Republic." Cleansing the reprobate South of the affliction of slavery would remove the last great obstacle to making America into the fully righteous Christian nation destined to lead the world into the millennial kingdom, and General Sherman was seen as God's "terrible swift sword" (a view not shared by the residents of Atlanta).

What actually crowned the triumph of the North was, however, something less than the opening of the millennium. As George M. Marsden puts it (1991, p. 10):

> What followed was the "Gilded Age." The era marked by the assassination of two presidents and the impeachment of another, a stolen election, and the reign of rampant political and business corruption and greed was well named by Mark Twain. A veneer of evangelical Sunday-school piety covered almost everything in the culture, but no longer did the rhetoric of idealism and virtue seem to touch the core of the materialism of the political and business interests. It was a dime-store millennium.

As the original vision of America leading the world into the millennium began to dissipate, the Evangelical community split along liberal and conservative lines. The liberals were ready to modify such basic beliefs as the reliability of the Bible and the atonement, and stressed social action and ethics. The conservatives stressed revivalism, strict adherence to the Bible, and put less stress on social action. It was out of this doctrinal split that fundamentalism was born.

Several religious trends that appeared after the Civil War fed into the theology of fundamentalism. One of these was dispensational premillennialism. Between them, dispensationalism and premillennialism embodied the opposite of the optimistic postmillennialism of traditional American Evangelicalism. Dispensationalism viewed history in the pessimistic terms of a series of dispensations from God in his efforts to save man from destruction. Each of these was frustrated by man's rebelliousness, which provoked God to end the age in an apocalyptic disaster of some sort. Though there were variations as to the number of dispensations, the first was generally seen as the Garden of Eden, ending in the Fall and the expulsion of Adam and Eve from the Garden. The last was to be the millennium. Before the millennium was our present era, the church age, which would end in a series of wars and disasters as man's apostasy increased, only to be terminated by the Second Coming of Christ—*before* the millennium. Different dispensationalists list varying numbers of dispensations. However, many would tend to follow the scheme of seven dispensations as set out below:

DISPENSATION   ENDED BY

1) Garden of Eden .... Fall of Man

2) Antediluvian World ..... Noachian Deluge

3) Post Flood Civilization .. Destruction of the Tower of Babel

4) Abrahamic Covenant .... Babylonian Captivity

5) Post Exilic Renewal ...... First Coming of Christ

6) Church Age .... Second Coming of Christ

7) Millennium .... Last Judgement

The idea that human beings were too fallen to bring about the millennium was an absolute rejection of the ante-bellum Evangelical ideal. The Gilded Age and every sign of secularization in society fed the hopes of premillennialists that the collapse of society, and with it the Second Coming, were imminent.

The premillennial view is dominant among today's fundamentalists, and its pessimism is evident in their view of the Christ of the Second Coming. For example, here is Raul Ries on the subject (*Manna For Today*, KKLA, November 16, 1993):

> The first coming of Jesus Christ was a coming with love and grace and mercies. The second coming of Jesus Christ is going to be a time of judgment. He's not coming to save. He's not coming to be a nice guy this time.

Nor is Ries alone in presenting the stern, judging Christ. David Jeremiah in his study of the Book of Daniel gives us two grim views of the Christ of the end-times. The first of these sees Jesus as the boulder that smashes the idol with a head of gold and feet of clay in Nebuchadnezzar's dream. Elsewhere in his study of Daniel (broadcast on KKLA October 27, 1992) Jeremiah uses the statue's representation of world history going from gold to clay as a slap at evolution. He sees the the world as decaying. This antagonism toward evolution fits the premillennial outlook, since both evolution and the postmillennial view partake of the notion of progress (*The Turning Point*, KKLA, November 2, 1992; *The Turning Point* KKLA, October 30, 1992):

> I want you to listen to these paradigms one right after another...The coming of the kingdom of Christ is smiting, not saving. It is ruin, not regeneration. It is pulverizing not purifying. It is smashing, not sanctifying. It is crushing, not cleansing.

> The sweet baby Jesus...is also the righteous judge. One day this old world which has rejected him and made him a laughingstock among the nations is going to see him come riding on a white horse. And he will smite the nations, and it will be severe.

The emphasis of fundamentalists on spiritual warfare and the Second Coming sets up a basis for mean-spirited, judgmental behavior. The Jesus they worship is part of a bait and switch scheme. Converts are lured in by the sanitized and rather Aryan Jesus with the soft-light halo frequently portrayed in Protestant churches. What they get is the harsh warrior-king—what my wife refers to as "Jesus in jack-boots."

End-Times Present

Though premillennialism succeeded postmillennialism among evangelical Christians early in the century, and fundamentalism avidly pursued detailed interpretations of the apocalyptic books of the Bible, for most mainline Christian denominations the Book of Revelation remained at best a poetic rendition in highly symbolic terms of something either far in the future or, if it referred to Rome, far in the past. At worst it was something of an embarrassment. Fundamentalist fancies predicting the end of the world in the year 2000 were generally relegated to the fringes until the resurgence of evangelical Christianity in the early 1970s.

Enter Hal Lindsey. His *The Late Great Planet Earth* (1970)—a slick, glib, pop-version of the premillennial scenario—rode the zeitgeist of late 20th-century anti-rationalism to the best-seller list. Arriving at a time when such works as *Chariots of the Gods?* (1968), *The Teachings of Don Juan* (1968) and *The Secret Life of Plants* (1972) were taken seriously, Lindsey's book exploited both the credulity of the period and the endemic American ignorance of world history. It also came out at a point when many of the nation's youth were switching from Krishna to Christ.

The premillennial scenario is as follows. The stage is set by the restoration of the state of Israel and the ongoing conflict between the Israelis and the Arabs. At the time of the seven years of Tribulation most of Europe will be united under a leader who will be, in reality, the Antichrist. He will conclude a treaty with Israel, guaranteeing its safety. Protected by this Neo-Roman Empire, the Israelis will feel secure enough to both disarm and rebuild the

Temple at Jerusalem. At this point, in concert with an Islamic alliance headed by Egypt, Russia invades Israel. The Arabic motive for the invasion is the outrage over the Israelis rebuilding the temple, which would necessitate the destruction of the Islamic shrine called the Dome of the Rock.

Russia's motive is a bit foggier. It has been variously given as a need for oil or food. Lindsey states that it will be the "great material wealth of the restored nation of Israel" (1970, p. 154). None of these is particularly convincing. Russia has vast petroleum reserves in Siberia and is an oil exporter. The Middle East is hardly a bread-basket. The Russians might well re-annex Ukrainia for food, but hunger would not lead them to Jerusalem. Nor is there wealth enough in Israel to make such a military adventure worth the cost. In *Prophecy 2000,* David Allen Lewis lists seven possible reasons for Russia's invasion of Israel. They are (1) because the Bible says it will happen, (2) because of Russia's desire for warm weather Mediterranean ports, (3) the mineral wealth of the Dead Sea, (4) the desire of Russia to punish Israel as the U.S. punished Iraq, (5) to seize Middle East oil wells as a way of bringing down the West, (6) pressure from Moslems within the Confederacy of Independent States (CIS), and (7) to use the war as a distraction from internal problems.

The reasoning behind the assumption that it will happen because the Bible says it will (at least according to the premillennial scenario) is rather circular. The desire for warm weather ports would more likely make Turkey the victim of a Russian invasion, particularly since they would want to control the Dardanelles. The supposed riches of the Dead Sea are mainly potash, sulfates, calcium chloride, magnesium, and bromine. Not only does Russia have deposits of all of these within its borders, particularly in the Caspian depression and the Caspian Sea, the mineral wealth of Siberia (which includes gold, lead, zinc, tungsten, mercury, molybdenum and antimony) as well as that of the Urals (copper, chromium, iron, uranium and sulfur), easily dwarfs anything that could be gained in Israel. Should Russia be driven to use force to gain mineral reserves beyond its borders, it would probably use it to reassert its hegemony over the Moslem states formerly part of the Soviet Union. The idea of "punishing Israel" is absurd. The U. S. did not attack Iraq to punish it. Rather, the Gulf War was fought to safeguard the world's oil supply. If Russia invades the Middle East to cut off the West's oil supply, said invasion would not be aimed at either Israel or Egypt as in the premillennial scenario. It would be aimed at the Persian Gulf. As to using a war to distract the people from internal problems, in order to think in such terms the Russians would have to forget their own history. Far from distracting the people, the extra stresses of World War I pushed internal pressures to the breaking point, resulting in the Russian revolution. That leaves pressure from the Moslem states as the only remaining motive for the attack on Israel. Considering that the Moslem states of the CIS are distracted by their own internal problems, even this seems a bit thin. However, in his latest comprehensive work to date, *Planet Earth —2000 A.D.*, Lindsey also sees the Russians being dragged almost unwillingly into the invasion because of entangling alliances with Islamic states, particularly those of the former Soviet Union. Despite Russia being pulled into the invasion however, the adventure becomes one of vast conquest, since the next step in the scenario is the Russian double-cross of its erstwhile allies as Russia invades Egypt.

At this point, the Russian commander hears that the Chinese are mobilizing and that the "Romans" (Western Europeans) are about to attack. He hastens back to Israel where the Russian army is decimated by "Roman" tactical nuclear weapons. The Chinese now invade from the east, the Euphrates river having dried up so that their army of 200,000,000 can attack the "Romans" at Armageddon. As we have seen, the "kings of the east" alluded to in Revelation were more likely to be the Parthians than anyone else. Nevertheless, it is hardly surprising that Lindsey interprets them as the Chinese, rather than, say, another horde of Moslems including the Iranians, Afghans, and the Moslems of the states formerly part of the Soviet Union. After all, no occidental paranoid fantasy worth its salt could leave out the ravening hordes of Asia, and Lindsey even calls his chapter on the orientals in his first book "The Yellow Peril." Not only is there great destruction at Armageddon, all the cities of the world are destroyed in what would appear to be a nuclear war. At the point when all the great world powers have destroyed each other, Jesus comes back and establishes the millennial kingdom.

Readers may have noticed that the United States is conspicuously absent from this scenario. If one considers that biblical writers had no knowledge of the New World, this is hardly surprising. Millenarians, however, assuming that the apocalyptic books are divinely inspired prophecy, have to account for why the world's leading power has no part to play, while Russia, the European Community, the Arabs and the Chinese are all involved. Usually, these modern prophets can only make the excuse that the U.S. will have been reduced to a minor power, a mere appendage of the new Rome, by the time of the Tribulation. This is a bit hard to buy in 1996 with the end possibly a mere four years off, and according to Lindsey's original estimate the Tribulation should have begun in 1988 (1970, p. 54). This would have put Armageddon in 1995, though since Lindsey first wrote he has modified the original parameters. Now he states that the start of the generation that will see the end should be in 1967, the year Israel captured Jerusalem, rather than 1948, when modern Israel came into being. The 40 years comprising a biblical generation would then be up in 2007. However, just as he hedged his original prediction with such modifiers as "seems to be," Lindsey has also allowed for a generation to be either 40 or 100 years. Thus, along with 2007, he has 1948 + 100 = 2048, and 1967 + 100 = 2067. So, if the United States does not go down the tubes in the next 10 years, Lindsey has two fall-back positions, both likely to occur after he is dead. Evidently, he has learned to avoid the Millerite error of setting too precise a date.

Israel and the End-Times

Leaving aside for the moment the anomalous position of the United States, let us examine some of the specific sections of this scenario starting with a consideration of the role of Israel. While the Middle East in general and Israel in particular have been the focus of many international crises, fundamentalists accord that land an undue level of importance. For example, David Jeremiah says (*The Turning Point* KKLA, December 21, 1992):

> Ever since the time of Abraham, the land of Israel has been the nerve center of the world. And ever since the time of Jesus Christ, the land of Israel has been the truth center of the world...As we look at our newspapers today, we discover at this time it's the storm center of the world.

Even granting some rhetorical leeway, none of Reverend Mr. Jeremiah's three assertions are correct. In the ancient world Israel's chief importance lay in its geographical position as the gateway between Egypt and the fertile crescent. Thus, invaders such as the Assyrians, Persians and the army of Alexander the Great had to pass through the land on their way to Egypt. Traders coming overland would also have to pass through. On the other hand, sea-going traders such as the Greeks and Phoenicians simply sailed to the Nile delta and bypassed Israel altogether. If any one location could have been said to be the nerve center of the ancient world in pre-classical times, it would have been Babylon. With the rise of Greece and Rome the peripheral nature of Israel remained the same, though the center of power in the ancient world shifted to the Mediterranean. With the defeat of the Turks at Lepanto (1571) by the allied fleets of the Italian city-states, and Spain and the defeat of the Spanish Armada (1588) by England, the power center of the western world shifted to the European states directly or indirectly bordering the Atlantic Ocean. And, of course, Israel was never a "nerve center" or power center of the great empires that flourished in India and China.

Nor has Israel been the "truth center" of the world since the time of Christ, particularly if we consider the "truth" Jeremiah is referring to as being Christianity. Paul saw to that by evangelizing the Gentiles and converting a Jewish sect into a new religion. The centers of Christianity quickly became Rome, Constantinople, Antioch, and Alexandria. The failure of Christians in Judea to join in the Jewish revolt resulted in the final separation of the followers of Christ from Judaism, and the destruction of Jerusalem by Titus in 70 C.E. effectively removed that city as a Christian spiritual center. The fall of Antioch and Alexandria to Islam in the seventh century further separated Christianity from Israel and effectively made it a European religion. As a Moslem fief, Palestine ceased forever to be what Jeremiah would call the "truth center" of the world.

Is Israel today the "storm center" of the world? Well, it is certainly one of them. Other "storm centers" are Korea, the India-China border, the India-Pakistan border, Iran, Angola, the Caucasus Mountains, Central Europe, Central America, and any other place where either endemic tribal hatreds or the intrusion of great powers has kept violence simmering just under the surface calm at all times. My attack on Jeremiah's statements may seem rather gratuitous. However, it is important to note that much of what premillennialists see as specific, fulfilled prophecy is based on a sloppy rendering of history often trimmed to fit their interpretations of apocalyptic literature. Hence the assumption that the end-time would focus on Israel. A nuclear armageddon based on the atomic arms race between the U.S. and the former U.S.S.R. focused far more convincingly on a confrontation between NATO and Warsaw Pact forces in Central Europe. As China becomes ever more important, the storm center of the world could be in the Pacific, a far cry from Israel.

Lindsey's view that the restored, modern state of Israel would be the focus of the end-times is based on his interpretation of the Olivet discourse, Ezekiel 37, 38 and 39, and the later chapters of Zechariah.

In Ezekiel 38, a restored nation of Israel, living at peace is attacked by Gog, prince of Magog. Lindsey links this with the prophecy of the "contemptible person" in Daniel 9 and 11 who makes a false peace with Israel and lulls them (in his interpretation) into giving up their arms in the belief that he (the Antichrist) will protect them. Leaving aside for the moment that it's a bit of a strain on the imagination to envision the Israelis is giving up their arms and trusting their defense to an outside power, let's consider when this is to happen. Referring to Jesus' statement in Matthew 24:34 that "this generation will not pass away until all these things take place" he asks (1970, p. 54):

> What generation? Obviously, in context, the generation that would see the signs—chief among them the rebirth of Israel. A generation in the Bible is something like forty years. If this is a correct deduction, then within forty years or so of 1948, all these things could take place. Many scholars who have studied Bible prophecy all their lives believe that this is so.

As I said earlier, this should have resulted in the seven years of tribulation starting in 1988, with Armageddon taking place in 1995. Of course, Lindsey was careful to hedge his bet by couching this prediction in vague terms: A generation is "something like" forty years. "If this is the correct deduction" these things *could* take place within "forty years or so." Despite all the hedging, Lindsey had to rework both the beginning of the tribulation and the length of a generation to avoid the embarrassments of the failure of the U.S. to fade as yet into a mere appendage of the New Rome, as well as the fact that the European Community still has not unified into a Neo-Roman super-power. Also, the charismatic leader—the Antichrist—has yet to be found among the mundane, pragmatic and rather uninspiring lot that comprise the major players in European politics.

Russia as the Enemy From the North

For all that premillennial scenarios depend on current events, they turn out to be wonderfully independent of unforeseen changes in them. For example, the fact that the Soviet Union—long identified with the essential apocalyptic bogey called the "Enemy from the North"—ceased being the evil empire to become the Russian republic, has not dampened millennial ardor in the least. Even before Zhirenovsky appeared on the scene, post-communist Russia was still viewed as the "Enemy from the North," perhaps even as fated to fill that role. Curiously, this consideration has not deterred fundamentalists from evangelizing the Russians. Thus they join a motley horde of proselytizers that includes Mormons, Moonies, Scientologists, New-Agers and Hare-Krishnas. This onslaught, along with Pepsi, pizza, and Big Macs, would seem to be America's most generous gift to this struggling nascent democracy: a surfeit of junk-food for the mind as well as the body.

Russia, as I have noted, is extremely important to Lindsey's scenario as the player making the opening move. While this scheme is supposedly based on events related in the Book of Revelation, the Gog and Magog prophecy, supposedly referring to Russia, is found only in Ezekiel. The "enemy from the north" referred to in the Book of Daniel is Antiochus Epiphanes and the Seleucid Empire. Since he is seen as representing the Antichrist, the king of the north in Daniel cannot possibly be Russia and still fit Lindsey's scheme. Yet, since Ezekiel 38 and 39 are part of apocalyptic literature, and since Gog and Magog were supposed to come from "the uttermost parts of the north," and since the Jewish historian Josephus identified Gog and Magog as the Scythians, Russia, as the current occupant of lands formerly held by the Scythians, inherited their mantle. This view was abetted by traditional prejudice against Russia, which was heightened in 19th-century Europe. Napoleon referred to the Russians as the "barbarians from the north," while the English and the Germans indulged in varying degrees of Eurocentric racism, regarding Russia as a semi-Asiatic power, hence quite beyond the pale. The saying, "Scratch a Russian and you find a Tartar," sums up the attitude historically held by western Europeans. Of course the polarization of world powers during the Cold War, when nuclear arsenals made the end of the world plausible, intensified the identification of the Soviet Union as a satanic power.

The reason Ezekiel viewed the Scythians as a terror was because of the Scythian invasion that devastated the Assyrian Empire between 641 and 617 B.C.E. (see Chapter 4). Since Ezekiel wrote between 593 and 563 B.C.E., the Scythian episode was known to him. That the Scythians might come again was not improbable. That they might bring other barbarous peoples from Asia Minor with them was a reasonable assumption. Thus, they were likely to have in their company the Cimmerians, whom the Assyrians called the Gimmirai and who are called the nation of Gomer in the Bible. They were also likely to bring the tribes of Meshech and Tubal (Mushki and Tabal), as well as troops from the city of Togarmah (Tilgarimmu), all located in Asia Minor (see Chapter 6). While some fundamentalists see Gomer as Germany, and Lindsey assumes that Meshech = Moscow and Tubal = Tobolsk (briefly the capital of Siberia), these speculations are based on nothing more than surface phonetic similarities stretched to the limit. Like his assertion that *Rosh* = Russia, they are without scholarly merit. The *Eerdmans Bible Commentary,* compiled by a conservative evangelical publishing company, says of Meshech and Tubal on page 682, "…their equation with Moscow and Tobolsk, and *Rosh* with Russia is insupportable."

None of this has any effect on the premillennial scenario. When ideology is involved, truth is the first casualty. I was given a lesson in just how little the truth impinges on the premillennial dogma when in 1992 I called in to a talk show on a fundamentalist radio station to ask their guest, Hal Lindsey himself, if, in light of the end of communism in Russia, he still thought that the Russians were the enemy from the north. He told me that he did, and the following exchange took place between us (*Live From L.A.* KKLA, September 15, 1992):

> Lindsey: [I] believe that it's the ethnic core Russians and always have been. They're the ones that are the enemy from the north, because Magog is the forefather of the Scythians, who are the modern Russians.
>
> Callahan: No, I'm sorry, you're absolutely wrong there. The Scythians were an Iranian-speaking people nomadizing on the steppes. They were wiped out, pretty much, by the Huns. And there's steppe empires over and over there. And the Russians…
>
> Lindsey: I don't know where you get your information, but I have reliable, scholarly information that says the Scythians are the modern ethnic Russian people.
>
> Callahan: Well, I suggest you look at any good history book and you'll find that the Scythians ceased to exist at about the time of the Roman Empire and that they were wiped out by the Huns. And the Russians are…
>
> Lindsey: You're absolutely incorrect.

Callahan: Well, I'll tell you what. Check out the Encyclopedia Britannica and see what they say.

Lindsey: I went beyond the Encyclopedia Britannica. The Encyclopedia Britannica also says that they're the forefathers of modern Russians, and so do all of the ancient scholars who were closer to the record, such as Herodotus, 5th century B.C., who did extensive…

Callahan: The Russians didn't even exist at the time of Herodotus. They weren't differentiated from the other Slavs.

Lindsey: Oh, you're from another planet! You don't even know where it's at, my friend. I don't know where you're getting your information, but it's tailored to your own prejudiced point of view.

Even without Mr. Lindsey's assertion that I was of extra-terrestrial origin, the reader can probably tell that the above exchange was getting heated. At this point, the show's host broke in and asked me what I thought Ezekiel was referring to and why I didn't think it was Russia. I pointed out that the nations mentioned as being with Magog were all identified in Biblical maps as being in Asia minor. Lindsey responded and had the last word:

Lindsey: Let me comment on that. I've done some extensive reading on this just recently, because we did a book called *The Magog Factor*. And first of all, the Russians have spent a great deal of money excavating the Scythian ruins because they are their fore-fathers and they know it. The Russians have spent a great deal of money excavating the area that's in the Ukraine. They show that the Scythians extended all the way to China. In fact, there's a reference that says that the thing we call the [Great] Wall of China today was originally called the Wall of Magog…

Later, after Lindsey had fielded questions from other callers who were both friendlier and more credulous, the host asked him, somewhat jokingly, if he was writing anything more about "that Scythian thing." Admitting that he was taken aback by my call, Lindsey said, "There are so many books that prove the Scythians are descendants of Magog and the forefathers of the Russians. But here is one that is really worth reading. It's called *Foes From the Northern Frontier* by Professor Yamauchi…."

To date *The Magog Factor*, co-authored by Lindsey and Chuck Missler, has failed to appear on the shelves of Christian book stores. However, had I still been on the air when Lindsey mentioned Professor Edwin Yamauchi's book, I could have pointed out that Yamauchi wrote the book as a *refutation* of Lindsey's view, not a support—this despite the fact that almost 25% of *The Magog Factor* appears to have been copied verbatim from *Foes from the Northern Frontier*. Lindsey and Missler did this without giving any attribution to Yamauchi, thus giving their work a spurious air of scholarship. When a reporter from the *Los Angeles Times* tried to contact the authors about this, they were unavailable for comment (see Rivenburg 1992). Since *Foes from the Northern Frontier* is out of print, Lindsey could claim over the radio that it supported his view without having to worry about any listener actually reading the book. When I finally ran down a copy at the Fuller Theological Seminary Library I found it to be a modest volume of 148 pages dealing largely with archaeological evidence of the Scythian episode that occurred at the end of the Assyrian Empire. There was nothing in the book that indicated in any way that the Great Wall of China had ever been called the Wall of Magog. This would have been highly unlikely anyway since the Great Wall was not built until 221 B.C.E. long after the Scythians had been superseded on the eastern steppes by the Huns. Further evidence that Lindsey was being disingenuous is the fact that when he was on the same talk show about a year earlier, a caller gave him Yamauchi's views in some detail (*Live From L.A.* KKLA, August 20, 1991):

> Caller: According to Christian archaeologist Edwin Yamauchi, Ezekiel 38, Rosh does not at all refer to Russia. In addition, he says that Meshech and Tubal refers to tribes that lived in eastern Anatolia, in Turkey and that Magog probably refers to the Scythians, who came from north of the Caspian Sea and fought with the Babylonians and Egyptians and Persians, even the Syrians. How does Mr. Lindsey respond?
>
> Lindsey: Well, first of all, you take the geographical coordinates at the time that the prophecy is to be fulfilled, and that's just before the second coming of Christ, when he sets up the kingdom of Israel. It says they would come from the extreme north. Well, you go to the extreme north of Israel and there's only one nation there...

Lindsey went on to cite 19th century Hebrew scholar Wilhelm Gesenius as his authority, but the caller persisted in asserting Yamauchi's views:

> Caller: Well, [Yamauchi] says the Hebrew word for chief, Rosh, was transliter-

ated by the Septuagint as a proper name. He also says that the addition of Rus didn't take place until 839 C.E. which was the first written reference...I think a modern archaeologist would take precedence over [Gesenius].

Lindsey: Well, I won't sit and argue with you about it. There are many historians who for centuries traced these people as settling in the north. I'm not saying that the Russian name came from Rosh.

(Note: This is not true. On page 65 of *The Late Great Planet Earth* Lindsey asserts in some detail that *Rosh* is the origin of the name "Russia.")

The caller persisted in attacking Lindsey's interpretation of Ezekiel by pointing out that Gog and Magog are spoken of as having bows and arrows. How could this be a reference to a modern army? Lindsey had the last word by stating that the Bible did not say arrows, but rather used the word "missiles." The caller was stopped by that one and retired in confusion. The verse in question is Ezekiel 39:3, which is rendered in the Revised Standard Version of the Bible as: "then I will strike your bow from your left hand and make your arrows fall out of your right hand." The Tanakh also translates the word as arrows, as does the Zondervan Amplified Bible, which Lindsey quoted from in *The Late Great Planet Earth*. Also, in the context of the verse, which also mentions the bow, even if "arrows" is changed to "missiles," it would have to be assumed that the missiles in question were arrows, as opposed to hand-held rocket launchers.

Lindsey's loyalty to Professor Yamauchi's expertise was easily shed in 1994, when I again had a chance to confront him on the air (*Live From L.A.* KKLA, October 28, 1994):

Callahan: Reverend Lindsey, you and I spoke together when Mike Ryan had this show.

Lindsey: [Yes?]

Callahan: And you said at this time that there was a book by Professor Edwin Yamauchi, Foes From the Northern Frontier, that validated your view on the Gog and Magog prophecy.

Lindsey: [Yes.]

Callahan: And I disagreed with you on that and I couldn't find a copy of it. So I finally wrote Professor Yamauchi. And he wrote a letter back [saying], "I was rather chagrined to learn that Hal Lindsey has quoted me to support his theories, as I had written to criticize some of his views." What is your response to that?

(At this point I was cut off. Thus I was unable to refute anything else that Lindsey said.)

Lindsey: Well, I didn't know that he had written to criticize that, but I know that in our research we found all kinds of evidence—not just Mr. Yamaguchi [sic]—but we found all kinds of evidence that...the tribe of Magog was the forefathers of the Scythians, and the Scythians are clearly the modern ethnic Russians. So there's a trail that's a lot broader than Mr. Yamaguchi, and I won't mention him again if that's the way he feels.

Warren Duffy (host): (Laughs) So take that, Mr. Yamaguchi! Thanks for calling, Tim. Thanks for your question.

This glib shedding of Yamauchi as a scholarly source, plus Lindsey's confession that he did not know that the professor had written to criticize his views and his inability to even get the man's name right, all underscore Lindsey's disingenuousness in using *Foes From the Northern Frontier* in 1992 to back up his scenario. In passing, I should note that Edwin Yamauchi is highly respected both as an archaeologist and as an evangelical Christian.

In addition, Lindsey's assertions that the *Encyclopedia Britannica* supported his view that the Russians were the descendants of the Scythians, and that the Russians know this to be the case, simply are not true. Both the *Encyclopedia Britannica* and the *Great Soviet Encyclopedia* agree that the Scythians spoke an Iranian language and that they were defeated by the Sarmatians, a related people who by the first century C.E. had deprived them of all but the Crimea. This remnant was conquered by the Ostrogoths in the third century, at which time the Scythians ceased to exist as a separate people. In 372 the Huns swept not only the absorbed remnants of the Scythians but their Sarmatian and Gothic conquerors out of the Russian steppes. Slavic tribes moved into the area gradually, but did not emerge as a dominant group until after the empire of the Huns collapsed in 454. The Russians did not emerge as a nationality distinct from other Slavic tribes until the Varangian principality of the Rus was unified by Prince Oleg in 880.

So how is it that the Scythians came to be identified with the Russians? The encyclopedias point out that the term "Scythian" was commonly used as a description of anyone living on the Russian steppes well after the Scythians had ceased to be a power. Thus, the Iranian-speaking Sarmatians, the Teutonic-speaking Goths, and the Altaic-speaking Huns were all likely to be called "Scythians." As I noted earlier, Ambrose saw the Goths and Huns as Gog and Magog. In fact, the Visigoths in Spain so accepted this view that Alfonso III (866-910), ruler of the fragment of Visigothic Spain still in Christian hands following the Moorish conquest of 771, believed that the Gog and Magog prophecy foretold of the day when the Visigoths (Gog) would drive the Moslems out and restore Spain as a Christian kingdom This view seems to have held wide currency in the Middle Ages (see Yamauchi 1982, p. 22) If one were to follow this particular line of reasoning to its logical end the Gog and Magog prophecy would have to have been fulfilled during the reign of Ferdinand and Isabella!

The Visigothic claim notwithstanding, "Scythian" remained a term easily used to characterize the Russians in the 19th century. As Napoleon approached Moscow and saw that it had been set afire he is said to have exclaimed, "They are Scythians!" To some degree this was said in grudging admiration. He had expected his capture of the city would utterly humble the Russians and was appalled at the degree of resolve they showed in burning the city rather than letting it fall into his hands. The Scythians also used a scorched earth policy against such invaders as the Persians.

Among the allies of Magog in Ezekiel is the nation of Gomer. As I mentioned earlier, the Scythians had, previous to attacking the Assyrians, been used by them to check the Cimmerians. The word Cimmerian is a Latinized version of the Greek Kimmeri. The same people were known to the Assyrians as the Gimmirai and are called the nation of Gomer in the Bible. Despite this bit of history, the nation of Gomer is commonly held by premillennialists to be Germany. In response to a caller who was confused as to whether Gomer belonged in Germany or Turkey, Lindsey explained (*Live From L.A.* KKLA, October 28, 1994):

> [I]n the initial stages, you can find all of these [tribes] in the greater middle-east, and then they fanned out from there and...Gomer became known as Ashkenaz...a name that is associated with some of the people in eastern Europe and Germany...It's virtually impossible to identify some of these powers. Others are much easier. I know Beth-Togarmah is one that can definitely be tied into Turkey and the five former Soviet Union Republics that are Islamic.

Here Lindsey has tripped himself up—or at least he would have if any of his audience had the slightest knowledge of history or linguistic groups, or even had the sense to question the alliance of Germany, Russia, and a host of Islamic nations in an attack on Israel. First of all, Gomer did not become known as Ashkenaz. In the table of nations in Genesis 10, Ashkenaz and Togarmah are sons of Gomer. The only people in central Europe known as Ashkenaz are the Ashkenazic Jews of Germany, Poland, and Russia (as opposed to the Sephardic Jews of the Mediterranean lands). Because the Cimmerians (Gomer) were thought to come from a western land of perpetual darkness, the Jews arriving in northern and central Europe referred to that land as Ashkenaz.

If Lindsey would have the Germans be Gomer and Togarmah be the Turkic peoples, he has a big problem in linguistics. German, like all other Teutonic tongues, is in the Indo-European family of languages. But Turkish and most of the languages spoken in the Islamic republics formerly part of the Soviet Union are in the Altaic family. Yet, despite the Germans and Turks speaking radically different languages, Togarmah, according to the Bible, is supposed to be the son of Gomer. Thus, for Lindsey to be right, the Turks have to have been derived from German stock. Nothing could be further from the truth.

Finally, the premillennialist scenario of Russia bringing with its own armies troops from Germany and other Central European nations worked only as long as the Warsaw Pact was extant and the Germans involved were East Germans. Now, with the Warsaw Pact a thing of the past, with the nations of Central Europe still resenting their all too recent occupation by Russian troops and particularly with German reunification, why would any of these nations join Russia in the dubious enterprise of invading Israel? Also, Lindsey's scheme only works with East Germany being Gomer, since West Germany, as a member of the Common Market and the European Community, would have to be—according to Lindsey's own scheme—part of the 10-nation Neo-Roman Empire, hence a different end-times player. Now that what was once "Gomer" has become part of the European Community, Lindsey's scheme is completely invalidated.

The final unraveling of Russia as the opening player in the premillennial scenario is that Gog and Magog are mentioned in Revelation in a way that is incompatible with Lindsey's assertion that they will be destroyed before Armageddon. Though the good reverend fails to mention it, Revelation 20:7-8 states:

And when the thousand years are ended, Satan will be loosed from his prison and will come out to deceive the nations which are at the four corners of the earth, Gog and Magog, to gather them for battle; their number is like the sand of the sea.

This satanic army besieges the new Jerusalem, but is destroyed by fire raining down from heaven. This is much like what the premillennialists envision happening to the Russian army, but the problem is that they have Gog and Magog attacking before Armageddon. The attack related in Revelation 20 takes place after the millennium. This is 1,000 years late. Clearly the Gog and Magog referred to in Revelation cannot be Russia. But if Gog and Magog can mean something else here, how can anyone be sure that they stand for Russia in Ezekiel?

The New Rome
Ten Nations (more or less) under the Antichrist

Since the Beast of Revelation is represented as having 10 horns representing 10 kings (and by implication, 10 kingdoms), and since the final beast from the sea in Daniel's dream of the four beasts has 10 horns and, finally, because the idol in Nebuchadnezzar's dream had 10 toes, it is assumed by a number of premillennialists that the revived Roman Empire of the last days will be a 10-part kingdom. As David Jeremiah puts it (1982, KKLA October 27, 1992):

> The Bible clearly teaches that in the end-times, during the time of the Antichrist, there will be a ten-nation confederacy that rules with the Beast during the final days. And many have seen in this prophecy a picture of the renewed Roman Empire in the end-time. We are living today as Christians and as Americans in the aftermath of the Roman Empire. No other empire has grown up since that one. There is no other world dominion since the Romans. And if you can find us as Christians in prophecy anywhere...we are in the aftermath of the Roman Empire, down in the legs somewhere of this Beast, down in the feet, mixed in with the...afterglow of the tentacles of Rome that still reach out. For we still operate much in a Roman way, We have, for instance, Roman law and even our popular religion in this country goes back to its Roman root—not Christianity but popular religion. So Rome is very much with us....

As I pointed out in an Chapter 7, only someone absolutely ignorant of world history—willfully or otherwise—could say that there has never been an empire greater than that of Rome since its fall. Among the many states Jeremiah consistently ignores are the Arab caliphates, the empires of the Seljuk and Ottoman Turks, and the Mongol Khanate. Leaving all this aside, what makes up this 10 nation confederacy of the new Rome? Speaking more to the point, Jeremiah says in another part of his study on the book of Daniel (1982, broadcast on KKLA December 10, 1992):

> And he has 10 horns on his head, We don't have to doubt that. For over and over again in Revelation 17, we are told that the 10 horns are 10 kings and 10 kingdoms. This beast is united with 10 confederate nations, which are a part of the European Common Market or the last and final bloom of the Roman Empire.

This is pretty much the party line among premillennialists. Hal Lindsey put it this way (1970, p. 94):

> We believe that the Common Market and the trend toward unification of Europe may well be the beginning of the 10-nation confederacy predicted by Daniel and the Book of Revelation.

At the time Lindsey wrote these words the Common Market only consisted of six nations. Thus, when they did expand to 10, it gave his writings a certain credibility. However, a closer look at the Common Market or, as it is more properly called, the European Economic Community (EEC or sometimes just the European Community or EC), shows that this credibility is only superficial. The EEC started out in 1946 as the European Coal and Steel Commission (ECSC). It was converted into the EEC in 1957 by the Treaty of Rome—something that should send shivers up many a premillennial spine. At that time it consisted of six nations: France, Italy, West Germany, Netherlands, Belgium, and Luxembourg. In 1972, only two years after the publication of *The Late Great Planet Earth*, Denmark, Ireland and the United Kingdom joined, bringing the number up to nine. When Greece joined in 1981, the 10-nation confederacy was complete, and Lindsey's prediction was validated—briefly. What the premillennialists failed to consider was that the EEC would not stop at 10. In 1986, Portugal and Spain joined, bringing the number up to 12. How then could David Jeremiah still refer to the Common Market as the

New Rome in 1992? Note that he referred to the 10 confederate nations as being "a *part* of the European Common Market." The fact that the EEC has expanded beyond 10 nations does not faze the premillennial crowd in the least. After all, what are a few facts against their interpretation of the Word of God? Here's how Raul Ries puts it (1988):

> We know that today there are 10 nations in the Common Market. The Bible says there's only going to be 10...the will make up the revived Roman Empire in a time to come...Most of the nations that are right now in the Trilateral Community of Europe...are from the old Roman Empire. Two have to drop out in order for there to become 10.

I have heard Ries refer to the "Trilateral Community of Europe" repeatedly. It would appear that either his flock is as ignorant as he is or that neither they nor his colleagues want to hurt his feelings by telling him that the Trilateral Commission, an unofficial advisory body made up of members from North America, Europe and Japan (hence trilateral), and the European Community are two separate entities. Leaving that aside, note how he blithely discounts the facts when they do not jibe with his cherished view that the EEC *must* only consist of 10 nations because the Bible says there will be 10 nations. Unfortunately for Ries and other premillennialists, far from showing signs of nations dropping away, the EEC continues to grow. Sweden, Finland and Austria were accepted into it in 1995, bringing the number of members up to 15. So now five must drop out!

Another problem for the premillennial view is that Turkey, identified by Lindsey as Togarmah (thus part of the alliance that joins Russia in the dubious military adventure of invading Israel), is an associate member of the EEC. As such, like Germany as Gomer, it is a member of two different, mutually hostile end-time power blocks. Should some of the more prosperous nations of Central Europe, such as Hungary or the Czech Republic join the EC, it will be interesting to see what mental gymnastics and what amount of fact twisting Lindsey and company will go through to fit the new circumstances into their prophecy.

Twisting facts to fit one's interpretation of the Bible is made easier by a considerable amount of ignorance on the part of fundamentalist authors. In his book *Apocalypse*, Grant Jeffrey points out that the new currency of the European Community has as its symbol a woman riding on a beast. What could this be but the Whore of Babylon riding on *the* Beast? Jeffrey asks the ominous question (p. 184), "Why would Europe choose this symbol for their new currency?" If this author would read any other mythology than his own, he would know that the woman riding a *bull* is Europa, who in Greek myth was carried off by Zeus in the form of a bull. Since Europa gave her name to Europe, she is a reasonable symbol to use on EC currency.

The Rapture

One might wonder how it is that anyone could look forward to all of the terrible things of the premillennial scenario, even if the earthly reign of Christ lay on the other side of the tribulation. In fact, most premillennialists do not think they will have to. The readers are bound to have seen bumper stickers that say, "In case of Rapture, this car will be unoccupied." The word rapture (as I noted in Chapter 8) derives from the Latin verb *rapere*, meaning to seize or snatch away. In the biblical context it refers to Paul's telling the Thessalonians that those Christians living at the end will be caught up in the clouds at the second coming of Jesus. That there is no mention of the Rapture in Revelation has led to a friendly debate among premillennialists. Thus, they divide according to when they think the rapture will happen with respect to the Tribulation. They are either pre-trib, mid-Trib or post-Trib. Lindsey favors the pre-Trib view, that is, that Christians will be caught up in the air before the rise of the Antichrist. The only people among the saved who will go through the Tribulation, according to this view, are those who convert to Christianity after the rapture. The other views are also well represented among premillennialists, however, with the late Dr. Walter Martin arguing persuasively for the post-Tribulation rapture. Whole books have been written and appear in fundamentalist bookstores arguing whether or not the church will face the terrors of the Antichrist.

Other than Paul's description of the rapture in 1 Thessalonians, the only allusion to anything like it is in Matthew's rendering of the Olivet discourse, where he speaks of two men in the field or two women grinding at the mill and "one is taken and one is left" (Mt. 24: 40-41). That what amounts to a few verses at most can cause such a controversy and be the subject of so much fervor and speculation is an indication of how far from the actual Bible supposedly Bible-believing fundamentalists can get when it comes to the apocalypse.

In reality, there is so little material in the Bible that relates to the Rapture that it should be of minor importance. That it has become a major portion of Lindsey's scenario, and that the dominant view with respect to the rapture is pre-Trib, is an indication that most premillennialists want to have their cake and eat it too. Having consigned the rest of us to agony and destruction, they reserve for themselves the sugar-coating of being caught up by God before anything gets unpleasant. Who can blame them? Their pre-Trib *deus ex machina* makes the whole scenario so much more palatable. And, after all, Lindsey and company would not want to set up barriers to belief.

Whose End of the World?

While "Babylon" is usually taken to mean Rome, there is an alternative view espoused by Charles H. Dyer in his book, *The Rise of Babylon,* that Babylon actually *means* Babylon. In this scenario Saddam Hussein becomes the Antichrist and his efforts to rebuild Babylon, far from being aimed at tourism, are for the purpose of moving his capital there from Baghdad. In Dyer's scenario Hussein becomes the great power in the world by eventually controlling the Persian Gulf and all its oil. Apparently, this will have to wait until "Stormin' Norman" Schwarzkopf is in an old age home. Some adherents of this view see Kuwait as doubling for Israel, allowing Iraq to be at once Babylon *and* the Enemy from the North. While such an interpretation is likely to offend most premillennialists, by combining two apocalyptic bogeys into one it does achieve a certain economy. Another potential "Babylon" is identified for us by Gary Kah in his book *En Route to Global Occupation* (1992, p. 65):

> Is New York destined for destruction? I don't have the answer to this question, nor do I wish such a fate on the people of that city. However, the parallels between New York and the great, but wicked, city described as Mystery Babylon in Revelation 17 and 18 are difficult to ignore.

If New York might be Babylon could there be a place in Bible prophecy for the United States after all? While it is a bit of a reach, some millenarians see a potential allusion to America in the Gog and Magog prophecy of Ezekiel, specifically in Ezek. 38:13 (KJV):

> Sheba and Dedan and the merchants of Tarshish, with all the young lions

thereof, shall say unto thee [Gog], Art thou come to take a spoil? hast thou
gathered thy company to take a prey? to carry away silver and gold, to take
away cattle and goods, to take a great spoil?

In case the reader missed the allusion, the United States is represented, so
some millenarians say, by the "young lions" of Tarshish. Generally speaking
Tarshish is thought to be either Tharrus, a city in Sardinia or the city of
Tartessus in southern Spain. Both of these were Phoenician colonies. Sheba
and Dedan were both Arabic kingdoms. How then can anyone read into this
that Tarshish has anything to do with America?

The answer is that, since the lion is the symbol of England, and since the
Phoenicians were known to have reached the British Isles, and since Tarshish
was a biblical symbol for the farthest west (see Jonah 1:3), all this means that
Tarshish = the English speaking peoples. Furthermore, in his book *Prophecy
2000*, David Allen Lewis, citing *America B.C.* by Barry Fell, claims that not
only did the Phoenicians reach America, but that Fell reports in that book that
a stone found in New Hampshire inscribed in Punic letters translates into
English, "Voyagers From Tarshish This Stone Proclaims." Well, what more
proof can we ask? If England is the lion of Tarshish, the *young* lions of Tarshish
must be England's offspring, i.e. the United States and Canada. These "young
lions," say the millenarians, are vigorously protesting Gog's invasion of Israel
in Ezek. 38:13.

All of this is a bit thin, but it gets thinner when we consider that it is only
in the King James Version of the Bible that we find the phrase, "merchants of
Tarshish and all the young lions thereof." In the English translation of the
Hebrew from the Masoretic text the phrase is rendered, "the merchants of
Tarshish with all the magnates thereof" and in the Revised Standard Version
it is "Tarshish and all its villages." Thus, even this tenuous link tying America
to Bible prophecy proves to be but a chimera.

The lion as a symbol of England and thus a way to link modern nations
to apocalyptic images is exploited again in the minority view of the four beasts
from the sea in Daniel 7. While the majority of fundamentalists see the
empires represented in this vision as being synonymous with those in
Nebuchadnezzar's dream of the idol, a fair number of them disagree, arguing
that there would be no point in repeating the same prophetic message twice.
Thus they see the four beasts as symbolizing a succession of power among

modern nations. The first of these, the winged lion, is obviously the British Empire. This is succeeded by a bear, which is (what else?) Russia. The leopard with four wings and four heads is seen as some power in Asia or possibly the Middle East. Of course, the fourth beast, with its iron teeth and 10 horns, is still the empire of the Antichrist, whatever it might be geographically.

Another prophecy recast in modern terms is that of the fall of Babylon. Since the conquest of the Chaldean Empire by Cyrus of Persia does not match the bloody slaughter predicted by Isaiah and Jeremiah, Chuck Missler, co-author with Hal Lindsey of *The Magog Factor,* sees it as yet unfulfilled. He sees the Kurds as the future executioners of Babylon, presumably in revenge for what they have suffered at the hands of the Iraqis. To fit them into the prophecy, Missler claims that they are the modern day descendants of the Medes. This is a little hard to believe since Xenophon and the 10,000 Spartan hoplites had to fight their way through the lands of the Kurds in 400 B.C.E. He tells us in the *Anabasis* that the Kurds had previously destroyed an army sent against them by the Persians. Yet at that same time the Medes were part of the Persian Empire and lived further east. Considering that Missler was a party, along with Hal Lindsey, to claiming support for his theory on the Gog and Magog prophecy from Edwin Yamauchi, when in fact the latter was writing to debunk it, and considering that he and Lindsey used Yamauchi's material without giving him attribution, it's safe to say that one cannot accept that the Kurds and the Medes are the same people based on his assertion alone.

What we have in these alternative readings of the apocalyptic works is the same shaky structure as is seen in the main fundamentalist scenario: a fragile framework of faulty scholarship, poor history and often outright fiction, which has been disguised by a blanket of sheer imagination. In the next and last chapter, we will see works of even greater imagination in the conspiracy theories linked to the end-times fantasies by the paranoia implicit in the millenarian world view.

BLACK HELICOPTERS, HONG KONG GURKHAS, & OTHER SIGNS OF THE NEW WORLD ORDER

Secular Conspiracy Theories

RUNNING PARALLEL TO THE PREMILLENNIAL SCENARIO and plugging into it at various points is the mythos of secular conspiracy theories. This is hardly surprising. After all, paranoia is the logical corollary to millennial fantasies. In many cases millenarianism and conspiracy theories are the religious and secular sides of the same coin, and they share so much in common that it is often hard to figure which grows out of the other in the minds of those harboring a conspiracy-based world view. The relationship is further complicated, as we will see, by the impact of technology on the premillennial scenario.

Modern Technology and Other Signs of the End

Just as the premillennialists try to stretch apocalyptic writings (that were about the politics of their time) to fit modern times, they also try to fit poetic pictures of destruction into modern technology. The most obvious of these is the idea that fire raining down from heaven means nuclear-armed missiles. Another is the idea that the phrase "every eye shall see him" (Rev. 1:7) refers to the return of Christ being seen worldwide on television.

Hal Lindsey has speculated that the demonic locusts, the plague of the fifth trumpet, actually represent helicopters. Here is the actual description of the locusts from Rev. 9:7-10:

> In appearance the locusts were like horses arrayed for battle; on their heads were what looked like crowns of gold; their faces were like human faces, their hair like women's hair, and their teeth like lions' teeth; they had scales like iron breastplates, and the noise of their wings was like the noise of many chariots rushing into battle. They have tails like scorpions, and stings, and their power of hurting men for five months lies in their tails.

In that their wings make a rushing noise, that helicopters could be said to look as if they have stinger-like tails and that the locusts' armor could be said to be a description of the metal skin of helicopters, the locusts could be stretched to fit these modern machines, if one uses a good deal of imagination. Hal Lindsey apparently took the locusts having faces of men as being the crew of the helicopters as seen in the cockpit from without. Just how it is that military helicopters would torture, but not kill, for five months is not explained. On the other hand, locusts commonly live for five months, and Joel's locusts were also like horses. It is also hard to figure how they could have come out of the smoke from the bottomless pit (Rev 9:3) or why their king would be Abaddon, the angel of the bottomless pit (Rev. 9:11).

Even if helicopters do not work that well in fulfilling the imagery of Revelation, they do figure in conspiracy theories. Listen to any fundamentalist radio station for awhile and you will hear reports of ominous black (i.e. unmarked) helicopters harassing good conservative folks. Supposedly they were hovering over the Branch Davidian compound in Waco just before the tanks went in. People have claimed that the helicopters are often filled with men wearing unusual uniforms, hence the speculation that they are carrying foreign troops and that these are trial runs for the U.N. takeover of the U.S., thus instituting the world government that will be ruled by the Antichrist. Among the people who claim to have been buzzed and harassed by low flying black helicopters are Christians who are home-schooling their children to keep them out of the secular school system. Despite the popularity and availability of video cameras and despite reports of repeated harassment, none of these sightings have ever been substantiated. This last minor fact has not reduced the fears concerning the infernal machines in the least. If anything, the ability of the black helicopters to avoid detection has added to their satanic mystique.

Another report of foreign troops being brought in to take away our rights was the assertion that the federal crime bill of 1994 had in it a provision for bringing in foreign police—specifically from Hong Kong—to enforce laws in America. The idea was that, unlike American cops, the foreigners would not have any compunction about firing on a crowd of American citizens. There was even one report that the police being brought over from Hong Kong were Gurkhas, troops with a reputation for savagery.

Reality was something else again. While there are about a thousand Gurkhas stationed in Hong Kong, they are used for border patrol only.

Members of this elite corps of the British army are not so much noted for savagery, but rather are famous for their honesty, trustworthiness, sense of personal honor, and most of all for their *valor*. Since 1911 Gurkhas have won 13 Victoria Crosses, the British equivalent of the Congressional Medal of Honor. The likelihood that these elite troops, so fiercely loyal to the Queen, would be loaned out to the U.S. to kill Americans is nil. However, there is just the smallest grain of truth to the rumor that the government was going to bring in Hong Kong police. On page 843 of HR 3355, section 5108 directed the Attorney General, the heads of the FBI and the Drug Enforcement Agency (DEA), along with the Commissioners of the Immigration and Naturalization Service (INS) and the Customs Service to recruit *former* Royal Hong Kong Police officers into Federal law enforcement positions. The true story is this. Hong Kong is shortly due to revert back to the People's Republic of China. Thus, the officers of the Royal Police will soon be without either a job or a home. The fact that the INS was involved in the recruitment plan should tell anyone that these officers would be brought in as *naturalized citizens*. Since Hong Kong is an international port, its police are experienced in coping with black market goods and drug smuggling, hence the participation of the FBI, the DEA, and the Customs Service in the recruitment program. This is a far cry from bringing in foreign police for crowd control. In any case, this recruitment plan was dropped from the final version of the bill.

Another horror story of the impending world government is that they have already subverted our money, planting occult symbols on dollar bills that hint at the drive to a globalist dictatorship. This was done during the (infamous) Roosevelt administration. The symbol in question is the pyramid with an eye on the back of the dollar bill. Below it is the Latin inscription *Novus Ordo Seculorum*, which translates as "New World Order." Or does it? What we have here is a compound error made up of bad Latin, bad spelling, and poor history. Those readers who, like myself, took some Latin in high school, might remember that the suffix "orum" is the genitive plural for nouns in the second declension. *Seculorum* would have to be plural and mean "of the worlds," which seems a rather clumsy phrasing. It certainly would be if in fact the word in question was "seculorum." Actually, in their desire to read an apocalyptic conspiracy into our currency, the millenarian crowd has added the letter "u" between the "c" and the "l" of the word printed on the dollar, which is *seclorum* or "of the ages." Thus, far from saying "New World Order," *Novus Ordo*

Two symbolic emblems that represent for some evidence of an organized world conspiracy: on the top, the reverse of the Great Seal of the United States as it appears on the back of a dollar bill, and on the bottom, the seal of the Knights Templar.

Seclorum reads "New Order of the Ages." Since this symbol and motto are on the back of our country's Great Seal and were put there when the nation was being founded, they represent the Revolutionary sentiment that by dispensing with kings, whose rule was autocratic and based on force, and replacing that system with a republic based on reason, balance of powers, and self rule, the founders of our nation were creating a new order for the ages.

Another phrase to be found on the back of the dollar bill, in fact one more prominently displayed than the Latin motto as well as being written in English is: "In God We Trust." For some reason this phrase and its obvious implications seem to be consistently overlooked by conspiracy theorists.

Other excursions into modern monetary subversion involve credit cards, bar codes, and other technologies that could potentially be a modern version of the Mark of the Beast. The most technologically sophisticated of these would be a computer microchip inserted under the skin either in the forehead or the back of the hand. Such technology is actually available and has been used to locate sheep and cattle grazing on range-lands. However, such solid state electronics are extremely vulnerable to electromagnetic fields, such as those generated by television screens. Sitting too near the boob-tube could erase the Mark of the Beast from many a couch potato.

There are, of course, other technologies that suggest themselves as potential Marks of the Beast. Whole books have been written on how the bar code is a prelude to it. The cashless society is another concept that fits into the idea of having to take the mark if one would buy or sell. Thus, credit cards in general and Visa cards in particular are candidates for the Mark of the Beast. In the case of Visa cards, we have a dubious excursion into numerology, which should, like astrology and palmistry, be anathema to fundamentalist Christians. The basic scheme of numerology is that every letter in the alphabet is assigned a number from one to nine as follows:

$$1 : 2 : 3 : 4 : 5 : 6 : 7 : 8 : 9$$
$$A : B : C : D : E : F : G : H : I$$
$$J : K : L : M : N : O : P : Q : R$$
$$S : T : U : V : W : X : Y : Z :$$

Then the numbers of each word or name analyzed are added up. If a two or three digit number results, those numbers are added in a column until a number from 1 to 9 is reached. These nine numbers have specific psychological characteristics assigned to them, much as do the 12 signs of the Zodiac. Applying this system to the word VISA, we get the following

V I S A

4+9+l+1=15   l+5=6

In the original numerological system, 6 stands for natural harmony as in the six colors of the spectrum. However, in order to make the Visa card come out as the Mark of the Beast, those fundamentalists who indulge in this sort of nonsense substitute biblical symbolism wherein 6 is the number of imperfection. Thus, by extrapolation, 6 means the same as 666. And *voila!* we have the Number of the Beast!

I will concede two items. First, while they do look for satanic conspiracies in many innocent aspects of the mundane world, very few fundamentalists involve themselves in interpretations as arcane as the numerological value of the Visa card. Second, the fear of some form of mandatory identification card and its misuse by a centralized government, even on the national level, is a reasonable one. While I like the convenience of my charge cards, untraceable cash transactions, which cannot be monitored by either a government or a corporation, constitute a democratically sound safeguard against intrusions into one's privacy. It is when these entirely valid concerns are linked to paranoid millennial fantasies that bizarre interpretations result, and if we must interpret every universal identification system in apocalyptic terms, then every American citizen, upon being assigned a social security number, has taken the Mark of the Beast.

So far I have dealt with supposed symptoms of the satanic New World Order. Let us now look at the institutions millenarians and others of their ilk see as the movers behind this globalist conspiracy.

Global Conspiracies

Those who see the world in terms of a system under Satan's control, who see themselves—as fundamentalists do—as being under siege, not only see a satanic pattern in world events of today, but see them as entrenched in history as well, particularly in the events of the twentieth century. They also see the conspiracy as having so pervasively infiltrated our system that virtually no one in power is untouched by it. For example, John McManus, present head of the John Birch Society, said that not only was the Reagan administration thoroughly infiltrated by agents of the New World Order, and that the public was brainwashed by the "liberal media," but that William Bennett and Rush Limbaugh were both brainwashed by the New World Order (*Live From L.A.* KKLA November 29, 1993). Since not even Rush Limbaugh can be trusted, it is not surprising that McManus also pointed out that the heads of CBS, NBC, ABC, the *New York Times,* the *Washington Post,* the *Los Angeles Times,* the *Wall Street Journal, Time, Newsweek, U.S. News and World Report,* and the *National Review* are all members of the Council on Foreign Relations (CFR), seen as one of the chief architects of the New World Order.

Besides media heads, who else is a member of the CFR? According to Gary Kah in *En Route to Global Occupation* (as well as other sources), former and present members of the CFR include Adlai Stevenson, Dwight D. Eisenhower, Cyrus Vance, Zbigniew Brzezinski, Paul Volker, Lane Kirkland, Henry Kissinger, George Schultz, Nelson Rockefeller, David Rockefeller, Alan Greenspan, Jeanne Kirkpatrick, George Bush, Richard M. Nixon, George McGovern, Michael Dukakis, Donna Shalala, Richard Cheney, Colin Powell, Jimmy Carter, John F. Kennedy, Robert Kennedy, Edward Kennedy, Jesse Jackson, and many others. That people whose political beliefs cover such a broad spectrum are all members of the CFR should tell anyone that the organization, in actual fact, has no particular political leaning of its own. In short, the membership is too broad, varied, and extensive to be an indicator of any significance. Rather than revealing an entrenched conspiracy, this partial membership list indicates a prestigious organization that people prominent in politics, education, the media, and finance frequently join. Kah admits that Dukakis only joined the CFR *after* his unsuccessful bid for the presidency.

Other organizations high on the enemies list in this basic conspiracy scenario are the Trilateral Commission, the Club of Rome, the Bilderberg Group, and lesser organizations such as The Aspen Institute. All of these share with the CFR the qualities of being unofficial advisory bodies with distinguished membership rosters.

Official government and international organizations in the supposed conspiracy include the Federal Reserve System (FRS) and, of course, the United Nations, the world government itself. Facts have little credence in minds of conspiracy addicts when it comes to the major players in their cherished scenario. That the UN is unable to control or bring into obedience one warlord whose clan controls one section of one third world city would seem to make it a paper tiger. The same is true of the European Community, the other major contender for the role of Empire of the Antichrist. That the EC is either unable or unwilling to intervene effectively in Bosnia, its own back yard, makes it a bit of a dud as the Neo-Roman Empire. Conspiracy theorists counter that the U.N. and the EC are allowing the conditions in Bosnia and Somalia to deteriorate for various reasons of their own, among them being a draconian program of population control. Of course, if either of these two institutions were to intervene effectively, these same theorists would use *those* events as evidence of the growing power of the UN and the EC. Thus, their belief is confirmed regardless of what happens, a sure sign of intellectual self-deception.

As Michael Howard points out in his 1989 book *The Occult Conspiracy:* "Conspiracy theorists regard the UN with with suspicion because of the alleged involvement of the CFR in its creation" (Howard 1989, p. 167). The Council on Foreign Relations was begun when the United States failed to join the League of Nations, which had been set up after World War I chiefly by President Woodrow Wilson and his special advisor Col. E. M. House. In 1919 Col. House met with members of a British group called the Round Table that was the brain-child of 19th-century diamond and gold magnate Cecil Rhodes. Rhodes was obsessed with the vision of a world government based on British values and had set up the Round Table as a means toward that end. (This, of course, makes Rhodes scholars suspect as agents of the New World Order.) Members of the Round Table agreed to set up a non-governmental advisory body aimed at influencing nations toward peaceful resolution of conflicts. In England it was called the Institute for International Affairs (IIA); in America it became the CFR. An unofficial Anglo-American advisory group or think-tank hardly fits the role of end-time bogey. However, the CFR does have a strong internationalist bent. In many ways the organization's lack of ideology has been used against it. As Howard puts it (p. 166):

> In the eyes of their opponents the CFR is currently dedicated to destroying the sovereignty of the United States, reversing the democratic process which instigated the 1776 American Revolution, promoting internationalism and the foundation of a world super state embracing both capitalism and Communism in a new political order. The evidence for this seems to be largely based on the neutral stance adopted by the CFR in American politics.

Formerly, the CFR was viewed by its critics as being an elitist right-wing power group and was even accused of financing Hitler's rise to power. No support has ever been found for this claim.

Next to the CFR, the Trilateral Commission is perhaps the most anathematized international advisory group in existence. Founded in 1970 and having a membership drawn from Japan, Europe, and North America, its stated goal is to "encourage closer cooperation among these three democratic industrialized regions" (item 15479, *Encyclopedia of Associations*, 1995). The Club of Rome has a broader appeal, being concerned with issues as varied as environmental degradation, overpopulation, economics, etc. The Bilderberg Group was originally founded in 1954 as an anti-Communist organization, but softened its stance in the wake of detente.

All of these organizations have properties that lay them open to attack from the more paranoid among us. First of all, since they are composed of an international elite, there is the suspicion, no doubt somewhat justified, that their members think that they know better than the common man or woman how the world ought to be run. Second, since they often discuss sensitive issues, they often keep their meetings secret. This implies covert operations and clandestine plots. Third, given that all of these organizations wish to draw upon people influential in the worlds of finance, politics and media, there is considerable overlap of membership among them. This gives the appearance of an international conspiracy. Certainly the potential for elitism and conspiracy exists among these organizations, but the varied political views of the members would tend to act as a safeguard against such an occurrence. Howard gives this word of caution with regard to such organizations (p. 163):

> In general, as far as it can be detected at all by those who are directly in contact with its working, this influence can be characterized as benign. However, the unpalatable fact must also be faced that in some instances the pursuit and exercise of power in the political arena can have a corrupting effect, especially when it encounters the inherent weakness of human nature.

Probably the greatest weakness of human nature seen in these organizations is in their inherent failure, because they are so much a part of the established system, to comprehend or anticipate what might variously be called novelty, chaos, or serendipity. As two examples of this failure to comprehend the curves thrown us by reality, consider that it was the professionals who got

In this depiction of George Wasington as a Mason, the line of type across the bottom of the picture proudly ranks his Masonic membership with his stint as Commander in Chief of the army and his term as President of the United States. The scroll in Washington's hand reads, "'The grand object of Masonry is to promote the happiness of the Human Race.' Washington." On the sash winding down the corinthian columns that flank Washington are the words, "Brotherly Love, Relief, Truth, Friendship, Temperance, Fortitude, Prudence, Justice," and "Charity." Detail of the painting *George Washington as a Freemason* courtesy of the Library of Congress.

us into Vietnam. Consider also that the experts were caught just as flat-footed as the rest of us at the break-up of the Warsaw pact and the fall of the Soviet Union.

The Federal Reserve System (FRS), along with any international banking system, is another source of paranoia for the conspiracy crowd. Any control or manipulation of the money supply is assumed to be part of a monetary conspiracy inimical both to individual freedom and national sovereignty. McManus has claimed that our nation's national debt is being deliberately increased to put us in hock to international bankers as part of the plan to destroy our national sovereignty and create the New World Order. The FRS, or the Fed, created by congress in 1913, has the function of controlling the money supply, which it does by buying and selling government bonds, regulating the rate at which commercial banks borrow money from the Federal Reserve Bank and regulating the requirements as to what percentage of commercial banks' assets are held in the Federal Reserve. If the Fed buys government bonds, reduces the discount rate to commercial banks, or lowers their Federal Reserve requirements, the money supply is increased, interest rates fall and inflation increases. When the Fed sells bonds, raises the discount rate or the Federal Reserve requirements, less money circulates, interest rates rise, and inflation is reduced. Obviously businesses are affected, often much against their will, by the policies of the Fed. Hence, it is not always well thought of, and among conspiracy theorists it has be come viewed as an agent of the New World Order, this despite the fact that its present chairman, Alan Greenspan, was a protege of the late Ayn Rand and is strongly influenced by Libertarian economic theory.

Templars, Freemasons and the Dreaded Illuminati

That those who see the world as rushing to its final doom are likely to see any group urging international cooperation as being an instrument of the Antichrist is understandable. Instead of seeing the CFR and the Trilateral Commission as idealistic and somewhat elitist brain trusts, millenarians see them as a network of semi-secret societies wielding power illegitimately, not merely to influence but to control sovereign national governments. But whence came these powerful shadow regimes? Conspiracy theorists trace them all the way back to the Knights Templar, who, starting out as crusaders

and protectors of pilgrims, supposedly fell under various influences including pagan mystery religions and the Assassins of Alamut. Having become corrupt and rich, the Templars tried to control the wealth of Europe but were
valiantly stopped by Philip the Fair of France (1268-1314). Upon being put to
the question the leaders of the Templars revealed that they worshiped a goat-
headed idol called Baphomet, which they anointed with the blood of unbap-
tized babies, that they ritually defiled crucifixes and that they practiced
sodomy in their secret rites. Kah and other conspiracy theorists report this
story with evident relish. The Templars, after all, make wonderful foils. As the
first internationalists whose wealth and banking system made them the cred-
itors of and potential powers behind the governments of rising national states,
they resemble the picture the theorists in their paranoia have painted of the
CFR, the FRS, the Rockefellers and the Rothchilds. That they were secretly
practicing satanic rites confirms the theorists in their assurance that their
modern counterparts are part of the kingdom of the Beast. All of us who grew
up reading Sir Walter Scott's *Ivanhoe* are predisposed to believe the worst of
the Templars from the start. After all, Bois-Gilbert and the other heavies in the
classic were all Templars.

But how much of this story is true? And how does it relate to modern times?
The Templars were obviously quite powerful and somewhat corrupt. By the
beginning of the 13th century, three crusading orders—the Templars, the
Knights of St. John, and the Teutonic Knights—between them controlled 40%
of Europe's frontiers and as such exerted considerable influence in the courts
of Europe. The Templars made money by ferrying crusaders and pilgrims to
the Holy Land and importing spices from there to Europe. As their wealth
increased, they became the bankers of Europe and they became increasingly
lax in fulfilling their religious vows. They conspired with the Sultan of Egypt
to thwart Frederick II's crusade, and by 1254 were at open war with another
crusading order, the Knights Hospitaler. When Acre, the last Christian strong-
hold in the Levant, fell to the Moslems in 1291 the Templars were expelled from
the Holy Land. Now they were no longer even nominally crusaders. In 1307
Philip the Fair found himself facing bankruptcy and owed the Templars large
sums of money. Thus, he made common cause with Pope Clement V to destroy
the order, whose increasing wealth and independence was alarming the
Church. The Grand Master of the Templars, Jacques de Molay, came to Paris
that same year to discuss a new crusade. He was arrested, and Templar lodges

and treasuries were seized throughout France. Pope Clement issued a bull ordering the arrest of all members of the order throughout Christendom. It was then that the Templars made their confessions either under torture or the threat of it. Considering that both the King of France and the Pope needed some criminal charge upon which to base the seizure of Templar treasuries, it is hardly surprising that the order was found to have become heretical. To this day it is unclear which charges if any made against the Templars were true. De Molay protested his innocence even as he was being burned at the stake in 1314.

The significance of the Templars is that there is a link between them and Freemasonry. Late in the Middle Ages powerful craft guilds flourished in Europe. But, as the result of the decline in the building of new cathedrals and the subsequent drop in guild membership, the masons began to allow men not involved in the trade to join as honorary members. These men became known as "free and accepted masons" or Freemasons. In some countries, after the fall of the Templars their remnants were absorbed into the Masonic Guilds. Much of the medieval tradition, however, was embellished in the 17th and 18th centuries when the Freemasons adopted the rites and trappings of various chivalric orders. Though the organization is not specifically Christian, it began with a distinctly Protestant, anticlerical bias. The Templars, seen as prototypes of Protestant martyrs, were taken as a chivalric ideal to aspire to. So it is in modern times that the Masonic club for teenage boys is called the DeMolay, and the Knights Templar is one of the advanced lodges in Freemasonry. Without going into a detailed history of the Masons, let me just point out that their system of secret lodges allowed for open discussion of politics in countries where voicing one's opinion could result in imprisonment or death. In Latin countries Freemasonry tends to attract free thinkers and anticlericals. This fact plus the association of the Templars with the Masons has laid the latter open to all the charges leveled against the former, not only by fundamentalists but by European and South American dictators. In volume 22 of the *Encyclopedia Britannica* the true significance of the Masonic lodges is mentioned in a discussion of the history of Italy in the late 1700s (p. 223):

> In the Italy of the old regime, there had been no representative political life. But the increase in the number of Masonic Lodges at the end of the 18th century demonstrated the desire for secret discussion of problems different from those that were agitating the academies and the agrarian societies. Not

all the Freemasons became supporters of the Revolution and the French, but many of them did so. The moderate and constitutional demands of the Masonic Lodges began to be accompanied by more democratic demands, and there were in Milan, Bologna, Rome, and Naples cells of Illuminati, republican free-thinkers, after the pattern recently established in Bavaria by Adam Weishaupt.

But were the Illuminati really such radicals? Indeed they were, and they were justly considered a threat by virtually every government in Europe. And what were the Illuminist beliefs that were so threatening to the governments of Weishaupt's day? Among them were such dangerous ideas as universal suffrage, equality of the sexes, and complete freedom of religion. Other Illuminist beliefs were of the utopian socialist variety. They included the abolition of social authority, private property and national states. Humanity, in the Illuminist vision, would live in anarchic harmony and universal brotherhood, and would enjoy peace and free love. This may make the Illuminati sound like a cross between Marxists and 1960's flower children, and is no doubt the image that so horrifies fundamentalist conspiracy theorists. But all such comparisons are doomed to error, because implicit in them is a disregard for historical context. To understand the Illuminati, one must understand the politics of Europe in the late 18th century, the time of the Enlightenment. In reaction to the excesses of the religious wars of the 1600s the intellectuals of the 1700s were rational, secular and anticlerical. The growth of science and rationalism provoked the thinkers of that day to question everything, and they found much that did not stand up well in the light of reason. Thus, in addition to being rational and secular, they were also democratic and egalitarian. And seeing the concentration of wealth and power in the hands of the nobility and the state religions, they considered the abolition of private property a necessary step to change what was clearly an unjust social order. Despite the prevalence of democratic ideals in the philosophy of the time, most of the states of Europe were ruled by kings who were absolute despots. (Remember that the American Revolution was just starting the year the Illuminati came into being.) These powers naturally resisted the democratic flow of their culture tenaciously, so tenaciously in fact that it took the rest of the 18th century, all of the 19th century, and part of the 20th to remove them. Thus it was not until late in the 1800s that the French were free of both the Bourbons and the descendants of

Napoleon Bonaparte. It was not until the end of World War I that the Hohenzollerns of Prussia, the Hapsburgs of Austria, and the Romanovs of Russia were removed, and the empires of Austria-Hungary and the Ottoman Turks broken up. Indeed, we are still today dealing with the aftermath of the persistence of these monarchies.

As a graphic indication of how the battle lines were drawn, consider that as part of the Illuminist initiation ceremony the candidate was led into a room containing an empty throne, a crown, a scepter, and a sword, and was invited to take them up. But, he or she was told, if they did so they would be denied entry into the order. The crowned heads of Europe were not likely to take kindly to a secret society harboring such sentiments, nor were the established religious authorities. This, coupled with the anticlerical and anti-Christian bias of the Illuminati, made them even better foils than the Templars had been in the Middle Ages. Thus they were branded as atheists, Satanists, assassins and whatever else would feed a sensationalist, fear-mongering campaign. (I should point out that as Marxist as the abolition of property sounds, a variant of that principle—land redistribution—was practiced in America when, following the Revolution, the estates of Tories were seized, broken up, and given to landless families. Since most of the newly independent colonies still limited voting rights to property owners, this meant that the number of voters was increased significantly.)

Are the Illuminati still active? Are they the unifying power behind the CFR, the Trilateral Commission, the Bilderbergers, and the Club of Rome? Are they the secret masters of worldwide Freemasonry? For the most part the Illuminati were absorbed into other revolutionary groups. No doubt many joined the French Revolution or shifted in the 19th century from utopian socialism to Marxism. There is no evidence that they exist today.

On the other hand the influence of Freemasonry is such that men holding to its ideals were instrumental in creating one of the 20th century's greatest powers, a power whose global influence and military might is greater than any known in the history of the world, a power viewed by many small nations as a distinct threat to their sovereignty. In fact, one of these nations has identified this power with Satan. This ominous power is the United States of America.

Most of the founders of our nation, including George Washington, were Masons. Such was the influence of Freemasonry that the back of the Great Seal, that symbol on our dollar bill that so terrifies conspiracy theorists, contains the pyramid with an eye in it, which is a Masonic symbol.

Humanists and New Agers

Not only were most of the founding fathers Freemasons, at least one, Benjamin Franklin, was a Rosicrucian. The Rosicrucians were supposed to have access to the teachings of Christian Rosenkreuz who was born in 1378 and lived for over 100 years. He had supposedly learned esoteric disciplines held by the ancient Egyptians, the Pythagorean philosophers of ancient Greece and other occult wisdom. In reality, the earliest Rosicrucian writings date from 1614. This secret fraternal order may actually have been founded by the Swiss physician and alchemist Paracelsus (1493?-1541). While it attracted many of the intelligentsia of the 18th century, the Rosicrucian order never seems to have developed as an organization of significant political influence to match the Freemasons. It was a common belief in the 18th century that ancient civilizations had held secret knowledge lost to people of their day. To some degree this was true in that, for example, the technology to make large panes of clear glass, lost since the fall of the Roman Empire, was not rediscovered until the 1600s. The supposed esoteric knowledge of the Egyptians, however, was more the stuff of which the legends of Atlantis were made. Fraternal orders used supposed access to ancient hidden knowledge as a means of self-validation. The Masons claimed descent from the masons sent by Hiram of Tyre to build Solomon's Temple. Naturally, these Phoenician masons brought with them secrets of the ancient Egyptians. Thus, fraternal orders developed a quasi-pagan mythology as part of their ritual. Fundamentalists in general and conspiracy theorists in particular have seized on this, anathematized the Masons and Rosicrucians, and see in their rituals a pagan revival.

Another pagan revival or intrusion of occult influences is that popular pastiche of westernized eastern religion, astrology, warmed over 19th century mysticism (theosophy and the like), revived paganism of dubious validity and general feel-good spirituality called the New Age movement. Of course, the phrase "New Age" is too close to "New World Order" to not provoke fundamentalist paranoia.

Both the pseudo-pagan rites of the Freemasons and the New Age movement excite millenarian fears as being the religion of the false prophet in Rev. 13:11-15. The facts that the New Age movement is patently silly, that the

Rosicrucians have been reduced to soliciting new members through ads in pulp magazines, and that the mumbo-jumbo of Masonic ritual is nothing more than the usual hokum of fraternal societies, have not blunted those fears in the least. And, since conspiracy theorists point out the great overlap in the ranks of professional politicians of Masons and members of the CFR, fears of the Illuminati are revived.

As an example of how absurd such fears of a pervasive *sub rosa* paganism are, I can offer my experiences with Masonic organizations, indirect though they were. Out of filial duty I attended a number of officer installations as my parents moved up the ranks as members of the Garden Grove chapter of the Order of the Eastern Star, a Masonic organization for women and married couples. Having met the other members of the lodge and heard their political and social views, I can safely say that, as staunch Nixon supporters in the Vietnam War years, these people were not Illuminist, neo-pagan revolution-aries. It is common at these installations for the newly installed officers to introduce the friends and family members who have turned out to support them. Many of these are from other Masonic women's or couple's organiza-tions, such as Daughters of the Nile or the Amaranth. Like the officers they had turned out to support, these women were quintessentially Orange County Republican. Thus, when one of the matrons introduced one of her friends as "the High Priestess of my White Shrine," momentary visions of these ladies indulging in pagan rites and child sacrifice dissolved in the face of their obvious middle-class conservatism.

What stretches credulity even further is the supposed link between New Agers and secular humanists, particularly since the later generally hold the former in absolute contempt. The prime mechanism of indoctrination into this pagan/humanist world system is seen by millenarians and conspiracy theorists as being the public school system. The main tactics are seen as dumbing down students to make them manageable and desensitizing them to such horrors as infanticide. The system's chief architect is generally con-sidered to be the late John Dewey, whom they hold responsible for modern failures in education The problem with this view is that Dewey's model of permissive education hit its peak in the 40s and was dealt a death blow by the pressure to emphasize math and science at the expense of the humanities fol-lowing the launch of the first Sputnik satellite in 1957. That the emphasis in science has not produced better educated students since then is a product of family breakdown, oversized classes, the encumbering of teachers with all sorts of baggage based on social agendas, the pervasive influence of television, and a host of other societal problems, none of which are demonstrably related to clandestine conspiracies.

As an example of fundamentalist fears that children are being desensitized to such horrors as infanticide, consider a brief article by fundamentalist author Berit Kjos (pronounced Chos) that appeared in a magazine called *Media Bypass*. Kjos told of a mother who was trying to restrict the use of a novel called *The Giver* in the classroom because it contained a scene in which a low birth-weight baby is efficiently done away with. The mother felt that it desensitized children to infanticide. Kjos (1995) says of the book:

> Laura's mother knew that *The Giver* fit into the flood of classroom literature
> that force children to think the unthinkable and reconsider the values they
> learned at home. It also models many of the pitfalls and supposed perfections
> of the utopian school-centered community documented in Goals 2000 and
> other blueprints for change prepared by the educational establishment.

And now for a dose of reality. I was so intrigued by Kjos's article that I went to the library and read *The Giver,* which was the winner of the 1994 Newbury Award. The novel is about a futuristic society which is seemingly utopian. As the story unfolds it becomes more and more evident that the society is quite sinister. Old people, incorrigibles and problem babies are "released." Up to the point of the climactic scene Laura's mother thought would desensitize kids to infanticide, release has by implication been a mystical letting go. When the hero actually views the "release" of a low birth-weight baby it turns out to be a horrific scene in which the baby is killed by lethal injection and disposed of down a garbage chute. Desensitizing? Hardly! The scene is traumatic. If anything it is likely to turn the kids into right-to-lifers.

Laura and her classmates were required to make their own decisions as to whether the society portrayed in *The Giver* was right or wrong, though how they could think it right is a bit hard to figure. Fundamentalists object to such exercises. This is curious since they are the first to complain about "dumbing down" in the school system. One would think that exercises that make kids examine why they believe what they believe would be the opposite of dumbing down. Yet, when it comes right down to it fundamentalists want their children taught by rote. This is fine as far as it goes. Multiplication tables, rules of grammar and proper spelling can and should be laid out in black and white terms. But children also need to exercise their minds. And here is the rub. People can only be taught to think for themselves by questioning the validity of ideas. People who question invariably start questioning the Bible or at least how their parents and other authorities interpret it. Since children who question things may end up questioning their parents' premillennial beliefs, fundamentalists, when it comes right down to it, really do not want their kids to think.

The Importance of Conspiracy Theories

As part of the crisis that provokes the creation of a world government, Gary Kah sees the possibility of a Syrian attack on Israel, with a possible nuclear exchange as part of the hostilities. He cites the failed, or as he puts it, as yet unfulfilled, prophecy of the destruction of Damascus in Is. 17:1 as possibly being fulfilled in this exchange, thereby validating both the prophecy and his scenario. That prophecies that clearly were not fulfilled are assumed to be awaiting fulfillment—someday—highlights the impossibility of falsification built into the fundamentalist scenario. There is in essence a basic dishonesty that pervades both millenarian prophecies and conspiracy theories. There may also be, among those who accuse the rest of us of being dupes or agents of a conspiracy, some hidden agenda of their own. Whether it is from sloppy research or sympathetic politics, Gary Kah has quoted extensively from so-called historian Nesta Webster to back up his assertion that the illuminati/Freemasons are responsible for Marxism and everything else of evil in the world. Michael Howard says of Nesta Webster (1989, pp. 161-162):

> Typical of these politically motivated conspiracy theorists was Nesta Webster, who wrote a series of best-selling books in the 1920s exposing the so-called Jewish world domination plan. She claimed that the Jews, working through secret societies and the international banking system, were the *eminences grises* behind the revolutionary movements of the eighteenth and nineteenth centuries...Webster believed she was the reincarnation of a countess who had been executed in the French Revolution and was convinced it was her duty in this lifetime to expose the secret societies who had plotted the 1789 uprising...Webster revealed her true political colours in 1923. Her books had

reviled Marxism as the modern cover for the "Jewish menace" and in that year
she went a step further by joining the British Fascist Party....

That dishonesty which makes prophecy unfalsifiable and fails either by
insufficient research or design to report the fascist anti-Semitism behind a
cited author may not be entirely limited to that of an intellectual nature. It
might well be cynically, cold-bloodedly monetary as well. While I cannot read
the minds of those fostering millenarian fears and thus cannot absolutely
prove a deliberate attempt to deceive on their part, there are ample motives
that might lead them to fan millennial paranoia.

Consider Hal Lindsey. According to the back cover of his book, *Planet
Earth— 2000 A.D.,* he has authored 11 books. All of these are on the end-time
and all are best-sellers in the Christian market. Their combined world-wide
sales exceeds $35 million. In addition to this Lindsey has speaking tours, talk
show appearances, etc. While I have no idea what portion of the sales goes to
him or how much of this money he devotes to charities, it is a sure bet that his
celebrity status makes for a more attractive life than merely pastoring a local
church would.

Then there is Don McAlvany, editor of *The McAlvany Intelligence Advisor,*
another conspiracy theorist who mixes stories of implanted biochips as the
Mark of the Beast with ominous predictions of impending economic collapse.
He advises his readers to buy gold and silver as a hedge against the coming disaster. Interestingly enough, McAlvany is a dealer in silver and gold. Could it be
that that his financial interests are to some small degree shading his prophecies?

While such end-times speculations as seeing the Mark of the Beast in the
bar code, Visa cards, and implanted computer chips, or fears that Hong
Kong Gurkhas will be imported into the U.S. for crowd control may seem
harmless and rather silly, the avid adherence to the belief that these are the
last days has serious consequences in that it motivates the way a sizable bloc
of American voters views both domestic and foreign policy. In his book *The
Mind of the Bible-Believer,* Edmund D. Cohen points out that it was extremely fortunate that the Soviet Union was run by atheists. Since they did not view
the world as being fulfilled in an apocalyptic vision and did not believe that
they had immortal souls that would survive a nuclear armageddon, they had
a built-in reason to avoid an atomic war. Hal Lindsey has many times boast-

ed that his lectures at places such as the Air Force Academy are always heavily attended and well received. Perhaps we should thank God that the Cold War ended before one of Lindsey's enthusiastic listeners pushed the nuclear envelope too far.

Even with the end of the Cold War, there are consequences that voters holding the premillennial mind-set may plunge us into. Consider that their belief in the end-times has not been in the least bit shaken by the end of the Cold War and consider that the sweeping Republican electoral victories of 1994 were accomplished by a shift of only 2% of the voters coupled with a low voter turnout. Since one of the voter blocs influencing that swing to the right consists of fundamentalist Christians looking forward to Armageddon, defense spending will likely not be based on rational considerations alone. Further, an aggressive, even bullying foreign policy could emerge, particularly in terms of our dealings with the Islamic nations and Russia.

While the influence of premillennialists may well prove a windfall for defense contractors, it could easily have a disastrous effect on how the government deals with internal issues. Consider the example of the infamous James Watt. As Secretary of the Interior, it was his job to enforce environmental regulations. As a premillennialist, however, it was his belief that there was no point in defending the environment since the world was going to end soon and the whole thing would be destroyed anyway. There is no end to the number of problems this rationalization could be applied to. Why worry about the problems of homelessness or drug addiction? The world is going to end soon. Why bother using our taxes to fund vaccinating school children? The world is going to end soon. Why bother reforming injustices? The Lord is coming back to institute a perfect society in a few years at most. Particularly when the financial benefits of more defense spending and less emphasis on environmental and social programs fit so nicely with the eschatology of the premillennialist voters, we will see how destructive are the fantasies woven by Hal Lindsey and others of his ilk.

EPILOGUE:

"Woe to those...who make the fatherless their prey!"

I F THE PROPHETIC AND APOCALYPTIC BOOKS of the Bible are indeed *not* reliably prophetic either historically or as a look into the future, must we abandon them? Skeptics are often accused of destroying spiritual truths in the process of debunking myths, thus leaving those who had believed in them with nothing to cherish and creating a void where there had once been something of value. Considering that the human mind is capable of infinite levels of self deception, a perception on the part of the newly undeceived that they will lose that which makes life meaningful should they accept the validity of the debunking could lead them to reject reason and continue to believe in that which is demonstrably false. Fortunately, this needn't be the case with respect to the prophetic and apocalyptic books of the Bible. We can answer the question, "Must we abandon them?" with a resounding "No!"

To see what we might keep while rejecting the historical validity of the prophecies, consider Isaiah 10:1,2:

> Woe to those who decree iniquitous decrees and the writers who keep writing oppression, To turn aside the needy from justice and rob the poor of my people of their right, that widows may be their spoil, and that they make the fatherless their prey!

This deep sympathy for the poor and the powerless continues a theme seen in Nathan's upbraiding of King David for orchestrating the death of Uriah so that David could take his wife, Bathsheba, for his own (2 Sam. 12:1-12). While we have no extrabiblical corroboration of this incident, the fact that such a tale would be deliberately preserved as a description of the proper course of relations between king and prophet is an indication that such a society did indeed exist in ancient Israel. Nor is this the only case of a prophet upbraiding a king. Samuel spoke in similar wise to Saul, as Elijah did to Ahab. It is notable that when Elijah had to flee for his life, it wasn't from the wrath of Ahab, but rather that of his foreign queen Jezebel. Isaiah was not alone among the prophets of the Assyrian period in condemning the powerful.

Amos 2:6,7 says:

> Thus says the Lord:"For three transgressions of Israel, and for four,
> I will not revoke the punishment,
> because they sell the righteous for silver,
> and the needy for a pair of shoes—
> they that trample the head of the poor into the dust of the earth,
> and turn aside the way of the afflicted;
> A man and his father go in to the same maiden,
> so that my holy name is profaned;
> they lay themselves down beside every altar
> upon garments taken in pledge;
> and in the house of their God they drink
> the wine of those who have been fined..."

The same condemnation is seen as well in Micah 2:1,2:

> Woe to those who devise wickedness
> And work evil upon their beds!
> When the morning dawns they perform it,
> because it is in the power of their hand .
> They covet fields, and seize them;
> and houses and take them away;
> they oppress a man and his house,
> a man and his inheritance.

This passion for justice and sense of outrage at the treatment of the poor continues into the later periods of prophecy as well. Jeremiah 5:28 condemns the rich and powerful in these words:

> [T]hey have grown fat and sleek.
> They know no bounds in deeds of wickedness;
> they judge not with justice

the cause of the fatherless, to make it prosper, and they do not defend the
rights of the needy.

Several verses in Ezekiel also condemn exploitation. Ezek. 22:29 is among
the more eloquent:

The people of the land have practiced extortion and committed robbery;
they have oppressed
the poor and needy and have extorted from the sojourner without redress.

After the return from exile the prophets continued to admonish the people to lead ethical lives. Zechariah 7:9,10 says:

Thus says the Lord of hosts, "Render true judgments,
show kindness and mercy each to his
brother, do not oppress the widow, the fatherless, the sojourner,
or the poor; and let none
of you devise evil against his brother in his heart."

Along with a passion for justice the prophetic writings also contain a sense of the grandeur of the cosmos, something which should resonate with us in the 20th century who by means of our powerful telescopes have caught a glimpse of the vastness of the Universe. Both Second and Third Isaiah speak of it in ringing poetry reminiscent of the Book of Job. For example, Isa. 40:22 describes God as:

It is he who sits above the circle of the earth,
and its inhabitants are like grasshoppers;
who stretches out the heavens like a curtain,
and spreads them like a tent to dwell in;

Isa. 66:1a gives a similar picture of God:

Thus says the Lord:
"Heaven is my throne and the earth is my footstool;

Even in condemnation the prophets, most of whom wrote their oracles as poetry rather than prose, spoke so powerfully that their words have transcended translation into English as in the famous words of Hosea 8:7a:

For they sow the wind,
and they shall reap the whirlwind.

And when the prophets speak of the last days poetry takes over. To insist that what is being said must be taken as a prophecy to be specifically fulfilled often degrades the beauty of the poetry and destroys the very spirituality that believers would seem to want so desperately to keep. Consider Joel 2:28 (3:1 in the MT) as an example:

> And it shall come to pass afterward,
>> that I will pour out my spirit on all flesh;
>> your sons and daughters shall prophesy,
>> your old men shall dream dreams,
>> and your young men shall see visions.

Any reference to the "last days," which, as we have seen, were thought of as taking place in the time of nations such as Assyria and Rome, should be taken as poetic and symbolic, lest any attempting to make them into specific prophecies be led either into the same error as the Millerites or into the absurdities espoused by modern premillennialists. The stories in Daniel, for example, needn't be literally true to invoke the heroism of the struggle of the Hasmoneans against the arrogance and power of Antiochus Epiphanes. The same is true of the dream-like narrative of Revelation. To pursue the meaning of such poetry with a book of doctrine in one hand and a timetable in the other is to invite folly.

So, my final word is that there is much of value in the prophetic and apocalyptic books of the Bible: a passion for justice, a sense of cosmic grandeur and truly wondrous poetry. How wonderful it would be if those so ardently pursuing a nuclear edge in the last battle would emulate the prophets they claim to revere by showing some compassion for the poor and needy!

Bibliography

Archer, Gleason L. 1982. *Encyclopedia of Bible Difficulties* Grand Rapids: Zondervan Publishing House.

Arnheim, Michael. 1984. *Is Christianity True?* Buffalo: Prometheus Books.

Augustine. *Confessions*. R. S. Pine-Coffin (trans). 1961. Harmondsworth, Middlesex, England: Penguin Books, Ltd.

Ball, W.P., G. W. Foote, John Bowden, Richard Smith, *et al*. 1986. *The Bible Handbook*. Austin: American Atheist Press.

Banks, Arthur. 1982. *Atlas of Ancient and Medieval Warfare*. New York: Hippocrene Books, Inc.

Bury, J. B., S. P. Cook and F. E. Adcock. (eds.). 1970. *The Cambridge Ancient History*. Cambridge: Cambridge University Press.

Baines, John and Jaromir Malek. 1980. *Atlas of Ancient Egypt*. Oxford, U.K.: Phaidon Press Ltd.

Cohen, Edmund D. 1988. *The Mind of the Bible Believer*. Buffalo: Prometheus Books.

Cheyne, T. K. 1895. *Introduction to the Book of Isaiah*. London: Adam and Charles Black.

De Camp, L. Sprague. 1972. *Great Cities of the Ancient World*. Garden City: Doubleday and Co., Inc.

Disselhoff, H.D. and S. Linne. 1960. *The Art of Ancient America*. New York: Crown Publishers.

Dyer, Charles H. with Angela Elwell Hunt. 1991. *The Rise of Babylon*. Wheaton: Tyndale House.

Gardiner, Sir Alan. 1961. *Egypt of the Pharaohs*. Oxford: Oxford University Press.

Gorman, Michael J. 1993. "Why Is The New Testament Silent About Abortion?" *Christianity Today*. January 11, 1993.

Grimal, Nicholas. Ian Shaw (trans.). 1988. *A History of Ancient Egypt*. Oxford, U.K.: Blackwell Publications.

Hall, H. R. 1963. *The Ancient History of the Near East*. Edinburgh and London: Morrison & Gibb Ltd.

Howard, Michael. 1989. *The Occult Conspiracy*. Rochester, VT: Destiny Books.

Jeffrey, Grant. 1992. *Apocalypse*. Toronto: Frontier Research Publications.

Jeremiah, David. 1982. "Series on the Book of Daniel." *Audiotape*. San Diego, CA: *Turning Point Ministries*.

Kah, Gary H. 1992. *En Route to Global Occupation* Lafayette, LA: Huntington House Publishers.

Kjos, Berit. 1995. "Serving a Greater Whole." *Media Bypass*. June 1995.

Langdon, Stephen H. 1931. *The Mythology of All Races. Vol. 6: Semitic Mythology*. Archeological Institute of America. Boston: Marshal Jones Co. Inc.

Larue, Gerald A. 1964. *Babylon and the Bible*. Grand Rapids: Baker Book House.

Lewis, David Allen. 1993. *Prophecy 2000*. Green Forest, AR: New Leaf Press.

Lindsey, Hal with C.C. Carlson. 1970. *The Late Great Planet Earth*. Grand Rapids: Zondervan Publishing House.

___. 1994 *Planet Earth-2000 A.D.* Palos Verdes: Western Front Ltd.

Lowry, Lois. 1993. *The Giver*. Boston: Houghton-Mifflin.

MacArthur, John Jr. 1982. "An Uncompromising Life." *Audiotape*. Panorama City, CA: Word of Grace Ministries.

Mack, Burton L. 1993. *The Lost Gospel: The Book of Q and Christian Origins*. San Francisco: Harper Collins.

Maenchen-Heflen, Otto J. 1975. *The World of the Huns*. Berkeley: University of California Press.

Matthews, Victor H. and Don C. Benjamin. 1991. *Old Testament Parallels*. New York: Paulist Press.

Marsdon, George M. 1991. *Understanding Fundamentalism and Evangelicalism*. Grand Rapids: Eerdman's Publishing Company.

Martin, Walter. 1988. "Series on Hermeneutics." *Audiotape*. San Juan Capistrano, CA: Christian Research institute.

McAlvany, Donald S. ed. 1994. *The McAlvany Intelligence Advisor*. August 1994.

McDowell, Josh. 1979. *Evidence that Demands a Verdict*. San Bernardino: Here's Life Publishers, Inc.

McEvedy, Colin. 1961. *The Penguin Atlas of Medieval History*. Harmondsworth, Middlesex, England: Penguin Books Ltd.

Missler, Chuck. 1995. "Update: Kurds." *Personal Update*. February 2, 1995.

Olmstead, A. T. 1951. *History of Assyria*. Chicago: University of Chicago Press.

Pfeiffer, Robert H. 1941. *Introduction to the Old Testament*. New York: Harper & Brothers Publishers.

Rawlinson, George. 1882. *History of Ancient Egypt. Vol. II.* New York: Dodd, Mead and Co.

Reddish, Mitchel G. ed. 1990. *Apocalyptic Literature*. Nashville: Abingdon Press.

Ries, Raul. 1988. "The Days of Noah in 1988." *Audiotape*. Diamond Bar, CA: Manna For Today.

Rivenburg, Roy. 1992. "Is the End Still Near?" *Los Angeles Times*. July 30, 1992.

Rogers, Jack B. and Donald K. McKim. 1979. *The Authority and Interpretation of the Bible*. San Francisco: Harper & Row, Publishers.

Ross, Hugh. n.d. *Fulfilled Prophecy and the Reliability of the Bible*. Pasadena: Reasons to Believe.

Saggs, H. W. F. 1962. *The Greatness That Was Babylon*. New York: Hawthorn Books, Inc.

Trigger, B.G., B.T. Kemp, D. O'Connor, and A.B. Lloyd. 1983. *Ancient Egypt: A Social History*. Cambridge: Cambridge University Press.

Wilson, Ian. 1984. *Jesus: The Evidence*. San Francisco: Harper & Row.

Wiseman, D. J. 1983. *Nebuchadrezzar and Babylon*. Oxford: Oxford University Press.

Yamauchi, Edwin M. 1982. *Foes from the Northern Frontier*. Grand Rapids: Baker Book House.

Encyclopedias

Encyclopaedia Britannica. 1995. Goetz, Philip editor-in-chief, Chicago and London: Encyclopaedia Britannica Inc.

Encyclopedia Judaica. 1971. New York: McMillin & Co. and Jerusalem: Keter Publications.

Great Soviet Encyclopedia. 1990. Waxman, Maron L. (ed.). New York: Macmillan Corporation.

The Jewish Encyclopedia Singer. Isadore, ed. 1916. New York: Funk & Wagnalls.

New Catholic Encyclopedia. Staff of Catholic University of America, (eds.). Washington, D.C. 1967. New York: McGraw-Hill.

Universal Jewish Encyclopedia. Landman Isaac (ed.). 1941. New York: Universal Jewish Encyclopedia, Inc.

Bibles

The Holy Scriptures According to the Masoretic Text. 1955. Philadelphia: Jewish Publication Society.

Jerusalem Bible. 1990. Wainsbrough, Henry, ed. New York: Doubleday Books.

King James Version. (originally translated 1611). 1970. Philadelphia: National Bible Press.

New American Standard Bible. 1978. Editorial Board of the Lockman Foundation (eds.). Nashville: Thomas Nelson Publishers.

*New Catholic Edition. (Confraternity- Douay Version.)*1960. New York: Catholic Book Publishing Co.

New International Version. 1986. Grand Rapids: Zondervan Publishing House.

Oxford Annotated Bible. (Revised Standard Version.) 1965. May, Herbert G. and Bruce M. Metzger (eds.). New York: Oxford University Press, Inc.

Revised Standard Version. 1952. New York: Thomas Nelson & Sons.

Tanakh. 1988. Philadelphia: Jewish Publication Society.

Tyndale Bible. 1990. Wheaton: Tyndale House.

Zondervan Amplified Bible. 1987. Lockman Foundation (eds.). Grand Rapids: Zondervan Publishing House.

Bible Commentaries

The Abingdon Bible Commentary. 1929. Eislen, Frederick Carl, et al. (eds.). Nashville: The Abingdon Press, Inc.

Eerdmans Bible Commentary. 1970. Guthrie, D., et al. (eds.). Grand Rapids: Wm. Eerdmans Co.

Index

Abaddon, 232
Abbasid Califate, 169
Abednego, 163
Abiathar, 19
Abinadab, 19
Abner, 20-22
Abortion, 31-32
Abraham, 10, 14, 18, 44, 113, 121, 125, 212
Achaean Greeks, 39
Achan, 139
Acre, 242
Acrostic, in Book of Nahum, 77
Actium, Battle of, 155
Acts of the Apostles, Book of 29, 117, 119, 124, 130, 187
Adar, month of, 172
Adrammelech, 62
Adrianople, Battle of, 204
Adventists, Seventh Day, origin of, 206
Aegean Sea, 26, 95, 160, 191
Ahab, 39, 57, 59, 69, 254
Ahaz, 25, 59-61, 66, 116
Ai, 139
Akitu festival, 131
Akkad, 107
Alamut, Assassins of, 242, 245
Alans, 91, 237, 241
Albanians, 91
Alchemy, 87, 101, 246
Alexander the Great, 27, 42-43, 66, 97-99, 101, 108, 136, 143, 150-151, 155, 212;
     in Daniel, 163, 167, 169, 170
Alexander, son of Cassander, 157
Alexandria, 26-27, 31, 161, 213
Alfonso III of Spain, 221
Almah, 115-116
Alphabet, 18, 194, 200, 235
Altaic-speaking peoples, 220, 222
Amaranth, 247
Amasis, 94

Amaziah, 57
Ambrose, 4, 204, 221
Amel-marduk (see also Evil-Merodoch), 22, 68, 104
Amen-em-ope, Instruction of, 25
America in end-times prophecy, 206-207, 213, 215, 225, 227-228, 232, 238-239, 245
Amillennial, 201
Ammon, Ammonites, 35, 37, 46, 56, 62, 71, 76;
     in Amos, 69;
     in Isaiah, 138;
     in Prophets of Chaldean Period, 91-93
Amon, 75
Amos, 10, 19, 37-38, 49, 69-70, 124, 195, 254
Anabasis, 229
Anagogical, 44-45
Anath, 11
Anatolia, 218
Andronicus, 160-161
Angel(s);
     Appears to Joseph, 125;
     Destroys Assyrians, 62, 68;
     in Daniel, 164,169, 170;
     in Olivet Discourse, 186-189;
     in Revelation, 195, 197-199, 200
Annals of Imperial Rome, see also Tacitus, 111, 173
Annunciation, 126
Anshan, 105
Antichrist, 109, 120, 168, 170-171, 191, 197-198, 200-201, 204-205, 209, 214-215, 223, 226-227, 229, 232, 238, 241
Antigonids, 159
Antigonus I, 42, 98, 108, 155, 157, 159
Antigonus Mattathias, 181
Antioch, 161, 213
Antiochus I (Soter), 159, 163

Antiochus II (Theos), 162
Antiochus III, the Great 160, 181
Antiochus IV, Epiphanes, 4, 38, 56, 143;
    Career of in relation to Book of Daniel 160-167, 170-171, 177, 215, 256
Antiochus V Eupator, 162
Antipater, Viceroy of Europe, 155
Antipater son of Cassander, 157, 159
Antipater founder of Herodean Dynasty, 181
Antitype, 116, 147
Antony, Mark, 155, 181, 195
Apocalypse of Peter, 18, 31, 32
Apocalypse, Four Horsemen of, 144, 195
Apocalypse of John (see also Revelation, Book of), 190, 193, 195,
Apocalyptic literature, 45-47, 64, 66, 70, 86, 124, 133;
    Daniel, 167-177;
    Epistles, 189-190;
    Ezekiel, 140, 143;
    Gospels, 183-189;
    Isaiah, 137-140;
    Jeremiah, 140;
    Joel, 144;
    Malachi, 144;
    Revelation, 190-202;
    Zechariah, 143-145;
    Zephaniah, 140;
Apocrypha, 27, 43
Apollo, 161, 163
Apologetics, 57
Apries, (see also Hophra), 76
Aquinas, 4
Arabath, 59
Arabia, 105
Arabic, 50, 210, 228
Arabs, 64, 92, 101, 209, 211
Aramaic, 27, 30, 44, 50-51, 151-152, 185, 191
Arameans, 76, 105, 126,
Ararat, 38

Archelaus, 126
Archer, Gleason A., 2-5, 22, 24, 34-36, 45, 53-57, 61, 93-95, 97, 102, 116, 126-127, 130, 139, 147, 153, 155, 183, 185-187
Arian, 31
Aristobulus, 181
Ark, 15, 33, 198
Armageddon, Battle of, 170, 191, 198, 201, 205, 211-214, 222-223, 251
Armenia, 136, 157, 195
Arnheim, Michael 116, 257
Arpad, 59, 61
Artaxerxes, 172, 176
Ascension, 119
Ashdod, 56, 61, 64
Ashkelon, 90
Ashkenaz, 221-222
Ashur, 81
Ashur-etil-ilani, 81
Ashur-uballit, 76, 81
Ashurbanipal, 41, 65, 75, 81
Ashurnasirpal, 83
Aspen Institute, 237
Assyria, Assyrians, 6, 10, 23 25, 37-39, 41-42, 46-47, 49-57, 59-60, 71, 75, 77, 84-85, 87, 90, 95 99, 106, 116, 121, 126, 133 138, 140-141, 143 145-146, 177, 212, 215-254, 256
    Fall of Nineveh, 81-84;
    in Isaiah, 5, 7, 61-70, 140;
    in Jonah, 146;
    in Micah, 138;
    in the Prophets of the Chaldean Period, 77-79;
    Scythians and, 216, 218, 221,
Astarte, 10-11
Astrology, 166, 235, 246
Astruc, Jean, 15-17, 21
Astyages, 42, 105
Atheists, 1-2, 5, 245, 250
Attalids, Attalus, 163
Augustine, 4, 14, 45, 204
Augustus, 127-128, 201
Austria-Hungary, 245

Azariah, in Daniel, 163
Azariah, King, 27, 57
Baal, 10, 140
Babel, 208
Babylon;
    Fall of, 101-109;
    in Revelation, 193, 198, 200
Babylonia, Babylonians, 15, 36-39,
41, 56-57, 62, 94, 131, 140, 152, 163-
165, 199, 208, 218
Babylonian Captivity, 4, 6, 10-12,
15-16, 18, 23, 25-26, 36-38, 44, 46,
49-50, 53, 55-56, 67-71, 76-77, 119,
126, 129, 133, 137, 145, 208, 255
    in Daniel, 149, 151, 171,
    174-175, 177;
    in Jeremiah, 84-87;
Bactria, 136, 159
Baibars, 90
Baphomet, 242
Bardiya, 135-136
bar-Kochba, Simon, 183
Barnabas, Epistle of, 31
Bartley, James, 146-147
Baruch, 22
Bathsheba, 253
Beast, The, 197-201, 223-226, 229,
242, 250
Beast, Mark of (or Number of);
    in Revelation, 200;
    in Conspiracy Theories 235-236,
    250
Beasts;
    in Daniel's Vision, 138, 167;
    170-171,223, 228;
    in Revelation, 191, 194, 199
Behemoth, 140
Bel, 27, 107
Belshazzar, (Bel-shar-usur);
    in history, 41, 103-107, 109;
    as depicted in Daniel, 164, 166-167
Belteshazzar, 163
Benjamin, Tribe of, 86, 113
Beth-togarmah, 140-141, 221
Bethel, Altar at, 109

Bethlehem, 117, 125-128, 137-138
Bethulah, 115
Bible Answerman Show, 26, 84, 91
Bilderbergers, 237, 239, 245
Biochips, 250
Bleek, F., 16
Bonaparte, Napoleon, 245
Bourbons, 244
British;
    as Lions of Tarshish, 228;
    as Winged lion in Daniel, 229
Budo de Stella, 205
Cairo, 93
Calendar, 172-175
Caligula, 201
Calvary, 108
Calvin, 5, 44-45
Calvinists, 205
Cambyses, 64, 93, 135
Canaan, Canaanites, 3, 10-11, 18, 22,
37, 39, 57, 63
Canon, 2-4, 13, 18, 23-25, 27-28, 30-
32, 34, 43, 136, 149
Carchemish, Battle of, 41, 76, 81, 93
Carrhae, Battle of, 195
Carthage, 160
Cashless society, 235
Caspian Sea, mineral wealth of, 210
Cassander, 155, 157, 167, 170
Catholic Church, 3, 4, 15-16, 27-28,
32, 34, 43, 136, 193, 205
Caucasus, 41, 75, 141, 213
Celts, 91, 194
Centeotl, 131
CFR, (Council on Foreign
Relations), 237-239, 241-242, 245,
247
Chaldea, Chaldeans, 6, 12, 18 22, 36-
38, 41-44, 47, 53-54, 57, 62, 65-69,
71, 75-77, 79, 81, 83-85, 87, 89-95,
97-99, 101, 102-107, 109, 133, 140-
141, 143, 145, 174 177, 229
    in Daniel, 151-152, 162, 164;
    164-168;
    in Isaiah, 99

Chandragupta, 157
Chanukah, 163
Charlemagne, 168, 194
Chemosh, 36
Cheyne, T. K., 50-51
Chi-rho symbol, 163
China, Great Wall of, 217-218
Chinese as "Kings of the East," 211
Christmas, 125-127, 163
Chronicler, 24-25, 85
Chronicles, Books of, 12, 22-25, 46, 68, 85, 118
Chronicles of the Kings of Israel and Judah, 22
Cimmerians, 41, 75, 141, 216, 221-222
Claudius, 201
Clement of Alexandria, 31
Clement V, 242-243
Cleopatra I, 160-161
Cleopatra VII, 155, 163
Cleopatra Thea, 163
Clogg, Bertram, 195, 197
Cohen, Edsmund D., 250
Colonia Aelia Capitolina, 183
Colossians, Epistle to, 30, 120
Constantine, 31, 163, 193
Constantinople, 213
Corinthians, Epistle to, 30, 189-190
Council on Foreign Relations, see CFR
Crassus, 195
Craterus, 155
Creationism, 5, 45-46
Crete, 17-18, 39
CRI, 13, 26, 91
Croesus, 42, 106
Cromwell, Oliver, 205
Crucifixion, 120, 122-124, 171-175, 177
Crusaders, 98, 241-242
Ctesiphon, 108
Cush, 95, 140-141
Cyaxares, 75, 81
Cynocephalae, Battle of, 160

Cyril, Cyrillic alphabet, 194
Cyrus, 42, 133, 135,152,153, 155, 229;
    as Anointed One in Daniel's 70
    Weeks, 171-172, 174, 176-177;
    ends Exile 84;
    and Fall of Babylon, 102-107;
    in 2nd Isaiah, 49, 53, 109-110, 143
D, Document, 12-14
Damascus, 25, 75, 181
    in Amos, 69;
    in Isaiah, 5, 59-61, 79, 249
Dan, Danites, 15, 153, 166
Darius (Darayawush),145, 155;
    accession of, 135-136;
    in Daniel as "Darius the Mede,"
    109, 152-153, 164, 167, 177
Davidic line of kings, 10, 42, 77, 86, 118, 121, 125-126, 128, 137
Davis, Edward, 147
DEA, 233
Delacroix, Eugene, 81
Delitzsch, Franz, 16
Demetrius, son of Antigonus, 108, 157-159
Demetrius (Seleucid), 160, 162-163, 170
De Molay, Jacques, 242-243
Deutero-isaiah, 49, 53
Deutero-pauline, 30
Deuteronomist(s), 12, 19, 22, 47, 138
Deuteronomy, 9, 12, 14, 123
Devil, 199
Dewey, John, 247
Diadochi, 108 155, 157
Didache, 31
Dillman, A., 16
Dionysus, 34, 162
Dispensationalism, 139, 190, 207-208
Dobson, Dr. James, 26, 166
Documentary Hypothesis, 9-18, 22, 24, 30, 49
Dodd, Charles, 30

Doederlien, J. C., 49-50
Dollar Bill in conspiracy theories, 233, 235, 245
Domitian, 38, 191
Dorian Greeks, 17-18, 39
Dragon;
    in Isaiah, 140;
    in Revelation, 191, 198-200
Drogheda, 206
Duffy, Warren, 220
Du Maes, Andreas, 14-15
Dyer, Charles, 227
E Document, 10
Ebionites, Gospel of the, 31
EC (European Community), 224-226, 238
Edom, Edomites, 14, 37, 42, 57, 59, 62;
    in Amos, 69;
    in Isaiah, 66-67, 138;
    in Prophets of Chaldean period, 71, 76, 91-92
EEC (European Economic Community), see EC
Egypt, Egyptians, 38-39, 41, 50, 61, 106, 161, 218, 246;
    in Ezekiel, 93-95;
    Gospel of, 31;
    in Isaiah, 63-65
Eichhorn, J. G., 15-16
Ekron, 62-63
Elam, 81, 107
Elath, 57, 59
Elephantine, 95
Elhanan, 24
Eliab, 19-21
Eliakim, 50, 76
Elijah, 37-38, 46, 57, 144, 198, 254
Elisha, 36-38, 46
Elohim, 10-11, 15-16, 19
Elohist, 10
Eltekeh, Battle at, 62
Elul, 172
End-times, 45-46, 133, 167, 183, 189, 195, 205, 208, 212, 214, 222-

223, 229, 250-251
Enkidu, 56
Enoch, Book of, 173
Enuma elish, 199
Environment, 140, 239, 251
Ephesians, Epistle to, 30
Ephesus, 28, 193
Ephod, 33
Ephraim, 10, 59, 61, 86
Epirus, 157
Epistles, 30-31
Esarhaddon, 64-65
Eschatology, 133, 205, 251
Esdras, Books of, 43
Esther, Book of, 3, 23, 25, 28
Ethiopia, Ethiopians, 62, 64-65, 94, 141, 143
Eumenes II, 163
Euphrates, 76, 103, 107, 195, 197, 211
Europa, 226
European Community and European Economic Community, see EC
Evil-merodach (see also Amyl-Marduk), 22, 68
Evolution, 44, 203, 208
Exile, see Babylonian Captivity
Exodus, 9-10, 12, 26
Ezekiel, Book of, 2, 6, 12, 19, 38, 42-43, 47, 66, 71, 85-87, 90-93, 95, 97-99, 149-152, 177, 194, 198, 214-215, 217-219, 221, 223, 227-228, 255
    Egypt in, 93-95;
    Gog and Magog in, 140-141, 143-144;
    Tyre in, 97-98
Ezra, 12, 15, 23-24, 42, 146
Ezra, Abraham ben Meir Ibn, 14, 49-50
FBI, 233
"Fed", 237 241-242
Federal Reserve System, see "Fed"
Flagellant, 205
Flood, 77, 79, 81, 138, 176, 208, 248

Franklin, Benjamin, 246
Fravartish, 135
Freemasons, 241-249
FRS, see "Fed"
Fundamentalism, 4-5, 10, 13-14, 16, 22, 57, 67, 85, 87, 89, 103, 108, 127, 146, 151, 166-168, 171, 173-177, 183, 187-190, 193, 195, 203, 206-207, 209, 216, 225-226, 229, 232, 235, 244, 246, 248-249, 251
Gabriel, 170-171
Galba, 201
Galilee, 29, 121, 126, 128, 179
Gall, 113, 120
Gareb, 87, 89
Gath, 24
Gauls, 90-91, 157, 159
Gaumata, 135
Gaza, 11, 61, 90
Gedaliah, 77
Geddes, Alexander, 16
Gedrosia, 160
Gehenna, 89
Gerasa, 29
Germanic Tribes, 41, 91, 194, 204
Germany, in Fundamentalist End-time Scenario, 205-206, 215-216, 221-222, 224-225
Gesenius, Wilhelm, 218-219
Gilead, 35, 37, 69
Gilgamesh, 56
Gimmirai, (see also Gomer, Cimmerians), 75, 141, 216, 221
Gnostic, 31
Goah, 87, 89
Gobryas, 107, 153, 155
Gog and Magog, 6;
    America in prophecy of, 227-229;
    in Ezekiel, 140-141,143-144;
    Goths and Huns as, 204;
    in Revelation, 201;
    Russia as 214-223
Goliath, 19-22, 24
Gomer, 75, 140-141, 216, 221-222, 225

Gomorrah, 69, 101
Gorman, Michael J., 31-32
Gospels, Origin of, 26 28-31
Goths, 6, 204, 220-221
Grace, 145-146, 165, 208, 257
Graf, K.H., 16
Graf-Wellhausen theory, 16
Great Disappointment, The, 206
Greece, Greeks, 11, 17-18, 39, 41, 61, 84, 94-95, 109, 141, 155, 159, 160-162, 167, 170, 181, 213, 224, 226
Greek (Language), 27-30, 44, 50, 115, 143, 151-153, 185, 190-191, 200, 221
Gregorian calendar, 173
Griesbach, Johann, 29
Griffith, D. W., 103
Grimal, Nicholas, 94
Gurkhas, 231-233, 236, 238, 242, 244, 246, 248, 250
Gyges, 6
Habakkuk, 19, 38, 71
Hades, 115
Haggai, 19, 38, 135-136, 143
Halys River, 104, 106
Hampden, John, 16
Hananel, Gate of, 87, 89
Hananiah, 163
Hanegraaf, Hank, 26, 84, 97
Hannibal, 160
Hapsburgs, 245
Har-megiddo, See also Armageddon, 198
Harmonization in fundamentalist hermeneutics, 3, 45, 186, 187
Harran, 76, 81, 105
Hashmon, House of, See also Hasmoneans, 162
Hasmoneans, 42, 126, 136 162, 179 181, 256
Hatamti Gate, 83
Hebrew, 3, 9, 19, 27, 36, 44, 50-51, 115-116, 121-122, 137, 143, 146, 151-152, 171, 200, 218, 228
Hebrews, Epistle to, 30, 114, 190

Hebrews, Gospel of, 31
Hebron, 15
Helicopters;
    as demon locusts in Revelation,
    231-232;
    Black, 232
Heliodorus, 160
Hell, 32
Hellenistic, 151-152, 160, 162, 169
Heritage, 117, 165
Hermeneutics, 43, 145, 183, 185
Herod the Great, 117, 125-126, 128,
174, 181
Herodotus, 103, 107, 217
Heshvan, month of, 172
Hezekiah, 38-39, 41, 50-51, 61-64,
66-69, 71, 85
Hiel of Bethel, 46-47
Hilary of Poiters, 204
Hilkiah, 50
Hinnom valley, see also Gehenna, 89
Hiram, of Tyre, 246
Hitler, Adolf, 97, 170, 239
Hittites, 38-39, 141
Hohenzollerns, 245
Home-schooling, 232
Homer, 17-18, 53, 84
Honya, see also Onias, 161
Hophra, 41, 76, 94-95
Hoplites, 229
Hosea, 10, 19, 38, 49, 69-70, 255
Hoshea, 61, 121
Hospitaler, Knights, 242
Howard, Michael, 238-239, 249
Humanism, 165, 166, 246-247
Humbaba, 56
Huns as personification of Gog, 6,
204, 216, 218, 220, 221
Hupfeld, H., 16
Huss, John, 205
Hussein, Saddam, 109, 227
Hussites, 205
Hyrcanus, 179, 181
Idumea, Idumeans, 42, 92, 179, 181
Iliad, 17-18, 53

Illuminati, 241, 244-245, 247, 249
Immanuel Prophecy, 59-60,
113,115-116, 137
Indo-European, 141, 222
Inerrancy, Biblical, 2-5, 13-14, 26,
30-32, 43-45, 130-131, 167, 188
Infanticide, 247-248
INS, 233
Ionian, 18, 61
Iphigenea, 35
Ipsus, Battle of, 157
Iranian-speaking peoples, 216, 220
Iraq as Babylon, 227
Irenaeus, 191
Isaac, 14, 18, 113, 258
Isabella, 221
Isaiah, Book of, 176, 255;
    Assyria in, 61-63;
    Divisions of, 49-57;
    Egypt in, 63-65;
    Embassy of Merodoch Baladan
    in, 67-69;
    Israel and Damascus in, 57-61;
    Judah's Neighbors in, 66-67;
    Tyre in 99
Ishmael, 77
Ishtar, 11
Islam, 92, 194,210-211, 213, 221-
222, 251
Israelis, 209-210
Israelites, 3, 35-36, 39, 61, 174
Iyyar, month of, 172
J Document, 10, 13-16
Jabesh-gilead, 35
Jacob, 10, 53, 113, 138
Jacquerie, 205
Jahaziel, 46
Jahveh, 10
James, brother of Jesus, 111,
Japheth, 141
Jason, 161
Jebus, 3
Jeffrey, Grant, 225-226
Jehoahaz, 76
Jehoiachin, 22, 68, 76

Jehoiakim, 76, 152
Jehoshaphat, 46
Jehovah, 13
Jephthah, 35, 45-46
Jerash, 29
Jeremiah, Book of, 10-11, 19, 22, 38, 41-42, 46-47, 66, 71, 76-77, 99, 113, 116, 125, 152, 229, 254;
    Babylon in, 101-103, 107-109;
    Egypt in, 93;
    Exile and Restoration of Jerusalem in, 84-87, 89-91, 171, 176-177;
    Israel's neighbors in, 92-93;
    "Latter Days" in, 140-141, 145
Jeremiah, David, 150, 164-165, 168-170, 174-175,193-194, 208-209, 212-213, 223-224
Jericho, 46-47, 139
Jeroboam I, 6, 47, 109, 173
Jeroboam II, 59, 69, 145-146
Jerome, 3-4, 14, 27, 31, 204
Jesse, 19, 21-22, 113, 118,
Jesus, 111-132; See also: Ascension, Crucifixion, Judas Iscariot, Nativity, Olivet Discourse
Jesus, Genealogy of, 125-127
Jezebel, 193, 254
Joachim, of Fiore, 205
Joah, 50
Job, Book of, 23, 25, 140, 149, 255
Joel, 19, 38, 136, 144-145, 195, 197, 232, 256
John Birch Society, 237
John the Baptist, 115, 125-126, 173
John Cassian, 45
John, Epistles of, 190, 203
John, Gospel of, 7, 28-29, 31, 50, 115, 117, 123, 125, 127, 129, 131
John of Patmos, 171, 190-200; See also Apocalypse of John
Jonah, 19, 25, 38, 136, 145-147, 228
Jonathan, 179
Jordan, 92, 121
Joseph of Arimathea, 122-123

Joseph, husband of Mary, 125-128
Josephus, Flavius, 111, 215
Joshua, Book of, 10, 12, 15, 19, 22, 46-47, 136, 138-139, 143
Josiah, 6, 11-12, 41, 47, 71, 75-77, 109-110
Judas Iscariot, 117, 125-131
Judas Maccabeus, 162, 179
Judea, 181, 213
Judean, 69-70, 163
Judges, Book of, 3-4, 11-12, 15, 18-19, 22-23, 35
Judgment, Last, 191, 197, 201, 208
Judith, Book of, 3, 27-28
Julian the Apostate, 204
Julian Calendar, 173
Kah, Gary, 227, 237, 242, 249,
Kaiwan, 69
Kantzer, Kenneth, 4-5
Karlstadt, Andreas, 14
Keranous, 159
Kethuvim, 9, 23, 27, 149
Kidron valley, 87, 89
King James Bible, 30, 115, 228
Kings, Books of, 6, 12, 16, 19, 22-25, 36, 46-47, 50, 57, 59, 62, 68, 94, 109-110, 145
"Kings of the East",
    in Book of Revelation 197, 200-201;
    in Fundamentalist Scenario, 211
Kings, Ten, who reign with Antichrist;
    in Book of Revelation 200-201;
    in Fundamentalist Scenario, 223-224
Kirjah-arba, 15
Kislev, month of, 172
Kjos, Berit, 248
KKLA, 108, 150, 164-166, 168, 174-175, 208, 212, 216, 218
Koropedion, Battle of, 159
Kurds, 109, 229, 258
L Material, 30
Labashi-marduk, 104

Lachish, 62
Laenas, Gaius Popilius, 161
Lahmi, 24
Laish, 15
Lamb of God in Revelation, 194-195, 197, 200
Lamentations, Book of, 23, 25
Lampstands, 144, 198
Laodicea, 30, 193
Le Clerc, Jean, 15
Lepanto, Battle of, 213
Leviathan, 140
Levitical Laws, 34, 174
Leviticus, Book of, 9, 12, 16, 85
Lewis, David Allen, 210, 228,
Lindsey, Hal, 47, 86, 133, 170, 203, 209-212, 214-222, 224-227, 229, 231-232, 250-251,
Locusts;
    Helicopters as, 231-232;
    in Joel 144;
    in Revelation, 197-198;
Lotan, 140
Louvre Museum, 94-95
Luke, Gospel of, 7, 28-30, 115, 117, 120, 123 125-128, 130, 174-175, 183, 185-188, 193
Lunar Calendar, 172, 198
Luther, Martin, 4, 14, 205
Lydia, 41-42, 104, 106, 167
Lysias, 162
Lysimachus, 155, 157, 159, 167, 170
M Material, 30
Maccabees, 3, 27, 31-32, 42, 55, 56, 92, 162, 179
Macedonia, 155, 157, 159-161, 181
Mack, Burton L., 30
Magi, 124-126
Magnesia, Battle of, 160
Magog, see Gog and Magog
Mahar-shalal-hash-baz, 59-60, 116
Malachi, 19, 38, 124, 136, 144
Malek, Jaromir, 94
Manasseh, 35, 71, 86
Manna For Today, 108, 166, 208

Marduk, 105-108, 199
Marduk-apal-iddina, See also Merodach-Baladan, 62
Mariamne, 181
Mark, Gospel of, 7, 28-30, 50, 117-118, 125, 127, 131, 175, 183, 185-188
Marked by God's Seal in Book of Revelation, 195, 197
Mark Antony, See Antony, Mark
Mark of the Beast, See Beast, Mark of
Marsden, George M., 207
Martin, Walter, 13-14 26, 43-45, 226
Marxism, 244-245, 249-250
Mary, 125-128, 131
Masons, see Freemasons
Masoretic Text, 9, 27, 34, 116, 120, 122-123, 151, 228
Massagetae, 204
Mattaniah, 76
Mattathias, 162
Matthew, Gospel of, 7, 9, 26, 28-30, 44, 50, 113,-115, 117, 123-130, 147, 174-175, 183, 185-189, 214, 226
Matthews, Victor H., 107
May, Herbert G., 25, 167
Mayans, 131
Mcalvany, Donald S., 250
Mcdowell, Josh, 57, 61, 66-67, 77, 79, 81, 83, 87, 89-90, 92-93, 97-99, 101-103, 108-109, 111-132
Mckim, Donald K., 5
Mcmanus, John, 236-237, 241
Medes, Media, 195, 229;
    and Assyrians, 38, 41, 59, 65, 75-76, 79, 81, 83;
    and Chaldeans, 104-106, 108-109;
    in Daniel, 103-104, 152-153, 164; 167-169, 177;
    in Isaiah, 102-103;
    in Jeremiah, 102-103;
Media Atropatene, 160
Media Bypass, 248
Medina, 105

Megiddo, 41, 76, 198
Melchizedek, 114
Memphis, 93, 161
Menahem, 59
Menelaus, 161
Merodach, 104, 107
Merodoch-baladan, 57, 62, 67, 68
Mesha, 36
Meshach, 163
Meshech, 140-141, 216, 218
Mesopotamia, 12, 26, 42, 56-57, 62,
71, 101, 105, 108, 155, 181
Messiah, 7 111, 113-114, 116-118,
121, 124-129, 131, 135-138, 140,
143-145, 147, 171, 175, 183
Methodius, 194
Metzger, Bruce, 18
Micah , Book of, 19, 38, 49, 69-70,
120, 125, 128, 137-138, 254
Michael, Archangel, 199
Michal, 6, 34
Microchip, 235
Mid-trib, 226
Millennium, Millenarianism, 47,
109, 189, 191, 203-250
Miller, William, 206
Millerites, 206, 212, 256
Minoan, 39
Mishael, 163
Missiles, 219, 231
Missler, Chuck, 217-218, 229
Mithraism, 163
Moab, Moabites, 25, 36-37, 46, 56-
57, 62, 71, 76;
     in Amos, 69;
     in Isaiah, 66-67, 138;
     in Prophets of Chaldean Period,
     91-93
Moloch, 25
Money-changers, 118, 124
Mongols, 97, 224
Montanism, 204
Morocco, 169
Mosaic, 14-15, 26
Moscow, 216, 221

Moses, 9-10, 12, 14-16, 18, 26, 28,
123, 198
Moslems, 14, 66, 97-98, 105, 169-
170, 210-211, 213, 221, 242
Mushki, 141, 216
Mycenaean, 17, 141
Naaman, 36
Nabatean, 92
Nabonidus, 104-106, 152, 164
Nabopolassar, 75
Nabu-kudurri-user, 152
Nabuchodonosor, 152
Nahum, Book of, 19, 38, 71, 77, 79,
83, 109
Napoleon, 170, 215, 221, 245
Nathan, 37-38, 57, 127, 253
Nativity, 125-129, 204
NATO, 213
Nazareth, 123, 126, 128
Nebuchadnezzar;
     (Nebuchadrezzar as referred to
     in Book of Daniel), 152, 163-167;
     Dreams of Idol, 167, 208, 223,
228;
     Madness of, 164, 166, 177
Nebuchadrezzar, 38, 41, 43, 68, 71,
76-77, 85, 92-95, 97-98, 104, 152;
     in Ezekiel, 93
Necho, 41, 65, 75-76, 94, 141
Negev, 92
Nehemiah, 12, 23-24, 42, 56, 146,
172
Neo-Roman Empire, 209-212, 214,
223-226, 227, 237, 238
Neriglissar, 104
Nero, 18, 191, 195;
     Nero redivivus, 197-198;
     Number of the Beast and,
     200-201;
Nes-hor, 94-95
Nevi'im, 9, 19, 23, 27, 179
New-agers, 215
Nicaea, Council of, 31
Nile, 26, 38-39, 63-65, 75, 93, 213,
247

Nineveh;
    Fall of, 41, 71, 75, 77-84, 109;
    in Jonah, 146
Nisan, Month of, 172
Noah, 15, 138, 149
Nuclear, 211, 213, 215, 231, 249, 251, 256
Numerology, 235-236
Obadiah, 19, 38, 71, 91
Odin, 35
Odyssey, 17-18, 53
Oleg, 220
Olivet Discourse, 43, 171, 175, 183-190, 199, 203, 214, 226
Onias, 161, 177
Opis, Battle of, 107
Origen, 31
Ostrogoths, 220
Othniel, 35
Otho, 201
Ottoman Empire, 169, 224, 245
P Document, 2-4, 11-14
Paganism, 56, 194, 204, 246-247
Paracelsus, 246
Parthenos, 115-116
Parthia, Parthians, 42, 108, 160, 181;
    as "Kings of the East" in
    Revelation, 195 197-198, 201, 211
Paul, Apocalypse of, 31
Paul, Epistles of, 26, 30-31, 43, 187, 189-190, 203, 213, 226
Pekah, 59, 121
Pekahiah, 59
Pele-joez-el-gibbor-abi-ad-sar-shalom, 137
Pentecostals, 7, 34
Pentateuch, 9, 15-16, 28
Pentecost, 115, 186
Pepuza, 204
Perdiccas, 155
Pergamum, 159, 163, 181, 193
Perseus, 161, 181
Persia, Persians, 38, 49, 53, 64, 133-137, 140,143, 145, 151;

and Chaldeans, 42, 104-109;
    in Daniel, 151-153, 155, 167, 169-170;
    and Egypt, 64, 93, 135;
    and Jews, 84-85;
    in 2nd Isaiah, 102, 109-110
Peter, Apocalypse of, 18, 31-32
Peter, Epistles of, 18, 31, 115, 203
Pfeiffer, Robert H., 55-56
Pharisees, 114
Philadelphia, 193
Philip III, 155
Philip IV, 157
Philip V, 160
Philip the Fair, 242
Philippi, 26
Philistia, Philistines, 11, 18-21, 24, 39, 56-57, 61-62, 71 76, 141;
    in Amos, 69;
    in Isaiah 66-67, 118, 138;
    in Prophets of Chaldean Period, 90-92;
    in Zechariah, 91, 145
Phoenicians, 39, 57, 59, 62, 90, 213, 228, 246
Phraaspa, 195
Phrygians, 39, 141, 204
Pietists, 206
Pilate, (Pontius Pilatus), 28, 111, 173
Plague;
    Bubonic 205;
    Revelation, 195, 197;
    Zechariah, 143-144;
Pompey, 181
Pontus, 157, 159
Porphyry, 4
Post-exilic, 11-12, 25, 50, 56, 70, 89, 91, 133, 135-137, 139, 141, 143, 145-147, 174
Post-trib, 226
Postmillennialism, 201, 206, 207-209
Pre-trib, 226-227
Premillennialism, 86 179, 190, 201 206-210, 213-214, 216, 222, 224-226, 231, 249, 251, 256

Protestantism, Protestants, 3-4, 15-16, 43, 136, 205

Psalms, Psalmists, 12, 23, 25, 77, 113-115, 117-124, 129, 140

Psamatik, 65, 75-76

Ptolemies, 27, 42, 159-162, 169-170

Ptolemy I, 155, 157,163

Ptolemy Eugertes and Philometer, 161-163, 167, 170

Punic Wars, 160, 228

Purgatory, 28

Pydna, Battle of, 181

Pyrrhus, 157, 159

Pythagorean, 246

Q material, 30,

Qarqar, Battles of, 39, 59, 61-62

Quelle, 30

Quirinius, 174

Qumran, 164

R Material, 12

Rabshakeh (also Rab-shaqa), 50-51, 62

Rachel, 86, 116

Racism, 215

Rahab, 139

Rapture, 175, 187, 189, 203, 205, 207, 209, 211, 213, 215, 217, 219, 221, 223, 225-227, 229

Rawlinson, George, 94

Reformation, 16, 28, 193, 205

Rehoboam, 10

Reincarnation, 249

Rezin, 59

Rhodes, 160, 181

Rhodes, Cecil, 238

Rhodes, Ron, 91

Ries, Raul, 108, 166, 208, 225

Rivenburg, Roy, 218, 258

Rockefellers, 242

Rogers, Jack B., 5

Romanovs, 245

Rome, Romans, 18, 29, 42, 69, 90-91, 141, 143, 188 204, 256;
    Census at time of Christ, 127-128;

in Daniel, 168-170;
and Hasmoneans, 180-183;
and Parthians 195, 198;
in Premillennial Scenario;
see Neo-Roman Empire;
in Revelation 200-201;
and Seleucids, 160-162

Rome, Club of, 237, 239, 245

Roosevelt, 233

Rosenkreuz, Christian, 246

Rosh, 216, 218-219

Rosicrucians, 246-247

Ross, Hugh, 46, 87, 120, 128-130, 143, 172

Rothchilds, 242

Roxanna, 155

Rus, 219-220

Russia, as "Enemy From the North" or Gog and Magog, 6, 141, 170, 210-211, 214-219, 222-223, 225, 229, 245, 251

Ruth, 23, 25

Ryan, Mike, 219

Rylands Fragment, 28

Sabbath, 12, 85, 171, 174

Sabeans, 143

Saggs, H. W. F., 104-105

Saite Dynasty, 65, 94

Sakkuth, 69

Samaria, 6, 10, 23, 39, 47, 60-61

Samaritans, 23-24, 146

Samson, 35

Samuel, Books of, 3-4, 6-7, 12, 16, 19-24, 33-35, 38, 117-118, 253

Samuel, Prophet, 33-34, 37-38, 254

Sardanapalus, 79, 81

Sargon, 39, 41, 61-62, 64, 121

Sarmatians, 204, 220

Satan, 124, 165, 191, 199, 201, 203, 222, 236, 245

Saul, 6, 19-22, 33-35, 254

Schliemann, Heinrich, 84

Schneller's Orphanage, 89

Scipio, Lucius, 160

Scorpions, 197, 231

Scythians;
  and Assyria, 41, 75, 81, 83, 90;
  as Gog and Magog, 6, 215-218, 220-221
Seba, 124
Sela, 57
Seleucia, 108
Seleucids, 27,38, 42, 108, 159-160, 162-163, 169-170, 179, 181. 215
Seleucus I, 108, 155, 157, 159, 167
Seleucus IV Phiopater, 160, 170
Seljuk turks, 169, 224
Sennacherib, 41, 50, 61-64, 68, 85, 106
Sephardic Jews, 222
Septuagint, 3, 26-27, 34, 115, 122, 219
Seventy Weeks, Prophecy of, 171-177
Shabaka, 62, 64-65
Shadrach, 163
Shalmaneser, 61
Shamash, 36
Shealtiel, 135
Shear-jashub, 53, 116
Sheba, 124, 227-228
Shebna, 50
Sherazar, 62
Shevat, Month of, 172
Siberia, 169, 210, 216
Sidon, 29, 57, 62, 76, 157
Simon the Cyrenian, 123
Simon (Hasmonean), 179
Simon, Richard, 15-17
Sin-shar-ishkun, 81
Sinai, 64
Sippar, 105, 107
Sivan, Month of, 172
Slavs, 194, 217, 220
Smyrna, 193
Socialism, 244-245
Sodom, 69, 101
Sodomy, 242
Sol Invictus, 163
Solar calendar, 172-173

Solomon, 10, 16, 19, 22-23, 25, 32, 39, 59, 127, 246
Solstice, 162, 172
Sorrel, 144
Soviet Union, 210-211, 215, 220-222, 241, 250, 258
Spain, as Gog, 221
Sparta, 41-42, 104, 106, 229
Spinoza, Baruch, 15-16
Streeter, Canon Burnett, 30
Stoner, Peter, 98
Suffering Servant, 131
Sumerians, 11, 18, 104
Susanna, 27
Synoptic Gospels, 28-29, 43, 115, 175
Syria, 36 39, 42, 59 62, 66, 75-76, 94, 104-105;
  in Isaiah, 5, 7, 57, 59-60, 249
Syriac, 50
Syrio-Ephraimite War, 25, 60
Tabal, 141, 216
Taborites, 205
Tacitus, 111, 173
Talmud, 108
Tammuz, 172
Tampering, signs of in prophets, 22-23, 68
Tanakh, 9, 27, 120-122, 219
Tanchelm of Antwerp, 205
Tarshish, 124, 227-228
Tartan, 64
Tartar, 215
Tartessus, 228
Teima, 105
Television, 231, 235, 248
Templar, Knights, 241-243, 245
Temple (First) 246;
  Book of Law, found hidden in, 11;
  Destruction of, 41, 77, 152
Temple (Second), 173;
  Building of, 24, 42, 136, 145, 171-172;
  Cleansing of, 179;